Contents

Policy Studies Institute

POLICIES FOR A CONSTRAINED ECONOMY

Policy Studies Institute

POLICIES FOR A CONSTRAINED ECONOMY

Charles Carter
John Pinder

 Heinemann Educational Books·London

Heinemann Educational Books Ltd
22 Bedford Square, London WC1B 3HH
LONDON EDINBURGH MELBOURNE AUCKLAND
HONG KONG SINGAPORE KUALA LUMPUR
IBADAN NAIROBI JOHANNESBURG
EXETER (NH) KINGSTON PORT OF SPAIN

British Library Cataloguing in Publication Data

Carter, Charles
   Policies for a constrained economy.—
      (Policy Studies Institute series)
   1.   Great Britain—Economic policy—1945-
   I.   Title   II.   Pinder, John
   330.941′0857   HC256.6

ISBN 0-435-84260-9

Phototypesetting by Georgia Origination, Liverpool
and printed by Biddles Ltd, of Guildford

Introduction

The idea behind this book is very simple. Like most people, we are greatly concerned about the poor working of the British economy, and in particular about its performance since 1970. That performance shows a double waste, both through a low growth of productivity and through a massive under-use of human resources and of capital. The period includes the greatest price inflation in British recorded history, and we still find ourselves faced by annual rates of inflation which would have been regarded as disastrously high in earlier years. British performance has been worse than that of most other advanced nations, and in consequence our country has moved far down the table which sets countries in order of production of wealth per head, with Italy rather than France or Germany now becoming our peer. Throughout the period it has been impossible to feel any strong confidence in the ability of government, whether Labour or Conservative, to find policies which will check the relative decline and lead towards reasonably full employment conjoined with price stability. Indeed, it is a striking feature of government policies that, despite the illusion of fundamental party differences which is produced by our adversary system of politics, what has actually been done by different governments contains large common elements; and what has been done has produced no adequate improvement, but rather a weakening of major parts of the economy.

Although the British problem is quite large enough as a subject for one book, we are not unmindful of the fact that – apart from Japan – problems of a similar kind (though so far generally less acute) are appearing in all the developed western economies. The British record in productivity growth, for instance, though grievously inadequate, is apparently not as bad as that of the United States. What we are describing may be a malady which is general to the 'mixed' economies (that is, those with a substantial element of private enterprise, but also a large welfare structure and considerable State intervention). Where appropriate, therefore, we shall need to look at developments in other countries, and we must avoid the implication that some peculiar British stupidity, laziness or ill-luck provides a full explanation of the economy's ills.

To the sickbed of the economy have gathered theorists of many types, including economists of several schools, sociologists, and students of industrial organisation, management and technical advance. Most have come with plausible prescriptions, but only to deal with a part of what is undoubtedly a very complex and deep-seated disease. Unfortunately the remedies they prescribe are not consistent with each other and the sales talk they purvey is liable to bring further confusion to the public mind. Thus, it is now implanted in the minds of many people that present high unemployment is solely due to the 'monetarist policies' of Mrs Thatcher. In fact, the policies referred to are not in any strict or effective sense monetarist at all, and they do not greatly differ from those pursued by the preceding Government, except in relation to incomes policy.

Our quarrel with most of the theorists, however, is that what they propound will work only if some inconvenient fact of the real world is first removed. Of course any theory has to ignore a great many facts of real life, since otherwise it would become impossibly complicated. It is important, however, that what is ignored should either be of little significance, or else be capable of change so as to be consistent with the theory. Facts such as the power of key workers to obtain rises in wages, or the political impossibility of putting the mortgage rate up to 30 per cent, are neither small nor capable of easy change.

What we contend, therefore, is that the best macroeconomic policy for Britain must be conceived as the best achievable within the known constraints. Such a policy is not likely to fit any tidy theoretical scheme, nor will it lead rapidly to an economic Utopia. It must rather be construed as the 'least-bad' solution to a problem, all of whose solutions are very imperfect. However, although some of the constraints may be incapable of being changed, and for others we may have no idea of how to induce a change, it must be an important subject of policy to produce a relaxation of those constraints which can by deliberate action be altered; otherwise we would be in danger of finding that even a 'least-bad' solution would fail to stem the economic decline. Therefore a part of our study must be to examine the time and ways in which some institutional and social constraints, unhelpful to an effective policy, can be altered; and how, in consequence, the 'least-bad' solutions can be varied so as gradually to become more powerful and effective.

The plan of the book is as follows. First we discuss – in a necessarily summary and elementary way – some of the alternative approaches to the management of the British economy; this helps us to define what are the difficulties about these approaches. Then we ask some questions about what was actually happening in the 1970s, and how all the efforts of well-meaning people have produced such a discouraging result. The central part of the book is about the fundamental factors which determine economic performance, and the way in which their operation is limited or distorted by constraints and institutional structures. We also consider how far the constraints are capable of alteration by deliberate policy, and over what period such an alteration could be effective. Finally, after briefly discussing the general idea of a 'least-bad' solution for a constrained economy, we set out the mixture of policies which we would ourselves favour for dealing with Britain's difficulties. In doing so, we necessarily have things to say about the 'policies' of non-governmental economic agents, such as firms and unions, as well as about public policy in its usual sense.

Our centre of interest is in policies for consistent application to develop the British economy over a period of, say, 20 years. We use the term development rather than growth, because we are concerned with the application of technology to improve the condition of the British people, in which the growth of gross national product as conventionally measured is only one, sometimes ambiguous, element. Thus technology can also be applied to reduce the number of hours worked in a lifetime, which appears in fact to have been the way in which people have used about one-third of the growth of productivity over long periods. Current advances in technology often make work more interesting or pleasant, and technology can be deliberately used to that end. It can also be used to improve the environment and the quality of life, and to reduce the use of non-renewable resources for each unit of output. The output we have in mind is, in short, not just the crude gross national product, but the sum total of benefits that the economic system may produce; and by development we mean the improvement, according to defined standards which may be those generally accepted in the society, of the relationship between the benefits and the inputs.

One important example of a distinction between development as we define it and growth, when we consider the long-term prospects of the economy, concerns the use of finite or non-renewable resources, the consumption of which clearly cannot grow exponentially for ever. If populations increase or essential resources have to be won with greater difficulty, Britain might have at some time to accept economic stagnation, and indeed a decline in the flow of wealth per head. The world will soon have six or seven billion inhabitants, and there is no early prospect that the resources could be found to provide for all this number even at the British material standard of living, let alone that of the United States or Sweden. From one point of view, therefore, economic near-stagnation is a form of involuntary virtue; at least we in Britain are not making things even worse for our poorer neighbours by increasing our rate of consumption of irreplaceable resources. But that, of course, is no reason for stagnating because of inefficiency or laziness.

Greater efficiency and higher production do not however necessarily imply a greater use of non-renewable resources. Our country is at present wasting resources in idleness that could produce wealth which the world needs, and which indeed is needed if we are to resolve some of our own social problems. Idle factories can perhaps be protected from decay, but unemployed men and women may be made less valuable by the experience of idleness. Furthermore, the experience of continued economic ill-success will, if it persists, undermine the political stability which has been one of Britain's great advantages, and may threaten internal order and the acceptance of democratic institutions. Producing material wealth is not an end in itself, but only a means of advancing human happiness and civilisation; and there is little likelihood that a Britain conscious of continuous economic failure would become happier and more civilised.

Our position is, therefore, that the factors which cause our economic system to work inefficiently, to leave usable resources idle, and to create social strains through inflation, must be identified and changed. In our medium-term perspective, this means a return to a higher growth rate; but we fully agree that it must be an early and major purpose of government to seek means by which the happiness of its citizens can be assured by a smaller use of resources – for instance, by measures to limit waste, to increase the life of durable goods, and to encourage conservation. The whole question of achieving a transition from the exceptional rates of economic growth of the last two hundred years to a state of little or no growth in the use of non-renewable resources (which, in the historical perspective, has been much more common), while still preserving and enhancing the contentment of citizens and the values of civilisation, deserves far more attention. The fact that we do not attend to it here does not mean that we lack appreciation of its importance.

Many people have helped us in writing this book (some without knowing it), and others have performed the invaluable service of criticising chapters as they have been written. Our grateful thanks are extended to all of them.

Charles Carter
John Pinder

Part 1
Policy and the Economy in the 1970s

1   Alternative Approaches

The necessary or inevitable effects of government on the economy are numerous and far-reaching. Even John Stuart Mill, after stating the principle that 'Letting alone . . . should be the general practice: every departure from it, unless required by some great good, is a certain evil',[1] went on to discuss numerous exceptions. The necessary functions of government, he said, are 'considerably more multifarious than most people are at first aware of, and not capable of being circumscribed by those very definite lines of demarcation which, in the inconsiderateness of popular discussion, it is often attempted to draw round them'.[2] The argument between those who would increase and those who would reduce government functions is still an active one, but it relates to ranges of movement up or down from a level of intervention immeasurably greater than in John Stuart Mill's day.

That intervention relates not only to the obviously economic variables such as taxation or the supply of money, but to disguised or indirect influences on the economy such as the support of research, the legal framework of trade union immunities, or the encouragement of a particular scope or content in education. Almost any theory of economic ill-success can therefore have attached to it a policy prescription, that is a list of measures to be taken by government which would be necessary if things are to be made better. On some theories, actions by government are necessary but not sufficient – that is, success depends also on some autonomous change of attitudes or procedures or institutions, not capable of being created by government. On other theories, action by government is seen as both necessary and sufficient; or, at least it is highly convenient to be able to persuade oneself that this is true. (But we are not ourselves so persuaded; which is why we give attention to changes needed to be effected by economic agents other than government.)

[1] *Principles of Political Economy*, Book V, ch. XI, §7.
[2] *Ibid.*, V, I, 2.

For our present purposes we can limit attention to those theories which are close enough to the real world to have a significant actual or potential effect on policy-makers. With the great increase in the number of practitioners of the social sciences in the last 30 years, there has come also a multiplication of theoretical models which, while they use words taken from the familiar world of affairs, are in reality only trivial exercises in pure mathematics; for they involve assumptions so different from reality that their inappropriateness as a guide to policy will quickly be discerned by practical men. We seek help in discerning which of the *economic* theories have any chance of relevance from Professor James Meade.[3] He divides the theorists into Non-Keynesian Monetarists, Keynesian Monetarists, Keynesian Non-Monetarists, and Non-Keynesian Non-Monetarists – the last being, in his view, an empty class. He then describes the Non-Keynesians as:

> 'those who believe that the best macroeconomic models are built on the assumption of flexible price mechanisms which continually clear markets, so that no excess unsold supplies or excess unsatisfied demands exist, one implication of this being, of course, that all unemployment is best treated as voluntary in the sense that the unemployed man or woman has chosen to remain unemployed rather than to cut his or her wage demand sufficiently to find a job. I find this assumption of continuous market clearing so unlike what goes on in most markets in our sort of developed economies that I would reject these Non-Keynesian models as being of no serious use in analysing our macroeconomic behaviour'.

This is a judgement with which we agree; the monetarist influences on policy, which are very real and important, stem from a much more practical and empirical version of monetarism.

An element of many of the Non-Keynesian models is a theory of rational expectations. If an economic agent (such as a private business man) possessed a complete and correct model of the operation of the economy, his expectation of (say) the price of his product next year would be the prediction made by the model, after using the facts known at the present time. (The prediction may be wrong because, before next year, a new unexpected fact enters the model; but it is *rational* for him to operate on his best expectation based on present facts.) But, of course, no one possesses a complete and correct model. If *either* the model is wrong *or* the formation of expectations is wrong, the business man will find systematic errors in his forecasts, and will then conceivably (though not necessarily) become able to make better forecasts in the future. Professor Meade finds this approach 'very implausible

[3] J. E. Meade, Comment on the Papers by Professors Laidler and Tobin, *Economic Journal*, March 1981, p. 49.

given the extreme complication of the real world in which we live'. We agree; it is an approach based on a misconception of the way in which expectations are in fact formed – a leading example of academic theorising unrelated to observation of actual behaviour. What the rational expectations school has done, however, is to provide a reminder of the potential importance of changes of expectations induced by changes of government policy. Of that importance we are in no doubt, though the process involved was much better described by Keynes and Shackle than by later theorists.

Professor Meade's further analysis of differences of approach extends to seventeen classes, but even then it is not complete, for it relates only to the purely economic theories of policy. For our present purposes, we can use a simpler classification, though recognising that there are many possible hybrids between the main approaches listed here:

(a) *The attitudinal school.* This sees the essential problem in such things as an aversion to hard work, a greed which demands more material wealth than is being produced, a failure to use intelligence constructively, a lack of daring entrepreneurial spirit, a tendency to load problems on to government without willing the means for their solution. Therefore, while it may be necessary to take short-term measures to abate symptoms like high inflation or high unemployment, no real success is to be expected until fundamental attitudes change. Government can assist this change through incentives and penalties, and through education and training, but the process is slow and the requirements not easy to define. Some, therefore, will argue the necessity of protection against foreign competition while the slow change occurs, lest there should be a complete collapse of the economy; others see foreign competition as an essential element in the incentives to change. A sub-class of this school is those who see the main problem as a sluggishness in exploiting new technology.

(b) *The structural school.* This group puts the main emphasis on faults in the institutional structure of the economy, such as having over-mighty trade unions, or excessively fragmented trade unions, or too large a public sector, or too many very large firms, or too many cosy understandings which restrict competition; or on weaknesses which have arisen in the democratic structure of society, which inhibit actions believed to be necessary to improve economic performance. There are various matters here which can be changed by government action, but generally rather slowly, so that this group also will accept a need for short-term measures in other fields, though not expecting that such measures will be very successful.

(c) *The comprehensive planners*. We include this school for logical completeness, though it is not strongly represented except at the extreme left of the Labour Party. Its members would see it as possible to deal with the problems of unemployment and inflation, as in parts of Eastern Europe, by setting up a comprehensive control system which requires all able-bodied people to work and all prices to remain stable. This implies a move, perhaps irreversible, from a mixed to a fully socialist economy, and observation suggests that it would substitute for present difficulties an enhanced problem of economic inefficiency, and also a considerable restriction of personal freedom.

(d) *The pragmatic monetarists*. This group sees the control of inflation as a primary object of policy, and regards it as an ascertained fact that there is a stable function of money in relation to income; so that, if the quantity of money grows by no more than the real rate of growth of the economy, prices should be, on average, more or less stable. It is recognised that the measures necessary to reach this situation, to 'squeeze inflation out of the economy', may cause a fall in output and employment: but it is thought that, once there is a reliable and generally held expectation of stable prices, the basis for forward planning will be improved, intelligent investment will be made easier, competition with foreign goods will be more effective, and the economy will therefore be able to move towards a higher growth rate and a fuller use of its manpower and other resources.

(e) *The demand managers*. This school regards the main problem as the under-use of resources and the low growth rate (which implies a paucity of opportunities to embody new technology). The centre of macroeconomic policy, therefore, is the control of demand so that it will be adequate, but not excessive, to bring forth the 'full employment' output of the economy. The quantity of money is seen as a secondary variable, to be sensibly regulated in relation to the transactions and other money needs of the growing economy; though some in the 'demand management' school doubt the existence of any reliable or stable relationship between money and income. A further line of argument would point to the inadequate rate of investment, which (so far as industry is concerned) can in turn be related to a very low rate of profit. This can be regarded as a manifestation of a 'vicious spiral' in an unsuccessful economy, or can be linked to institutional factors which have caused the share of labour in the national product to be excessively high; or it can be taken as evidence of a lack of effective management or entrepreneurial spirit. So inadequate investment can appear within other approaches, operating both as effect and as a cause of further problems.

Since our interest in this book is in the management of something like the present mixed economy of Britain, we do not further consider the 'comprehensive planners', who are concerned with a quite different economic system. It might be thought that a choice between the other four approaches could be made by an appeal to the facts; but the matter is not to be so simply resolved.

The reason for supposing that some long-run attitudinal, educational or structural cause lies behind the poor performance of the British economy is that the trouble can be traced back a long way – for more than a century – and in that period there have been a great variety of external circumstances and of government fiscal and monetary policies. The argument that other nations have run ahead of us because they started their industrial revolution later – taking advantage of our experience – might have looked plausible in 1900, but hardly in the 1980s. The disadvantages of being on the winning side in two world wars cannot explain events before 1914, nor the deep trouble we have experienced 35 years after the second world war. Nor are there convincing arguments based on Britain having a poor endowment of natural resources or an unfavourable geographical situation; compare us to Japan. It looks, therefore, as if there is some persistent 'X-factor' (or a lot of them) causing a stunting of economic growth.

But – as the description of approaches (a) and (b) implies – X has been identified in a great many ways. None of the identifications is, in a scientific sense, anything more than conjecture. Thus, it sounds plausible to say that British education does not encourage a high appreciation of wealth-creating activity. It would be equally plausible to say that Japanese education does not encourage creativity; but one hears less of such an argument, because the Japanese are so evidently successful. (One is tempted, therefore, to suggest that the conformity produced by Japanese education must be highly appropriate to a modern interdependent economy.) In fact, if one looks at the attitudes, culture and institutions in different countries, it will always be possible to find some which seem likely to favour economic success and some which do not. Therefore the fact that one can observe some unfavourable factors in Britain falls far short of a proof that *they* are the main cause of an economic performance worse that that of other developed nations.

But neither can one prove the converse. Common sense suggests that the qualities which are associated with economic success remain as Samuel Smiles listed them, 'Attention, application, accuracy, method, punctuality, and despatch . . . steadfastness, purpose and indefatigable industry'. 'National progress', he said, 'is the sum of individual industry, energy and uprightness, as national decay is of individual idleness, selfishness and vice'.[4] In so far as the desired qualities are capable of being affected by policy – by the education system, for instance, or by the incentives offered for good work and the disincentives for idleness or bad work – it is no doubt sensible to use national policies to try to move things in a helpful direction. In so far as forms of organisation get in the way, for instance by feather-bedding inefficiency or idleness, or by diverting attention to internal squabbles, or by creating unwieldy structures beyond our powers of successful management, it is no doubt sensible to try to change those forms. In other words, it is not an argument against *trying* to shift long-term factors in an evidently desirable direction that we do not know if this *by itself* would solve our problems, and that we are ignorant of the extent to which these factors are amenable to change by public policy.

There is undoubtedly a danger that the vagueness of the long-term factors, and the uncertainty about our power to influence them, will lead to their undue neglect. Therefore we pay much attention to them later in this book. Nevertheless, most people hold that good shorter-term economic management also needs attention, either to create a favourable environment in which appropriate changes in the long-term factors can be made, or even as itself the principal determinant of economic success. It is therefore necessary to look at the differences between the pragmatic monetarists and the demand managers, in order to understand how these differences arise.

Demand managers and pragmatic monetarists

That there is a new attitude to macroeconomic policy is strikingly illustrated by the fact that in 1960 the reaction to a slump would undoubtedly have been to stimulate demand and increase State spending – so far as the balance of payments constraint allowed – while 20 years later the reaction was to try to reduce State spending and to do nothing active to stimulate demand. The policies of the 1980s look much like those which were rather unsuccessful in the 1920s.

The simple textbook argument to justify the 1960 policy reaction was

---

[4] Samuel Smiles, *Self-Help*, passim.

as follows. Let an extra £1 million per week be injected by government into the economy – whether by a direct handout, or by reducing taxes, or by commissioning extra work to this value to be done with government money, or by stimulating private industry to invest more by lowering interest rates, or in any other way. A part of the £1 million will be saved, a part taken in taxes, and a part will be spent overseas (possibly, however, creating incomes in Britain by stimulating exports). The remainder of the new income will be spent at home, and will, assuming (since we are envisaging a slump) a general existence of high stocks and idle resources of manpower and capital equipment, first cause a run-down of stocks and a fall in the indebtedness of those who held them, and thereafter an increase in home production of goods and services, involving the paying out of further new incomes (wages, salaries and profits). These new incomes will in turn be saved, taxed, spent overseas or spent at home, the home spending creating another round of new incomes. Thus the initial stimulus is multiplied, and (if it comes directly from government) is in part self-financed through the creation of extra tax revenues; the extra saving helps to pay for the extra borrowing: indeed, if the spending on imports were to make possible an equal increase in British exports, the whole process would be potentially self-financing, with at the end a higher flow of wealth and the employment of resources which would otherwise have been wasted in idleness.

It was always recognised that so desirable a scenario depends on a general availability of idle resources, and that, as one approached full employment, bottlenecks would begin to appear and some prices would rise. It further became apparent that the institutional habits of the economy would tend to magnify and continue any price rise which occurred; income-receivers would demand and obtain compensation for rises in the cost of living and price-fixers would tend to work on a cost-plus basis, passing the cost of the higher income payments to the purchaser – and usually being able to do so because the purchaser's income would rise further. Thus 'cost push' was added to 'demand pull' as a cause of inflation of prices. It was made worse by the principle of maintaining customary differentials, which spreads wage increases obtained, not just to compensate for price rises, but as a consequence of productivity improvement or of the exercise of sheer trade union power, to other groups of workers, including some whose productivity is static or declining.

The existence of cost-push tendencies certainly made it dangerous to expand demand too much. Nevertheless, through the 1950s and 1960s the British economy was so managed as to be reasonably close to the point of full employment (with, indeed, an expanding labour force), and with rates of inflation which, after 1952, were generally below 5 per cent per annum. Inflation was then seen as a consequence of pressure on resources; no one supposed that we could pass, as we did in the 1970s, to the condition with the ugly nickname of 'stagflation' – static output, high unemployment, *and* rapidly rising prices.

Now it was always possible that the effect of distributing money to stimulate demand would not be to cause people to buy more real things (and thereby to set in motion the multiplier process), but simply to push up the prices of what those people already bought; the money passing initially into profits, but not being effective in producing a new round of spending. It is indeed evident that if one distributed money *only* usable to buy houses, the immediate effect would be to push up the price of second-hand houses; it could only be after a time-lag that more builders could be employed to add to the stock of houses, and if all the new money had first been absorbed in paying the higher prices of second-hand houses – that is, had passed into the savings of those no longer needing a house – the incentive to start new building would be much reduced. This example suggests that the key to the situation may lie in the *relative speeds* of the output response and the price response. There is evidence that the British economy is rather sluggish in its output response – that is one reason why we provide such a 'soft' market for foreign imports. On the other hand, we have just been through a period of very high inflation. Every business man therefore knows that it is dangerous to be sluggish in putting up prices; every wage and salary earner hopes for a rise at least once a year. Therefore, while Keynes could assume that it was not necessary to discuss price rises except near the point of full employment, it is now possible for the price reaction to displace the output reaction even during a slump – and, having done so, to have a multiplier of its own produced by the institutional cost-push influences (which are analysed in chapter 4 below).

Thus, while Keynes wrote in 1944 'how slow dies the inbred fallacy that it is an act of financial imprudence to put men to work!'[5], he would today find powerful resistance to spending in order to create employment. This appears constantly in Ministerial speeches:

'(The Rt. Hon. Gentleman) made a plea for a return to the illusion that there is no situation that cannot be made better by ever-increasing handouts of taxpayers' money ... By printing and spending more and more money, we would be perpetuating a fiction that the nation can afford a steadily improving life style within a declining

[5] J.M. Keynes, *The Collected Writings of John Maynard Keynes*, Vol. XXVII, *Activities 1940–46, Shaping the Postwar World, Employment and Commodities*, (Macmillan, London, 1980), p. 367.

performance . . . The only formula which (the Hon. member) gave was that in which so many of my Right Hon. and Hon. Friends indulge – spend, spend and spend . . . We have a positive policy – call it monetarism; call it what one will – and we have a Government who are not prepared to see past mistakes repeated through premature reflation of the economy or through a wild orgy of senseless spending (leading to hyperinflation and increasing unemployment).' (From a debate on 18 March 1981.)

The idea that spending during a slump might actually *increase* unemployment appears to be based on the belief that the effect would all go into prices, and thence into a reduction of exports and an increase in imports. This is clearly overstated; if, for instance, the government directly orders the building of more houses or roads or battleships, it would require a tortuous argument to lead to the conclusion that employment must go down.

The general view of the demand-management school about the control of the stock of money was that this is a quantity very difficult to define (for 'money' is whatever people may choose to use as money); that it is also difficult to control; and that (as suggested above) the relation between money stock and money income is imprecise and variable. Therefore money was to be provided in accordance with the needs of the economy, and was a secondary or passive variable. The interest of the demand managers was in controlling money *flow*, and for most of this school the primary instrument was fiscal – the variation of taxes and subsidies. This did not rule out the occasional use of interest rate variations, but these were more difficult to control (having, for instance, implications for international capital flows) and less certain in their effect.

But if the effect of a tax cut goes largely into prices rather than output, this means that demand management offers no effective policy for the control of either unemployment or inflation. Consequently it becomes necessary to have a prices and incomes policy, that is, to use direct controls (or firm understandings between employers and workers) to prevent fiscal measures running to waste by affecting the wrong variable. Professor Meade, in the article already cited, ingeniously claims to be a 'monetarist' as well as a Keynesian because he wants to control money flows; and he distinguishes his position from that of the demand managers who simply want to expand demand to create full employment, by suggesting that policy should 'keep the level of the flow of total money expenditures on goods and services on a steady growth path', but there should also be a 'reform of wage-fixing arrangements' which would promote employment in the various sectors of the economy (see p. 96). This appears to mean that wages should be kept down so that more people can be employed. But, though this helps to illuminate 'the absurdity of dividing economists crudely into Keynesians and Monetarists', the policy implications are not greatly different from those of grafting prices and incomes control on to a system of demand management by fiscal variation. Some may, for instance, doubt whether one could reform wage-fixing arrangements to promote employment by keeping wages down, without also having some control of (at least) administered and monopoly prices.

It follows, incidentally, that stimulation through monetary expansion could also create inflation while being ineffective in reducing unemployment – unless it is accompanied by an effective prices and incomes policy. Looking at the matter generally, it appears possible that the effects of altering money flows – given our present institutions and habits – have become unsymmetrical, being highly effective in increasing inflation, moderately effective in reducing it, somewhat ineffective in increasing activity, but more effective in reducing it.

If one could suppose that the hypersensitivity about prices and incomes, created by the experience of the 1970s, would die down in five or ten years, so that we could return to the relatively successful demand management of the 1950s and 1960s, then a medium-term prices and incomes policy would seem to be an attractive option. But it is very possible that the sensitivity would continue, having given rise to changes in institutions which allow and cause it to continue. This is where the approaches which require an incomes policy, if they are to be effective, encounter their main difficulty; for a *permanent* prices and incomes policy, if it is not to obstruct desirable change in the economy, needs to simulate some at least of the relative movements of wages and of prices which would take place if the economy was freely responding to market forces. Thus some people's pay has to be depressed relative to other people's pay, which is hard for an administered or corporately agreed incomes policy to achieve. Yet a prices and incomes policy which is *not* expected to be permanent simply builds up expectations of large changes to take place as soon as it ends; so that much of any good it may do will then be nullified. We consider these problems and some possible solutions in chapter 9.

A demand management policy supported by price and income controls administered in detail by officials has the extra disadvantage that it implies a further enlargement of the role of the State, and there have been signs, in Britain as in other developed countries, of some public nervousness about the size of existing State intervention. The pragmatic monetarists start with the advantage of a philosophy which fits a reduced role for government, whose economic management would take the distant and general form of the control of money supply, leaving prices and incomes to settle themselves within the constraints which monetary control would provide. But there are large difficulties. First, how is it proposed to get reasonably full employment of resources, and a satisfactory rate of economic growth? This is not a problem to the theorists (mentioned and dismissed on p. 2) who believe in continuous market clearing; but those who acknowledge the existence of numerous imperfections in markets have to take refuge in a vague belief that once inflation is conquered, the British economy will work properly. There is no historical period, like enough to the present, to which one can appeal in support of this belief; we do not know what the 1950s and 1960s would have been like without demand management, and the 1920s and 1930s are hardly a promising example.

Next, it is not literally true that one can leave prices and incomes to settle themselves, because government has decisions to make about the pay of its own employees and about the pricing policy to be permitted in nationalised industries. If it were possible to make a very large reduction in the size of the public sector, these decisions would not be so influential; but, as things are, the government's own actions are bound to have a large effect on other economic agents, and also an effect on its own ability to be strict in controlling the money supply.

There is furthermore a problem in deciding which monetary aggregate one is trying to control. Different definitions of 'money' provide figures which move in somewhat different ways; but the issue is not just a technical one, of deciding on a definition which is in some sense most nearly 'right'. Money is whatever people choose to use as money, or as means of credit; and whenever you choose a particular definition as a basis for constraint, the market shows both speed and ingenuity in finding new sorts of 'money' which are not constrained. However, the pragmatic monetarist claims no more than a rather general connection between the main stock of money and income, so perhaps definitional vagueness and dangers of leakage do not matter too much. What does matter, however, is the difficulty of achieving effective control. The British practice has in recent times been to control the quantity of money indirectly by controlling its price, and this must introduce some additional uncertainty into the process; it is indeed rather odd to lay much stress on the importance of a money aggregate which is a derivative of what you are actually controlling. But the more serious difficulty is that, both for interest rates and for the stock of money, the government is not truly free to pursue any consistent and precise policy at all.

For interest, one problem is that the interlocking structure of rates which is influenced by rates for short-term money includes a politically sensitive item, the mortgage rate. This affects a great many people – well over half of houses are owner-occupied, and the proportion approaches 65 per cent for the 30–44 age group, nearly all of whom must rely on mortgage finance. Attempts to isolate the mortgage rate when other rates rise simply lead to a drying-up of the flow of money for house purchase, and thus to a random injustice to potential buyers and sellers. Therefore governments are inhibited about using interest rate variations freely, if the situation seems to require very high rates. There is in addition, of course, strong objection to high rates from those who need to borrow large sums of money to finance business. But this may in practice be more easily overcome; business men may be expected to be more conscious than individual house buyers of the fact that rising prices can justify expensive borrowing. It is significant that for considerable periods in the last decade real rates of interest (that is, after correction for the price rises actually experienced – which is not necessarily the same as those *expected*) were negative. Yet, if one believes that monetary policy will work, by quickly bringing down rates of inflation, high rates may be a serious drag on activity. It is odd to use a policy instrument which avoids harmful side-effects only if people do not believe that it will work.

It is possible to control the quantity of money only if there are no prior open-ended commitments to finance large borrowers. If there are such commitments, the likelihood of being able quickly to achieve compensating variations in money used by other people is small. Experience shows, however, that there are two commitments which are inconveniently open-ended. One arises from the negotiation, at an earlier date and perhaps in very different business circumstances, of overdraft limits for particular businesses. Such overdraft rights commonly exist to protect a business on the days in the year when cash flow is particularly adverse, and different businesses will use them at different times. But when there is a general and severe recession, businesses may go into debt to their banks for a much longer period, and use their overdraft rights as a means of getting tiding-over finance. In terms of the way in which the money supply is being regulated, this means that a part of the supply has little response to rising interest rates; for a business in distress may have no prospect of getting finance elsewhere, and in the short run it will pay almost any rate in order to buy time. It is, of course, open to the banks to curtail the open-ended commitments (up to existing overdraft limits) by new agreements with their customers, but they are unlikely to be able to do this during a recession, when severity would simply cause more businesses to close.

The other commitment is that to finance the deficit of government, even if there are problems about doing this by long-term borrowing.

There are two important factors which enhance this commitment. One is that the structure of central and local government spending includes some very large items – in particular, social security and health expenditure – which tend to rise. Add to this a political commitment to increase finance for some other areas – say, defence and law and order under a Conservative government, or education and housing under a Labour government – and compound the problem by the automatic tendency for expenditures on aid to nationalised industries and on unemployment benefit to rise in a recession, and it becomes very difficult for any government to achieve a large cut in public expenditure, and at times impossible to prevent a rise. In fact, the only realistic prospect of a considerable fall in public expenditure would come from a transfer of major functions to the private sector; the idea, common among many outsiders who press for lower expenditure, that enough can be achieved by cutting out waste in existing services, is an illusion. On the other side of the account, governments (of all parties) have become increasingly nervous about increasing taxation. This is in part, of course, because most parties make foolish promises about reducing taxes; but it is also due to an increasing realisation of the harmful side-effects, the distortions and evasions, created by taxation levels of the kind now common in the advanced countries, and perhaps to a sense that the public is increasingly likely to revolt and demand reductions.

These are factors which help to explain the strenuous efforts of both Labour and Conservative Chancellors of the Exchequer to reduce the public sector borrowing requirement (an action which, to the demand management school, may be perverse) – and also the frequent lack of success in achieving desired reductions, particularly during a recession. But if public sector borrowing remains high, there is a *danger* of having to increase the money supply to help to finance it. It may, of course, be covered by voluntary long-term lending, backed by a high level of personal and business saving; but this cannot be relied on. Admittedly, Professor Laidler says that monetarist doctrine 'tells one that there are severe limits to the extent to which public sector borrowing can be financed by money creation',[6] and Ministers who talk as if *all* extra spending has to be financed by 'printing money' – regardless of the effect of that spending on the real economy – are talking nonsense. But there is certainly a residual potential problem for monetary policy.

What all this shows, however, is that the accurate conduct of a monetary policy intended to achieve and maintain long-run price

[6] D. Laidler, Monetarism: An Interpretation and an Assessment, *Economic Journal*, March 1981, p. 20.

stability is beset by many problems. Professor Laidler, in the article cited, admits that (up to 1980) only in Canada had the authorities succeeded in maintaining pre-stated monetary growth targets over an extended period. He cites Germany and Switzerland as examples of countries which have had difficulty in sticking to money supply targets for yet another reason, namely concern over the behaviour of the exchange rate; though (for whatever reason) these countries have certainly succeeded in having a low rate of inflation. Recently, high interest rates in the United States have forced other countries either to hold their own interest rates higher than they would like, or to alter exchange rates in a manner which may destabilise their economies.

But, despite all its problems, the pragmatic monetarist approach has, in two ways, a significant effect on expectations. First, by advancing the control of inflation to a position of primacy, and showing that, during its dominance, inflation can fall quite rapidly (despite failure to contain the money supply), it creates an expectation of more gentle price rises for some time ahead; at least among those who have forgotten that we also had pragmatic monetarists around when inflation was rising sharply, a few years earlier. Second, by proposing policies which in fact fit best with a reduced role for government, the approach may help to strengthen the sense that enterprises must stand on their own feet, and that automatic support in times of trouble through an extension of the role of government cannot be relied on.

The effects of these changed expectations are, however, difficult to judge, for they may not follow any clear pattern of rationality. As Keynes said 'Most, probably, of our decisions to do something positive, the full consequences of which will be drawn out over many days to come, can only be taken as a result of animal spirits – of a spontaneous urge to action rather then inaction'.[7] There are those who profess to see the British economy emerging from depression into a world of more stable prices, lean, tough and competitive, and ready at last to move forward at a satisfactory rate. There are those who expect it to be debilitated, cautious, unbelieving about the permanence of low inflation, and liable to decline (relatively) even faster than before. Which of the main shorter-term approaches, demand management or monetarism, does most to stimulate 'animal spirits'? Or will neither succeed in doing so?

Conclusion

To sum up: the long-run approaches, seeking to alter attitudes or structures, have a strong attraction, and one can make plausible judge-

[7] J. M. Keynes, *The General Theory of Employment, Interest and Money*, ch. 12, VII.

ments about them, even if there is at present no means of proving the appropriateness of any particular selection from the many possible factors which have been suggested, nor of making a credible claim that specific policies will have an assured beneficial result. The main competing schools of thought on shorter-term management both face very considerable difficulties in showing that they have a feasible solution. This is a discouraging conclusion, but not really at all surprising; the real world does not fit into neat and ascertainable models of behaviour. The right policy, as we suggest in chapters 8 and 9, combines elements from several approaches. It is wholly undogmatic; it does not assert that there is a plain answer which has been staring us in the face, nor that reliance on one or two instruments will free us from the necessity of thinking about others. It is necessarily tentative, because nobody has all the answers and the effects of policy are not all predictable.

2 What Was Happening in the 1970s?

This chapter is not intended to provide a political and economic history of the recent past, but rather to remind the reader of a few key facts, relevant to the discussion of future policy, and especially of those facts which tend to be remembered in a distorted form.

From 1959 to 1969 the output of the British economy (defined as the gross domestic product at constant factor cost) increased by some 35 per cent. From 1969 to 1979 (just before the onset of the recent severe depression) it is recorded as having increased by 20 per cent, of which about 4 per cent was contributed by the growth of the North Sea oil industry, but this slowing down of growth is probably slightly overstated by the official statistics, because of the increasing size of the 'black economy' whose output is not recorded. Undoubtedly the record of the 1970s was much worse than that of the 1960s; yet its relative badness, in relation to other periods and to other countries, should not blind us to the fact that even 20 per cent per decade would multiply output four times in an average lifetime. Nor was such a rate of increase exceptionally low by historical standards:

Table 2.1   *Percentage increase in gross domestic product at constant factor cost by decade, 1859–1979*

1859–69	18
1869–79	22
1879–89	30
1889–99	24
1899–1909	8
1909–19	13
1919–29	7
1929–39	20
1939–49	16
1949–59	27
1959–69	35
1969–79	20

Note: These figures are to a minor extent affected by the inclusion of Southern Ireland up to 1920.

Source: C. H. Feinstein, *Statistical Tables of National Income, Expenditure and Output of the UK, 1855–1965*, (Cambridge University Press, 1976), and National Income Blue Books.

Was the slower rate of increase in the decade 1969–79 caused by a break in 1974, when the shock of the increase in oil prices had hit the world and helped to accelerate inflation? In order to judge this, we take five-year periods from 1959:

Table 2.2 *Percentage increase in gross domestic product at 1975 factor cost by quinquennium, 1959–1979*

1959–64	19
1964–69	13
1969–74	11
1974–79	8

Sources: *National Income and Expenditure,* (HMSO, London, 1981).

This table does not suggest that the slide into ill-success can be dated solely from 1974. The economy seems to have first decelerated from the high rates of growth achieved in the early 1960s (which were better than those of the late 1950s). Looking at year-to-year changes, we observe a cycle of a good year, followed by three or four moderate years, and then another good year, up to 1973 (when the gross domestic product rose 6 per cent above the previous year); but then there was a fall in output for two years, moderate performance for four years, and a further fall in output in 1980. The quinquennium 1959–64 contains two good years; those of 1964–69 and 1969–74 one only (the latter also including a year of decline); 1974–79 contains no very good years, and a further year of decline. So the events of the 1970s can be blamed for producing, by whatever means, actual declines which have interrupted the normal cycle of greater and smaller increases.

Let us, however, return to the long view over the decades since 1859. The figures for domestic product relate to periods with very different rates of increase of the employed labour force; there was, for instance, a 20 per cent increase in the period 1879–89. The increase in gross domestic product per member of the employed labour force has in the last 120 years generally been in the range 10–20 per cent per decade, with lower figures in 1899–1919 and 1929–39, and a single higher figure, over 30 per cent, in 1959–69. Thus part of our malaise arises from comparison with a quite exceptionally good period by British standards; even for 1969–79 this figure, a sort of overall 'productivity' increase, was actually well above the average for the 120 year period.

The record for industrial production, however, was more disturbing. The increase here was no less than 41 per cent from 1959 to 1969, but (excluding North Sea oil) less than 5 per cent from 1969 to 1979, the peak having been reached in 1973. Industrial production in 1980 was 12 per cent down on 1973. For manufacturing alone the increases were 43 per cent and less than 7 per cent, with a 13 per cent fall from 1973 to 1980. The only decades in the last 120 years with anything like so bad a record for industrial production as 1969–79 were 1899–1909 (5 per cent) and 1909–19 (7 per cent) – and the latter figure was distorted by the nearness of 1919 to the ending of the first world war.

It is familiar ground that the British record is poor compared to that of other advanced countries: this can be clearly seen from diagram 2.1. Some commentators in fact date the disappointing record back to the middle of the last century. However, from 1850 to 1910 an appearance of relative weakness could perhaps be ascribed to the overtaking of a mature industrial country by new and thrusting competitors; and, although the recovery from the first world war was sluggish, British performance in the 1930s was (considering the special difficulties of the times) quite good, the decade showing some notable progress in developing new industries. The decade of the 1950s is hard to inter-pret, because both our West European neighbours and Japan started a long way back after the devastation and disruption of war, and a faster growth in these countries was not therefore surprising. But it is clear that since 1960 British relative performance has been poor, to a degree which cannot be ascribed either to the different problems of 'catching up' after the war or to the effects of newly industrialising countries.

The comparisons remain, however, full of pitfalls. Diagram 2.1, by using *per capita* figures, avoids the problem of different rates of popu-lation growth, but there are other important demographic influences, such as the age distribution, which vary from country to country. Migration trends differ, and Germany (in particular) has made flexible use of a large amount of temporary immigrant labour. Several countries have gained advantage (at least in terms of the valuation used for national income) by shifting manpower out of agriculture, a process already substantially complete in Britain. The size of public services is different, and there is therefore a different impact of the peculiar problems of measurement of their output.

None of these factors can explain the extraordinary success of Japan, whose industrial production multiplied by seven between 1958 and the 1973 peak – in which period British production rose by about 50 per cent. In the 1960s Japanese domestic product grew more than four times as fast as ours. But the statistical problems mentioned in the last paragraph suggest the value of a less aggregated approach. D. T. Jones showed that, while in the late 1950s and 1960s the growth rate of output per person in *manufacturing* was lower in Britain than in the major

Diagram 2.1 Gross domestic product per head, 1961 = 100

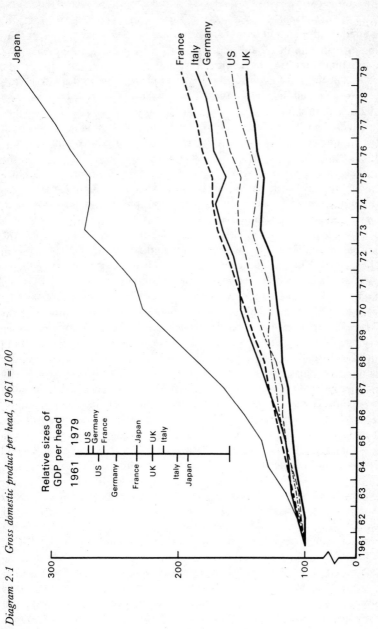

European Community countries, it was catching up, and in the period 1967–73 had reached the EC average (and exceeded the rates in Canada and the United States).[1] But it was, of course, much lower than the growth rate in Japan; and after 1973 UK performance once again fell behind that of other countries.

The profiles of economic development in the advanced countries are very similar: all did well in the 1960s, and have suffered setbacks since 1973. The best summary of the relative position of Britain is that her behaviour has been that of a chronic invalid, struggling towards better health in good times but quickly relapsing as a consequence of new stress.

Diagram 2.2 shows, for the period since 1965, the course of employment, unemployment and inflation. Despite a significant rise in unemployment from 1974 on, the employed labour force in Britain, just before the onset of the deep 1980 recession, was at a near record level. Indeed, if account is taken of the probable incidence of 'moonlighting' and of unrecorded jobs in the 'black economy', it is clear that the job-providing propensity of the economy was really rather good. But within the total of jobs the private sector had declined over the decade by nearly a million, with a corresponding increase in central and local government employment. Manufacturing employment fell over the decade by 1.2 million, indicating a productivity increase of some 24 per cent. This is a trend of productivity which must continue if British manufacturing is to compete against imports or in export markets, and it is likely to cause further falls in employment even if sales increase; but the compensating increase in government employment may have come to an end, partly for ideological reasons ('getting government off our backs') and partly because there is resistance to higher taxation and objection to increasing State borrowing.

Over the decade from 1969, unemployment rose by 160 per cent, and it has doubled again since 1979. Through most of the 1970s, however, employment opportunities for women were good enough to encourage a considerable increase in those offering themselves for work. The social trend towards the employment of married women moved fast, and the ratio of the working population (including those registered as unemployed) to the total population went up from 45.8 per cent to 47.1 per cent. The rise in unemployment is evidence that this change was more than the economy managed to assimilate; but in fact, up to 1979, that rise is almost wholly accounted for by the rise in the working population. Women were getting employment (especially

[1] D. T. Jones, Output, Employment and Labour Productivity in Europe since 1955, *National Institute Economic Review*, August 1976, pp. 72–85.

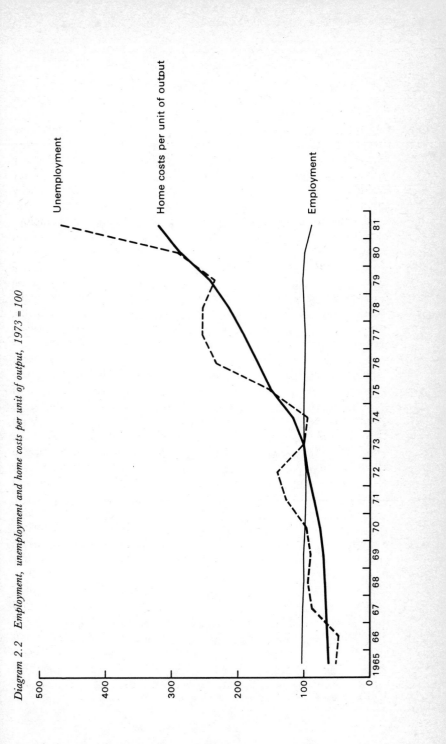

Diagram 2.2   Employment, unemployment and home costs per unit of output, 1973 = 100

in service industries) and men were being displaced (especially from manufacturing) into unemployment.

Looking ahead to the 1980s, the number of people entering the working ages will be falling, as a consequence of the decline in the birth rate from the mid-1960s. But the number leaving on retirement will be lower than the entrants, and will fluctuate considerably, as a consequence of the pattern of births during and after the first world war. The population of working age will grow substantially in the early 1980s, and then at a declining rate up to 1991, when the entries and exits will be almost equal. What is difficult, however, is to estimate the *activity rate*, that is the proportion actually seeking work. This is affected by certain social trends, such as earlier retirement and the increasing propensity of married women to work outside the home; indirectly by the birth rate, which (when it rises) reduces the number of mothers available for employment; but above all by the rate of unemployment itself, because some people do not look for work if they think it unlikely that they can get it. Department of Employment estimates[2] suggest that from 1981–86 the labour force may rise by 700,000 if unemployment can be held at 2 million, but by a million if unemployment in 1986 is down to $1\frac{1}{2}$ million. No estimate is offered for more optimistic assumptions on unemployment, but it may be conjectured that, with unemployment down to half a million (as it was in 1969), it would be necessary in the period to find some $3\frac{1}{2}$ million more jobs than were available in 1981. Recorded job creation in the period 1969–79 (twice as long as 1981–86) was only a quarter of a million. This shows that the combination of economic, demographic and social trends creates in the 1980s an employment problem of great difficulty; and that it will be unwise for any politician to suggest that he knows a policy capable of solving this problem.

In the decade 1959–69 consumers' expenditure rose by 28 per cent, government final consumption by 23 per cent, and gross domestic fixed capital formation by 74 per cent, all at 1975 prices. In the following decade the increases were 27 per cent, 27 per cent and 10 per cent respectively. But in fact nearly all of the small increase in capital formation can be accounted for by North Sea Oil. Within the remainder, investment in dwellings, in public services and in public utilities fell, that in manufacturing was fairly constant, while in the service industries investment rose substantially. This implies a shift within the total of capital formation in favour of 'productive investment', that is investment which yields marketable commodities and services. But *net* investment (that is, capital formation less capital con-

---

[2] Labour Force Outlook to 1986, *Employment Gazette*, April 1981, p. 167ff.

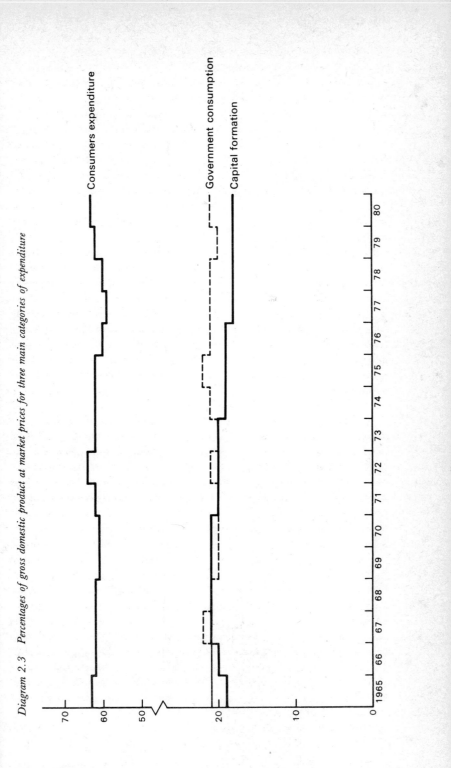

Diagram 2.3 Percentages of gross domestic product at market prices for three main categories of expenditure

sumption) fell substantially, except in oil, mining and service trades. There is good ground to suppose that we were investing far too little to secure a satisfactory competitive position and growth of output.

Diagram 2.3 shows the relation of consumers' expenditure, government consumption and capital formation ('investment') to the gross domestic product at 1975 market prices. These figures show a remarkable stability, but with some decline in the proportion of capital formation and a fluctuation in that for consumer expenditure. There is no evidence of marked change, induced either by the oil crises or by the recession in 1980; nor indeed of any great reaction to the differing policies of governments. But, as suggested in the last paragraph, the gentle decline in the proportion for gross capital formation conceals a more serious problem. Diagram 2.4 shows the trends for net investment (in £ million at 1975 prices), with investment in houses and social and public services and investment in manufacturing shown separately from the rest (which is predominantly the non-public services and the oil industry). There are statistical problems in measuring capital consumption, so not too much weight should be put on the figures in this diagram; but the conclusions, that net investment overall has fallen heavily since 1973, and net investment in manufacturing since 1970, while the ratio of public to private investment has fallen very greatly since 1976, are all likely to be broadly correct.

However, it is too simple to suggest that consumption and government current expenditure 'crowded out' investment. There were under-employed resources both of labour and of capital; if more decisions to invest had been taken, more new capital could have been created. It is true that within government expenditure, which is constrained by nervousness about increasing taxes and by problems about increasing borrowing, the big current spenders tended to have priority over government-financed capital programmes, particularly that for housing. In the private sector, however, we must look for the causes of any inadequacy of capital expenditure in the factors which produced low profits (see chapter 4) and high uncertainty.

The word 'inadequacy' in the last sentence would in some quarters be questioned. Thus, Mr Christopher Johnson[3] points out that *gross* investment in plant, machinery and transport equipment in the UK was in 1978 a slightly higher proportion of gross domestic product (9.2 per cent) than in France and Germany, and significantly higher than in Italy and the US; it was, however, less than the Japanese proportion, 10.9 per cent. He then claims that there is in any case only a weak connection between the investment/GDP ratio and economic growth;

[3] *Do we invest too much? Lloyds Bank Economic Bulletin*, No. 33, September 1981.

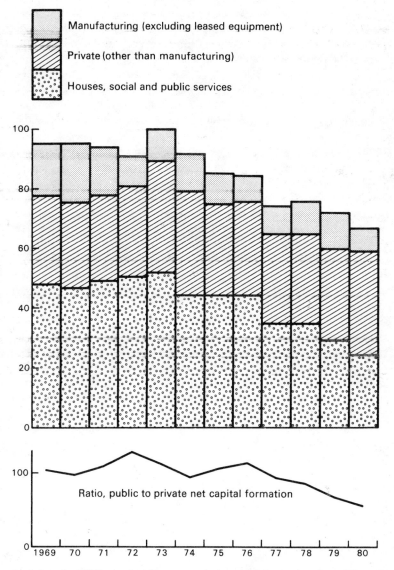

Diagram 2.4 *Net domestic fixed capital formation at constant prices, percentages of 1973 total*

Manufacturing (excluding leased equipment)

Private (other than manufacturing)

Houses, social and public services

Ratio, public to private net capital formation

and that the UK's capital/output ratio is too high, not too low. There is an element of overkill in these arguments. Certainly there is a great deal of wasteful and misconceived investment, so one would not expect the relation to output growth to be regular and close. But *gross* investment is in any case affected by the amount of capital equipment which requires replacement; one would expect the relation to extra output to be closer with *net* investment, or with the larger total of 'gross capital less retirements' – the owners of capital do not dispose of it as fast as the statisticians deem it to have been consumed. Furthermore, the need for investment depends on the point from which you start. We would assert that in manufacturing in particular, but also in some other sectors, there is in Britain too much out-of-date plant and machinery, and too little opportunity to embody new technology in new plant; and that the recovery of competitiveness cannot possibly be achieved on the basis of a declining investment.

The problem of private sector investment can readily be understood if one examines what has been happening to profits. From 1969 to 1979, the net profits of manufacturing companies, after the depreciation allowances permitted for tax, increased by 120 per cent; there was a notably sharp jump of both gross and net profits between 1975 and 1976. But over the same period retail prices multiplied more than three times, and the cost of capital goods by nearly four times. There were heavy increases in interest payments and in profits due abroad. It would not be surprising, therefore, if internal funds available for *new* investment were limited, and indeed if companies were tempted to economise on the timely replacement of their capital stock. Putting the matter another way, the real before-tax rate of return on trading assets (excluding North Sea Oil) was around 9 per cent in 1970, but down to 3 per cent in 1980. It still does not follow, of course, that adequate investment was *impossible*; some companies achieved it, and, for much of the period, lending institutions were complaining about the lack of good propositions seeking finance. But investment by ploughing back profits will always appear easier than incurring the costs and the conditions of new borrowing. (It should be noted, however, that there was some alleviation of the situation by the rapid spread of arrangements for leasing capital equipment; thus in 1980 the financial sector spent some £600 million on plant and machinery for leasing to manufacturing, equivalent to an addition of over 10 per cent.)

Some further light on the problem of profits is given by diagram 2.5. This shows how the *gross* profits of companies lost ground immediately after 1974, when the proportion going in wages and salaries jumped up, and again in 1980. The proportion going to companies remained, throughout the 1970s, below the levels in the 1960s – in 1960 it was 16 per cent. Since capital depreciation consumes a substantial part of gross profits and does not change greatly from one year to the next, the balance available for new investment has been cut very much more sharply, as the figures given in the previous paragraph show. The

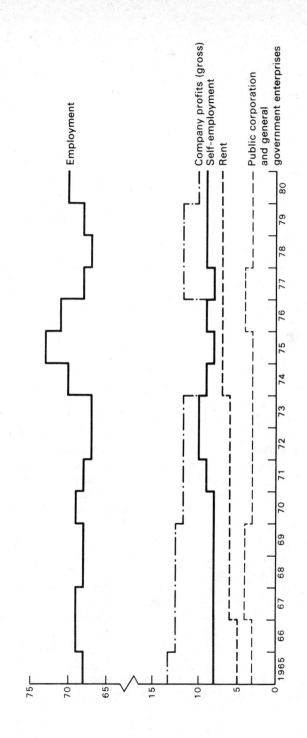

Diagram 2.5   Division of sector incomes after providing for stock appreciation, percentages of gross domestic product

issues raised by this are further discussed in chapter 4.

The fall in net investment in most sectors was associated with a decline in the ratio of research and development expenditure (R and D) for non-defence purposes to national product. The relation between research and development expenditure and economic success is a complicated one, and it is possible that the change indicates no more than a judgement that the effort of the late 1960s was wastefully large; or alternatively it might be produced by a decline in the relative importance of some of the very costly areas of research. But there is ground for suspicion that in Britain (and also in the United States) R and D was too low to support an adequate rate of technical change. Since much development is concerned with process improvements which enhance labour productivity, the following figures give cause for thought:

Table 2.3   Real gross domestic product per employee, 1978

	Index (1967 = 100)
United States	113
Canada	122
United Kingdom	128
France	148
West Germany	152
Japan	195

Source: US Bureau of Labor Statistics, (Washington, 1979).

Direct international comparisons of R and D expenditure are difficult, but it is clear that by 1975 non-defence expenditure, as a proportion of national product, was substantially higher in Japan and West Germany than in either the UK or the US.

Since new investment is often the occasion for embodying technical change, a decline in development expenditure (which is the greater part of the combined total of research and development) is likely to be an associate of a decline in net investment, the causal links operating in either direction, and both declines might well have been influenced by the unsatisfactory state of profits.

It is very possible, however, that the uncertainty associated with high inflation was a dominant influence in restricting investment and development; for it is well established that uncertainty tends to cause a postponement of major decisions to a hoped-for future time when expectations can be clarified. The effects of the inflation of the 1970s could well have been (for Britain) very great, for it was the biggest general inflation in our whole recorded history. Prices for consumer goods rose by a factor of $2\frac{1}{2}$ from 1914 to 1920, but 1920 was a peak year, after which prices rapidly receded. From 1974 to 1980 the rise was also by a factor of $2\frac{1}{2}$ but with the increase continuing. The inflation of the decade 1959–69 was (on various measures) of the order of 40 per cent; that for 1969–79 was well over 200 per cent, and for 1971–81 nearly 300 per cent. In the Napoleonic Wars and their aftermath, prices doubled over the 27 years from 1793 to 1820. The course of prices in the great Tudor inflation is more difficult to chart, but over the whole period from 1500 to 1650 the increase was much less than that of almost thirty-fold since 1913.

Violent price movements, coupled with expectations that they may continue and perhaps get much worse, create difficulty in assessing the value of any business proposition or contract extending over time. The uncertainty is compounded, for all businesses which export or use or compete with imports, by the fact that the fluctuations of prices in over-seas countries are different in both amount and timing, and are not necessarily made more even for British firms by fluctuations in ex-change rates. Over significant periods, sterling has appreciated against other currencies even though British costs have been rising faster than those of our main competitors.

Rapid inflation also has the effect of importing a greater uncertainty into negotiations about wages, and a greater likelihood of conflict, unless indeed some automatic indexation can be agreed. The result of this in the 1970s, however, may have been favourable to labour-saving investment, not only because employers have become pessimistic about their future ability to contain labour costs, but because they want (if they can) to reduce the relative importance to their business of the conflict area.

However, the general conclusion remains that it has probably become more difficult to modernise the British economy, to sustain international competitiveness, and to achieve a high growth rate, because of the effects of high and unpredictable inflation. Although the reason for elevating the 'fight against inflation' to be the main deter-minant of British economic policy was no doubt a judgement about the worries of voters, it may also have been justified as a condition for obtaining a more successful economy.

As is well known, that fight was conducted in the 1970s in part by a great variety of short-term expedients for controlling incomes and prices. The effects of these are visible as fluctuations in the curves, but there appears to be no basis for a judgement of their cumulative effectiveness. The con-ventional wisdom is that any temporary control simply pro-duces, like a compressed spring, a violent reaction to normality (or beyond) when it is released; and that while the control is effective it is very likely to produce distortions in the economy which lower its efficiency or lessen its rate of adaptation to the necessities of the world in which it operates. These are common sense conclusions, but perhaps tend to be a little overstated, because controls produce distortions (relative to the free market situation) in labour or product markets which are already heavily distorted by their various imperfections. It is not therefore self-evident that a further distortion will make things worse rather than better.

There were also attempts at deflation by tax increases or by making cuts in government expenditure. Diagram 2.6 shows the relation of total tax revenue, including national insurance contributions, to national income, and it also shows that, in the mid-1970s, the public sector borrowing requirement grew to large proportions.

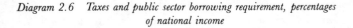

Diagram 2.6   Taxes and public sector borrowing requirement, percentages of national income

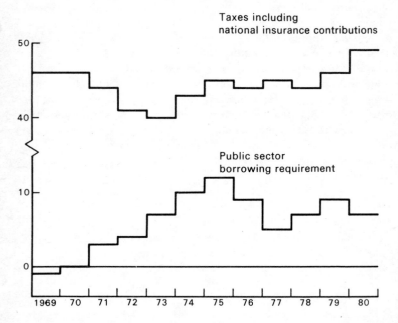

The diagram shows a significant fall in the relative level of taxes prior to the great inflation, but also a considerable rise at the end of the 1970s. But the level of taxes needs to be related to the expenditure which government sought to finance. The borrowing requirement, which was negative in 1969, then started a steep rise to a peak (relative to national income) in 1975. It was cut back substantially in 1976 and 1977, but then rose again. These heavy requirements of finance are relevant in relation to the conduct (shortly to be discussed) of control of the money supply. They also illustrate a problem which became of great importance in the 1970s: government expenditure proved diffi-cult to control (and contained several items with an in-built tendency to increase), while for political reasons, and because of increasing fears of harmful side-effects, tax increases to support the higher expenditure were not considered possible and therefore the fiscal control of the economy to hold back inflation became unusually difficult.

At the end of the 1950s the 'goods and services' element of government current expenditure was nearly 58 per cent of total current expenditure. By the end of the 1960s it was around 54 per cent, and by the end of the 1970s rather over 51 per cent. This change was not pro-duced by the burden of debt interest, which in the 1970s rose *slower* than government final consumption, but by the increase in transfer payments – influenced by demographic forces (e.g. the rising number of pensioners), but also to a major extent by the desire to make transfer payments more generous. However, although final consumption was a decreasing proportion of the whole, it was rising in almost all years. There were attempts to cut government expenditure, but they tended to be presented as changes in programmes – that is, as cuts in previously expected increases – and this made them appear more dramatic than they really were. Even the Labour Government's expenditure cuts between 1976/77 and 1977/78 (which were much greater than those subsequently proposed by the Conservatives) pro-duced only a minor fluctuation in the tendency for government final consumption to rise in real terms (and thus for total current expenditure to rise faster); this is shown in diagram 2.7.

Diagram 2.7   General government final consumption, year to year percentage changes at 1975 prices

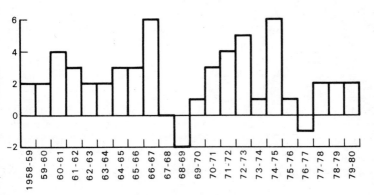

From early in the 1970s, however, governments were plainly anxious to cut back expenditure, and they did so in the area most readily reduced without upsetting ongoing programmes – namely, capital expenditure. At 1975 prices, gross capital expenditure rose between 1969 and 1970, and sharply between 1972 and 1973, but fell in every other year of the decade, so that by 1980 it was less than 54 per cent of its 1970 level. There was a moderate fall in the public housing pro-gramme – though, as it was cut back repeatedly, further reductions of expenditure were still expected – and a heavy reduction in 'other new buildings and works', especially those related to social services.

The course and effects of monetary policy in the decade are particularly difficult to chart. There is, to start with, no close relation between the statements of politicians and what actually happens. The modern Conservative Party does not mind being called 'monetarist', while Labour politicians tend to regard it as a term of abuse; but the real difference in actions has been very much less than the political rhetoric suggests. Domestic credit expansion [4] had a sharp peak in 1972-74, but the annual amount then fell for four years before beginning a long and steep rise in 1978. The changes in the money stock figure Sterling M_3 followed a similar course. The stock figure M_1 (notes and coin in circulation with the public, together with UK private sector sterling sight deposits) went up closely in line with the price level. The M_3 measures, which differ mainly by adding time deposits, went up rather faster than prices. 'Private sector liquidity (2)' appears to have risen since 1975 by rather less than prices or the value of output of the private sector. None of these figures is satisfactory as a measure of what is usable as money, a concept which changes as the ingenuity of the financial community provides new forms of credit or government policy allows their use.

The data are not inconsistent with the hypothesis that, in practice, money was supplied to meet transactions and other needs at the price level of each period, the course of the money stock being affected in addition by a variety of institutional and behavioural changes. The

[4] *Domestic Credit Expansion* is the sum of the public borrowing requirement, sales of public sector debt by the UK private sector (other than banks), bank lending in sterling to the private and overseas sectors, and certain Bank of England Issue Department holdings of commercial bills and promissory notes. The second item is generally negative; that is, the private sector meets part of the PSBR by buying public sector debt. The money stock M_1 consists of notes and coin in circulation with the public and UK private sector sterling sight deposits. *Sterling M_3* is M_1 plus UK private sector sterling time deposits and public sector sterling deposits (that is, M_1 is roughly notes and current accounts, but also covers other deposits available on demand, including money at call and overnight money, while M_3 is roughly notes and current and deposit accounts). *Private Sector Liquidity (2)* is a wider total including (for instance) building society shares and deposits.

monetarists claim, however, to find in the figures evidence that increases in money stock precede increases in prices, and can therefore be supposed to cause them (or to allow the operation of a natural tendency to price increase). The data are not inconsistent with this hypothesis either, though the special features of the period were such that it could hardly be expected to provide any strong proof. (And price movements in earlier periods were so much smaller that they provide no satisfactory supporting evidence.) It is certainly relevant that, at various times, Ministers have *believed* that they were helping to curb inflation by monetary restraint. However, it must be remembered that the system provides, not a direct control of the amount of money, but an indirect one by varying its 'price'; and that the government must so operate that the public sector borrowing requirement is met. Over a large part of the 1970s, the 'real' cost of money was low or negative; that is, if one had been able to predict with fair certainty the rise in prices for the ensuing year or so, it would often have been a good business proposition to borrow money and buy goods, and this would seldom have involved grave loss. In such circumstances, the degree of limitation achieved in the stock of money must be questionable, except to the extent that borrowers were deterred by uncertainty instead of cost, or were unwilling to tie themselves to long-term commitments at high money interest rates.

It is thus arguable that – until very recently – no clear policy of monetary restriction existed; for a course which consists of controlling the amount of money largely through the *uncertainty* about prices and interest rates can hardly be regarded as a policy at all. Perhaps, if interest rates had gone to 35 per cent in 1974, we would now have useful evidence about the effects of the monetary weapon. But governments in the 1970s did not feel free to do anything so drastic; after all, they had their own urgent borrowing to provide for, they were conscious of the political sensitivity attached to the house mortgage rate, and the impossibility of isolating that rate from the general structure of interest rates, and they were sensitive to the employment implications of a large rise in interest rates.

One final feature of the decade of the 1970s deserves attention, namely the behaviour of saving. The ratio of personal saving to personal income, which was 6–7 per cent through the 1960s, started to rise after 1971, and attained 12 per cent in 1979 and 1980; even fluctuations produced by the recession seem likely to leave personal saving at a historically high level. The savings of companies and public corporations consist of their profits, rents and non-trading income, less dividends, interest payments, taxes, and additions to tax reserves and (for public corporations) dividend and interest reserves. These savings

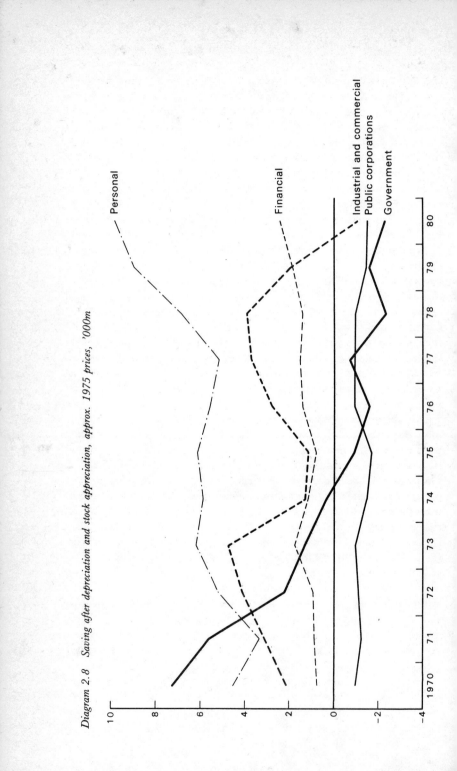

Diagram 2.8 Saving after depreciation and stock appreciation, approx. 1975 prices, '000m

also rose sharply over the decade, particularly in the case of financial companies and institutions. Government, on the other hand – as is implicit in the rise of the public sector borrowing requirement – moved from a position of net saving to one of considerable dissaving. But a considerable part of saving is notionally required to make good the depreciation of capital and to provide for the increasing cost of stocks. The course of saving *after* providing for depreciation and stock appreciation, roughly deflated, is shown in diagram 2.8.

This shows very clearly the rising surplus of the personal sector, the erosion of the real position of industrial and commercial companies, the continuing deficit of saving by public corporations, and the swing in the government position.

But the situation, as seen by savers, looks rather different. As every investor knows, it was very difficult during the 1970s to find any home for savings which did not involve a loss in real terms. In fact until 1980 new personal saving was inadequate to offset the erosion of the real value of existing assets, and no doubt the realisation of this prompted the increase in the personal savings ratio (with consequential effects on the level of demand). On the other hand, the company sector benefited from the effects of inflation on its monetary liabilities (which outweighed the loss on monetary assets of financial institutions). Government also benefited from inflation: it could have large financial deficits without increasing the real burden of debt. Inflation benefits borrowers at the expense of lenders, and diagram 2.8 shows the attempt of lenders to offset this disadvantage. While it would be unkind to suggest that these are facts which import hypocrisy into the attitude to inflation of governments, public corporations, and borrowing companies, it is certainly relevant that the financial interests of the individual citizen as lender (directly or through insurance companies and pension funds) run counter to those of government and of some corporate bodies, as borrowers.

Part 2
Constraints

3 What Determines Economic Performance?

The last chapter has told the sad story of the British economy in the 1970s. If we are to make the story of subsequent decades a happier one, we must first understand why performance in the 1970s was so poor. For this, we have to seek answers to two large questions. Why has the performance of almost all industrial countries deteriorated so much since 1974? And why has the development of the British economy been so much more sluggish than that of other industrial countries, not just in the 1970s but in the preceding hundred years as well?

The main approaches that economists employ to answer such questions were outlined in chapter 1. Those which are influential in contemporary Britain can be divided into the approaches concerned with attitudes or institutions and those that focus on the management of money or demand in the economy as a whole.

The significance of attitudes and institutions can hardly be in doubt. The question is, rather, how they relate to the structure and development of the economy. The modern economy is far more capital-intensive, skill-intensive and specialised than were the economies from which the models for most of our economic thought have been derived. This has caused markets to diverge more and more from the model of perfect competition, in which one product could be substituted for a multitude of similar products made by different producers and one worker could be substituted for a similar worker without cost or delay. The typical market is now less impersonal, more imperfect (in the economist's sense – no correlation is suggested between skill-intensity and moral imperfection) than this, and therefore more influenced by such determinants of personal or social behaviour as attitudes and institutions. Together, the economic structure and the social behaviour can have a big effect on economic performance.

These market imperfections are apt to cause difficulties for macroeconomic management. Numerous economists who concentrate on the management of the money supply or of global demand assume, implicitly, that the economy will perform well if they get the money supply or the global demand right: either markets are already perfect enough to allocate the money or the demand to a sufficiently productive use, or they will, after people have spent a period in the purgatory of unemployment and deindustrialisation, become nearly enough perfect for a satisfactory performance to be assured. Yet reflection about social behaviour in imperfect markets combines with experience to suggest that, in the contemporary economy, macroeconomic policy on its own will have no such fortunate result: that money tight enough to stop inflation will also stop the development of the economy; and that demand ample enough to allow full employment will also cause an only too ample inflation. The first chapter suggested that what 'most of the theorists . . . propound will work only if some inconvenient fact of the real world is first removed'. Imperfect markets are highly inconvenient facts that will undermine any scheme of macroeconomic management unless the markets can be made more perfect or behaviour adapted so as to be compatible with good performance in the imperfect markets.

This part of the book is about some of these inconvenient facts and their impact on economic performance. There is no shortage of such facts; the contemporary British economy seems to have specialised in their production. It is necessary to select; and those selected for consideration here are the ones thought most likely to shed light on the two main questions, about the poor performance of the industrial countries since 1974 and about the particularly poor performance of Britain, not only in that period but also in the century before it.

The first set of inconvenient facts concern the impact of bargaining power on pay and prices. Markets for both labour and products are imperfect, and are influenced by the behaviour of workers, managers, unions and firms. Their interaction, it will be argued in the next chapter, distorts pay and price formation in such a way as to generate inflation and squeeze the profits on which the development of the economy and the creation of new employment depend. It is possible that much of the 'stagflation' in industrial countries since 1974 can be explained by this. It is not likely that sin originated in that year, or even that human nature abruptly changed for the worse. But it is possible that the forces making for stability of many labour and product markets had been undermined by the growth of capital-intensity and specialisation that accompanied the growth of the industrial economies in the previous quarter of a century; and the oil price shock of 1973–74 could then have jolted such unstable markets into a spiral of strong pay push and somewhat weaker price push.

While this may account for at least some of the difficulties since 1974, it is not likely to explain the slow growth of the British economy in the previous century or the declining performance since the early 1960s – although the squeeze on profits has been a major additional constraint on development in the recent period. In order to throw light on the secular stagnation of the British economy compared with others, chapters 5 and 6 then consider the costs of industrial development and the inhibitions against incurring them. Here again, while economic structure or social behaviour may each separately be significant for economic performance, together they appear to have a powerful explanatory force, whether we examine the organisation of production within the firm, the influence of education, training and differentials on the acquiring of skills, the advance of technology through research, development and diffusion, or investment and the shift from older to newer lines of production. Chapter 7 considers how the picture is further developed when we take account of Britain's place in the international economy.

Thus the next four chapters concern various aspects of the interaction between economic structure, imperfect markets and social behaviour; and they suggest that these may explain many of the constraints on economic performance that we are seeking to understand. We then proceed, in Part Three, to consider some consequences for theory and the practical implications for British policy in the coming years.

4 Pay, Prices, Profits and the Impact of Bargaining Power

Over the eight years to the beginning of 1981, prices multiplied by 3.1 and income from employment by about 3.6; a sustained inflation, as chapter 2 has shown, without parallel in British history. The most common explanations are that people became greedier and trade unions stronger or that governments were lax in their management of money or demand. But the causes and effects of inflation will not be understood if we consider only people's behaviour or governments' macroeconomic management and ignore the consequences of the changing structure of the economy for producers' bargaining power.

PAY

In the 1930s, the theory of markets which are not perfect was developed in different ways by Edward Chamberlin and Joan Robinson.[1] But the subsequent focus of interest has been on the behaviour of firms – their ability to administer, or 'make', the prices of their products, instead of taking them from the market, and the peculiarities of their behaviour when faced by a small number of competitors. For a long time, the implications for wages were also seen to relate to the superior power of employers, and so to their ability to fix wages. This approach goes back beyond Marx to Adam Smith, who observed that the masters could force the workmen

'into a compliance with their terms ... In all such disputes the masters can hold out much longer. A landlord, a farmer, a master manufacturer, or merchant, though they did not employ a single workman, could generally live a year or two upon the stocks which they have already acquired. Many workmen could not subsist a week, few could subsist a month, and scarce any a year without employment. In the long run the workman may be as necessary to his master as his master is to him; but the necessity is not so immediate'.[2]

---

[1] Edward Chamberlin, *Theory of Monopolistic Competition*, (Harvard University Press, 1933); and Joan Robinson, *The Economics of Imperfect Competition*, (Macmillan, London, 1933).
[2] Adam Smith, *The Wealth of Nations*, ch. VIII.

Firms in the modern economy do indeed sell most of their products into imperfect markets; and the employer still has substantial sources of bargaining strength in his relations with employees. But the structure of this economy has given many employees a new source of power in bargaining with employers, quite apart from any changes in institutions or behaviour. No diagnosis of the causes of inflation can be useful unless it takes account of the economic or technological causes of this change in the balance of bargaining power.

The balance of bargaining power

The bargaining power of a group of workers in relation to the firm in which they work is represented by the cost to the firm if they withdraw their labour, set against the cost to themselves if they forego their pay. The cost to the strikers is not, of course, to be evaluated only by counting up the pay they lose; one has to consider, as Adam Smith did, the hardship they incur as a result of its loss. Subsistence for a week or a month is not so difficult as it was in Adam Smith's day. There are supplementary benefits for families, strike pay from unions, savings and other assets, loans from friends and relations: in short, a whole range of resources that stem from greater prosperity and from the workings of the welfare state.

These resources have undoubtedly played a significant part in shifting the balance of industrial power. Many strikers can realistically reckon that if the reduction of their incomes during the strike can be re-couped from higher pay after a settlement, they will have gained as a result of their action without enduring too much hardship meanwhile. But the emphasis that has been placed on the resources available to strikers, and on those derived from the welfare state in particular, has distracted attention from the more important change in the balance of bargaining power: the increase in the cost to the firm if labour is withdrawn. For it is this that has done most to improve the employee's prospects of getting more money as a result of a strike, and hence of regarding any inconvenience or hardship that he and his family may suffer as worthwhile.

Manufacturing production has, in the last 30 years, become much more capital-intensive. The capital costs of a factory, which are incurred whether it is working or idle, have risen correspondingly, giving the firm a strong motive to keep the factory at work. Other fixed costs which are met when a factory is idle, such as the pay of managerial, administrative, sales and a variety of specialist staff, have likewise risen in line with the growing complexity of industry. Yet the growth of these fixed costs may by itself be less important than the interdependence of the different aspects of a modern production process. Like the movement of a complicated clock, the failure of one small part to work can bring the whole to a stop. In assembly line production, the paint-shop at the end of vehicle assembly became a notorious example: one or two dozen people who work in the paint shop can, if they strike, bring the whole factory employing several thousand workers to a halt. Production worth several hundred or even thousands of times the strikers' pay can thus be prevented. If the firm continues to give the other workers their pay, it is bearing the whole of this cost, as well as the fixed costs already mentioned, during the period of the strike; if it ceases to pay any of the workers, that part of the cost is borne by them, and by the society as a whole in terms of lost taxes and increased social security benefits. But whatever proportion of the cost can be shifted from the firm to non-striking workers and to society as a whole, the cost to the firm as such is likely to remain grossly disproportionate to the cost incurred by the strikers and still more disproportionate to the cost of any concessions that may be sufficient to get them back to work.

Both Adam Smith and Marx emphasised the importance of the division of labour. But neither foresaw how this would be carried to a point where it could reverse the balance of bargaining power. Nor is the paint shop in vehicle assembly an atypical example. There are many different groups who can bring assembly line production to a halt; and this type of production has become normal for a whole range of consumer durables and standard items of capital equipment. Even if the assembly line has passed its zenith, it will for years ahead remain one of the principal methods of industrial production. Nor is it unusual in the degree to which it creates interdependence among the different groups of workers in an industrial establishment. Process industries such as chemicals, oil refining, glass, paper, iron and steel, cement and much food manufacture are just as dependent on continuous working by those who keep the process going, and so are utilities such as electricity, gas and water, as well as production and distribution chains for perishable products. That part of the economy which is not concerned with manufacturing or with primary industry but with services and administration, which provide the majority of jobs, has also experienced growing capital-intensity and has become increasingly vulnerable to major cost and disruption through selective strikes, for instance in computer installations. Most of this chapter relates directly to industry, and in particular to manufacturing industry, because this is the sector of the British economy which seems most to need improvement in its performance. But many of the references can equally be applied to service sectors, including government departments and other public bodies. We further consider the special problems of public sector pay in chapter 9.

In a large part of industry, then, the tremendous development of production since the war has increased the proportion of fixed costs and the interdependence of numerous groups of workers to the point where the prospect of a strike by one of these groups confronts the firm with an acute dilemma. If the managers resist and those workers strike, the firm incurs costs, including capital costs, the pay of many who are not on strike and a loss of sales (that may become a permanent loss of market share), which may be large in relation to the resources with which the firm can finance them. If this happens too often, the firm can be driven to bankruptcy. The costs are, in any case, likely to be disproportionate to the cost of meeting whatever demands the strikers may make, so that it seems logical to meet their demands – particularly if a similar process is likely to be raising costs among the firm's competitors, so that less ground would be lost through resulting price increases, which the competitors will also have to apply, than by a period of absence from the market during a strike. Yet if this logic is used in a series of demands and concessions, it may eventually become impossible to pass on all the higher costs in higher prices, because of resistance from anti-inflationary policies or competition from firms whose workers have exploited their bargaining power less, including in particular foreign competitors. The firm then loses sales or profits or both, goes into a decline and, again, eventually collapses.

In some well-known cases and many less well-known, this is not a caricature but what has actually happened. More often, workers have made less extreme use of their potential bargaining power. It is, after all, easy enough to see that most employees will be worse off if the firm goes bankrupt; nor is it excessively hard to understand that everybody can be better off if the firm prospers and increases the value added which is the source of pay. All that is needed, evidently, is for each employee to remember all the time that all can benefit if all work continuously and co-operate in improving methods of production, without quarrelling over changes in work patterns or the distribution of the fruits. Nor is this a caricature, but what has actually happened in many firms in Japan, enabling the employees' real incomes to rise for long periods by as much as 10 per cent a year, or about four times as fast as in Britain. But the foregoing analysis of the interdependence and fixed-cost-intensity of modern industrial structure has shown that this must be a function of institutions and behaviour, not of a hidden hand which combines the self-interest of each in the general interest of all. The self-interest of each is to use his bargaining power to enlarge his share of available resources and to reduce any inconvenience he may suffer from the way in which production is organised; and for many groups in a modern industry this bargaining power is, as we have seen, very great. It is, perhaps, not so easy in a country whose industrial revolution was generated by individuals giving free rein to their acquisitive instincts, and where economic thought and policy were founded on the assumption that this would automatically result in the general good, for people to refrain from using a bargaining power that will bring them immediate and tangible gains, in the interests of the longer-term benefits of co-operative effort. It is at least understandable if the British, with this background, take more convincing than some other people that these benefits will materialise and that each will get a share of them that he regards as reasonably fair. To the extent that a worker is not convinced of this he may be inclined to use his bargaining power to achieve a short-term gain – or at least to avoid a short-term loss through failure to keep up with a general rate of increase of pay. If the future benefit of co-operative behaviour carries no conviction at all among a number of the employees of a firm, the bargaining power may be exploited until the firm is at the precipice of bankruptcy or even over it. More likely there will be some degree of conviction, so that bargaining power is pressed only to the point where a firm is making less profit, selling fewer and dearer products, and improving its production methods less rapidly than some of its main competitors among whom bargaining power is used in a way that keeps the market regularly supplied and leaves more room for profit, investment and development; and these competitors pull steadily ahead, earning higher incomes, making better products and selling more of them, until they have gained a decisive advantage.

This is not intended to be a complete explanation of the loss of competitiveness in British industry or of the decline in British real incomes relative to those of other industrial countries. But it is put forward as one element in a diagnosis; and when we come to consider remedies we will bear in mind that the problem has been caused less by changes in social arrangements and attitudes than by a profound technological change that has created interdependence among large numbers of producers and hence greatly increased the need for co-operation among them. Individualistic behaviour which may not be regarded as bad in itself, and might have been admirable in the context of earlier technologies, has become incompatible with the successful application of the mainstream contemporary technologies. It is not so much that British attitudes and institutions have changed and need to be restored to a state of bygone virtue, as that technologies have changed and the attitudes and institutions need to adapt.

So far we have considered the relative costs of a strike to the strikers and to the firm, and the implications which changes in this relationship may have for the firm's performance. But if in many cases the costs to the firm have become disproportionate to the private costs to the striker, the costs to the society as a whole have become still more disproportionate. For not only does the society pay some of the costs of the strike itself, in benefits paid to strikers' families and tax on their earnings foregone; but the interdependence and fixed-cost-intensity that have changed the balance of costs within the firm have also changed the structure of the economy as a whole, so that costs are incurred elsewhere in the economy as a result of the suspension of production in the firm where the strike takes place. This may be because that firm makes components which are required in making some other firms' products; or the strikers' product may be widely needed by industry as well as by consumers, for example coal, electricity or gas; or the strikers may be able to stop a means of transport such as rail, lorries, shipping or airlines; or they may provide a general service such as customs clearance. In each case the withdrawal of these goods or services can impose costs on the economy and society far beyond the costs incurred by the organisation in which the strikers work, and *pro tanto* beyond the costs to the strikers. Thousands or even millions of other people may have to suspend their work, and behind them will lie fixed costs in line with the capital-intensity and complexity of the economy and society as a whole.

After a major strike by miners, electricity workers, lorry drivers, merchant seamen, dockers, air traffic controllers, steelworkers or engineering workers, to name some of those that have had the greatest impact on the British economy in recent years, estimates appear in the press that the cost to the country has been so many tens, hundreds or even billions of pounds. Any such calculation must contain a large element of judgement, even if it is confined to the costs to the firms in which the strikes take place. A firm's expenditure during the strike will be easy enough to measure. But how much of that contributes to future production despite the strike? How are we to account for the cost of capital that has been reinvested by the firm? How much of the production lost during the strike can be made up after it? What is the extra cost of doing so? What is the value of the market share that has been temporarily or permanently lost? What effect will a reduction of profits have on the firm's future development? How far will productivity suffer or prices rise in the future because workers follow the example of strikers who have made money as the result of a strike, or because managers accept employees' demands for higher pay or immobility regarding work practices in order to keep production going? Having started in the realm of accountancy, the answers to these questions have moved through those of econometrics and qualitative economics to that of a broad judgement of industrial and human affairs. But figures produced by the accountants and in the more sober reaches of econometrics could almost certainly be large; and the effects to which numbers can less readily be attached may not be less significant. The effects on the economy as a whole are yet harder to evaluate, for similar questions must be asked about all the other firms whose production is impeded or stopped as a result of the strike, as well as the inconvenience or hardship suffered by consumers. Given the number of firms and consumers who can be affected, the economic and social costs must sometimes be enormous. Yet this remains no more than unquantified judgement, because economists have not made serious attempts to measure the costs.

Given the importance of strikes in the contemporary economy, this seems to be a strange omission, and it is worth while to consider some possible reasons for it. Economists are generally ill at ease when confronted by the question of bargaining power. Many are so immersed in macroeconomic models that they have no time to study how the economy's constituent parts behave, even if inability to understand that behaviour has deprived the models of much of their usefulness. Some of those who recognise the importance of bargaining power regard its study as part of the province of sociologists, although such power is central to the performance of the contemporary economy and neither its causes nor its effects can be understood without an economic framework. Others deny the significance of bargaining power on the grounds that the price of labour is determined by impersonal market forces, whose decree no resistance on the part of workers can do more than delay. This latter has become a politically important belief, because it underlies the reliance on control of the money supply to bring the labour markets and hence pay, prices and profits into a productive equilibrium. The price that the market is usually said to assign to labour is the marginal worker's product: that is, the additional output that the firm can produce when that worker is employed or, conversely, the output it will lose if the firm dispenses with his work. But the concept of marginal product is hard to apply in the interdependent production unit in which each of a number of groups of employees must continue to work if production is to proceed at all. Since any one of those groups can stop the production, the marginal product of each of them, in the sense of the difference between production when they work and production when they do not, is equal to the whole of that unit's output. Since this is true of a number of groups in many of the typical plants of the contemporary economy, their marginal product can clearly not be the basis for determining their pay. Marginal analysis is not much use when the margin covers the whole page. Marginalists may answer that it should be possible to replace a recalcitrant group by other workers from a labour market in which the norms are set by activities in which diminishing returns do apply, even if such replacement, or a change of behaviour due to its possibility, may take a long time. But the marginalists cannot sustain their argument without that detailed analysis of the factors that influence the exercise of bargaining power, which economists are so reluctant to undertake.

Nor are economists likely to be encouraged to analyse bargaining power by any of the established interests. Leaders of trade unions may fear that research or writing on the subject will lead to the denunciation of over-mighty subjects and to calls for new legal curbs or statutory incomes policy or both; or alternatively that the autonomy of shop floor groups will be stressed, undermining what authority and credibility the unions' central leadership may have. It does not require much knowledge of industrial relations in Britain to understand that bargaining power is distributed among a multitude of groups in hundreds of thousands of establishments up and down the country, subject to an influence from their union headquarters which ranges from strong to very slight. For all its heterogeneous distribution, however, the power which the shop floor groups and the union leaders wield between them is, for the reasons given, great; and a natural prudery warns most people against too open an admission of such power. If others realise that you have it, this may bring an advantage in helping you to get your way; and it was noticeable, during the strikes by civil servants' unions in the winter of 1980–81, that the leaders of those unions, which are usually regarded as lacking muscle (i.e. the power to impose costs on their organisations or the economy), were tempted to point out how much they could inconvenience the citizen. But at the same time there is the fear that the strike and the union will become unpopular and that demands for control of unions will strengthen, if the power to impose costs on others is made too explicit.

Conversely many industrialists, although apt enough to complain in a general way about trade unions, are not so keen on discussion about the economics of bargaining power because it would expose the weakness of their position. Why publicise the costs that a strike can cause the firm, when that may incite some workers who may still be unaware of the extent of their bargaining power to use it against the company? For those who support the prevailing monetarist doctrine, moreover, there is the hope that monetary policy will weaken the bargaining power of unions enough to solve the industrialists' problem, so that there is no need to go into the vexatious details.

Even those who do not represent these interests tend to share the views, and hence the inhibitions, of one or other 'side' of industry, or to recoil from probing too deeply into such a sore point in Britain's uneasy class relationships. Many readers will doubtless feel that our analysis of constraints has started off on the wrong foot by stressing this most inconvenient of facts, which is better kept out of sight. But we cannot agree that either of the main industrial interests, let alone the society's general interest, can benefit from a refusal to analyse such a crucial fact in our economy, however inconvenient it may be. For without an adequate understanding of the fact of bargaining power, economists and politicians will fail to penetrate the principal cause of stagflation and will therefore continue to rely on nostrums that are unable to cure the disease.

Pay push, stagflation and the difficult search for a cure

We have seen that the structure of modern production gives many workers a great deal of power to push up their pay, and thus to increase their firm's prices or reduce its profits or both. Aggregated to the economy as a whole, the increase of prices becomes inflation; the reduction of profits, through the consequent decline of investment, becomes stagnation; and a combination of the two, which since the 1970s has become normal for the industrial countries, is the condition which has earned the ugly name of stagflation. The proportion in which the rise of prices and the squeeze on investment are combined determines the character of the stagflation, or more precisely the rates of inflation and of unemployment or growth; and this proportion depends on the behaviour of prices, which will shortly be examined. But first, it seems useful to consider some of the ways in which economists and politicians have hoped to deal with pay push; for the notion that there is some trend in the economy or some macroeconomic policy that is likely to solve the problem is surprisingly widespread, and distracts attention from the need to understand the nature of the markets in which both pay and prices are determined.

One way of escape from the constraint of pay push would be a trend in technology that reduced the workers' bargaining power. The technologies which have given such a high gearing to this power are, as has been shown, widely used in those parts of industry that have led the postwar development of the industrial countries. Now that this phase of development seems to have run out of steam, will technology take another turn, towards less capital-intensive, less interdependent forms of production, and consequently towards a reduction of the workers' power?

There may well be scope for designing less interdependent forms of production, if technologists are asked to do this in order to reduce the monopoly power which interdependence gives to some groups of workers. It may cost more to incorporate 'alternative pathways'[3] which will enable the system to operate if one pathway is blocked, but managements may judge the extra expense worthwhile. Workers may on the other hand react by trying to block all the alternative pathways. But what if microelectronic technology decentralises production so much that the workers' organisation cannot keep up? And will the microprocessor, which offers such a cheap means of data processing and of speedy and accurate process control, reduce the capital-intensity of industry which is the other technological source of workers' power?

While microelectronics will certainly change the face of industry during the rest of this century, it is far from certain that it will weaken interdependence and still less probable that it will reduce capital-intensity. It seems just as likely to continue along the path of other advances in technology and increase both. The assembly line and the process industry will anyway remain important throughout this period, even if the number of people on the assembly line is eventually reduced to the order of magnitude that is now to be found in the process plants. The numbers may be less, but the interdependence and ratio of capital to labour costs are more. This is especially true for Britain, where technology and capital-intensity have fallen behind the levels of competing countries, which have gained a corresponding advantage in their standards of living. Quite apart from the eventual effect of microelectronics, the British people are not likely to forego willingly the increase in their living standards that progress towards the higher level of technology can bring. Thus neither an unwinding of interdependence nor a reduction of our already inadequate capital equipment is likely to remove the technological basis of workers' disproportionate bargaining power.

If new technology will not solve the problem for us, most economists are only too ready to rely on the familiar remedies of macroeconomic policy. One idea which may once have sounded plausible but now seems self-indulgent is that expansion of global demand to secure and maintain full employment will be sufficient, because it will lead to a growth of production and hence of real incomes which will satisfy people's demands, so that they cease to push for inflationary increases of pay. It has become evident, however, that extra demand leads to

---

[3] Dr. Stephen Bragg, presidential address to the engineering section of the British Association, reported in the *Financial Times*, 2 September 1981. One such alternative pathway is to carry high stocks, which adds greatly to the expenses of some British firms.

higher prices as well as higher production; and examination of the nature of bargaining power within the firm and the economy shows why this is so, and why the impact on prices may be greater than that on production.

The new demand will improve the market position of many firms. They will sell more and their profits will increase. As the market for their products tightens, they may take the opportunity to raise their prices; but whether they do or not, their employees will be well placed to press for higher pay. With profits rising, there will be resources from which pay increases can be financed; in strong markets, the firms will be able to pass on at least part of the pay increases in higher prices; and those groups of workers who already have disproportionate bargaining power will find it yet further enhanced because the firms both have greater capacity to pay and also dare not lose production, and thus forfeit market share, perhaps permanently, to their competitors.

Given the opportunity and the bargaining power, some groups will push for pay rises beyond the growth of productivity. They may feel that they fell behind in a previous wage round, either because others secured increases beyond the growth of productivity or because the others' productivity rose, through no special effort or merit on those others' part, particularly fast; they will want to recover any increases in the cost of living; they may just feel a strong desire for more. There will also be motives of a less financial kind. They may be annoyed with their employers; the leaders of the group may want to establish their position by making a successful or even a spectacular bargain; some may hold an ideological view of relations with employers that justifies the use of muscle regardless of its effect on the firm, which is the most accessible part of the capitalist system; many will feel, without recourse to formal ideology, that if you do not get the better of the employers, they will get the better of you. Even in the (most improbable) absence of any of these motives, it will be difficult for workers to estimate the underlying growth of productivity within which the growth of pay should clearly be confined. The underlying growth of labour productivity is hard enough to estimate, even for economists who spend a lifetime trying to measure it. For the employees and their representatives, it will be a yet more elusive concept.

Since the bargaining power of some groups is so great, it is not easy to set a logical limit to the rises they can secure. Of course most people are not trying to reach logical limits, nor are they ideological, or even excessively greedy. But a fair number of rises will be obtained which are substantially above the growth of productivity, however it is measured; and in firms or sectors where productivity growth is above the average for the economy, the discrepancy with that average will be that much greater. Those who got less will then want to catch up, and will become increasingly annoyed if they do not. This annoyance is fed when directors and senior managers award themselves generous pay increases and fringe benefits at times when they are asking for restraint from others. Japanese industrialists set a better example.

How far can the different groups which we are discussing make their wishes effective? Some will lack the power to do so. But in the major industries in which the groups with most bargaining power are located, the other workers also have substantial power, if only because of the fixed costs that the firm must continue to pay even if they are all on strike. So in these industries, rises obtained at first by a minority will in due course become a going rate that is obtained by all; and the longer this process takes, the more production will be disrupted by disgruntled workers who have fallen behind.

As the pay rates in these industries increase, the firms will as far as possible raise their prices in order to maintain profitability, without which they cannot develop or even survive. In this way the additional money injected into the economy in the course of expanding demand will have stimulated higher prices as well as, or perhaps even instead of, higher production (see p. 8). Those who work in sectors of the economy where the workers have less power to impose costs on firms or society will have to pay the higher prices and will do what they can to ensure that their pay catches up. With full employment and tight labour markets, and with the support of Wages Councils and a variety of political and social pressures, most of them will do so. But by then some of the more powerful groups will be ready to set the process going again.

As it became increasingly clear, through the 1950s and 1960s, that pay push was associated with full employment, proposals for incomes policy were developed to counter this push directly and thus make full employment compatible with stability of pay and prices. If the use of bargaining power could be controlled so as to keep pay rises down to the rate of growth of productivity, inflation would be prevented and all would be better off. The incomes policies were, however, introduced by successive governments to meet urgent macroeconomic needs, and thus based on decisions taken in a hurry with varying degrees of support from varying numbers of union leaders. But bargaining power is distributed very widely through the economy, in factories, offices and other establishments and in small groups within those establishments, so that the push from these groups has to be controlled as well as that from the leaderships of several score unions. It is difficult enough to secure compliance with pay controls on the part of union leaders if they do not want to be controlled. The power of some of them to impose costs on the economy and society is, as we have seen, great; and governments cannot lightly take a risk that such costs will be incurred, or t⊦ ⋅ᵗ the public will hold them responsible for the costs if a major strike continues for any length of time. But this problem is simplicity itself compared with that of securing compliance on the part of the multitude of groups in establishments throughout the country. For although union leaders have a good deal of influence over them when calling them out on strike, in most British unions they have much less power to prevent the groups from taking action themselves. Thus control over the groups' pay push through the union leaders is not usually effective. Yet direct control over them by statute is equally insecure, given the costs they can impose on their firms if they do not co-operate in production, and the complications in the detail of pay which make statutory enforcement difficult if neither workers nor firms wish to comply with it. Thus the dispersal of power and the complexity of pay are impediments to the effectiveness of incomes policy which are particularly telling when the policy has been initiated by decisions rushed through in London, without thorough preparation in the country as a whole.

It is not surprising, then, that three major episodes of incomes policy, starting in 1964, 1972 and 1975, each succumbed after two or three years to the pressures inherent in this structure of bargaining power. The policy launched by George Brown in 1964 gradually melted away after a freeze in the second half of 1966. The episode which Edward Heath initiated ended spectacularly with the miners' strike leading to the change of government just after the decision by the Organisation of Petroleum Exporting Countries (OPEC) to quadruple the price of oil in November 1973. This cost push from oil then demonstrated the instability of almost all the industrial countries' systems of pay and price formation, which converted the energy price increase of a few percentage points on the cost of living into a pay-price spiral at rates ranging, according to the country, from about 10 per cent to 30 per cent a year. Only in Japan was the inflation brought down from a rate of over 20 per cent to single figures within a year and kept there. In Germany inflation was kept within single figures, although even the Germans with their anti-inflationary institutions and attitudes could not hold it down to its earlier levels, and could not even approach those levels without policies restrictive enough to cause high unemployment and slow growth. Most of the other industrial countries had with much difficulty reduced their rates to figures around 10 per cent a year by 1979, when the sudden push from the oil price again upset the unstable equilibrium in their pay and price systems. For the experience of the 1970s has shown that pay push is not just a product of British arrangements for industrial relations. Most other countries find the strength of workers' bargaining power hard to countervail, even if many of them find it less hard than the British.

The intrusion of the first oil price thrust, which was a bigger exogenous shock than had been experienced for at least two decades, into the then overheated full employment economies of the industrial countries exacerbated and accelerated the process of high pay demands by powerful groups, followed by a push by others for equivalent rises at a going rate, which had been developing in the previous period. Those who pressed for increases two or three times as high as the previous conventional limits showed that those limits were indeed conventional, in that market forces did not stand in the way of rises of, in Britain, up to 30 per cent or more. It was probably inevitable that the imbalance of bargaining power would eventually be demonstrated in this way, when the unstable equilibrium was given a sharp enough jolt. Having been demonstrated, the danger is greatly enhanced that not only exogenous cost push but also expansion of demand will tend to generate more inflation than hitherto. There are now precedents for a malign distribution of additional money in the economy between a rapid rise in prices and only a small rise in production; and because of the structure of bargaining power, the proportions of this distribution are set by convention rather than imposed by an impersonal market force.

The Labour Government that replaced that of Mr. Heath early in 1974 at first pursued a macroeconomic policy which accommodated the pay-price spiral in order to maintain employment, until it became clear in 1975 that the rate of inflation, already well over 20 per cent, was still rising fast. Reckoning that incomes policy would counteract the pay push with much less damage to employment and production than reliance on deflation alone, the government fixed the limit to pay rises at £6 a week, with the backing of the most powerful union leaders and wide support among the public. The simplicity and widespread support for this measure made it remarkably effective; and before the end of the second year, through which the policy was prolonged if in a somewhat less simple form, inflation had fallen from the rate of nearly 30 per cent down into single figures. But in the third year the usual strains appeared. The policy was opposed by a number of union leaders and by many groups on the shop floor, and its collapse was again associated with the loss of an election, this time to a government committed to a monetarist remedy for inflation.

The question of how far the monetary and fiscal policies of this monetarist Government differ from those of the preceding Government has been considered in chapter 2. Here we are concerned with the monetarists' belief that inflation will be conquered by control of the money supply: that if inflation is too high at the start (and the Government inherited a rate of inflation a little over 10 per cent), a restrictive monetary policy will be the only efficient way to bring the inflation down. However strong the bargaining power of workers and their organisations may be, the monetarist argument has been that it can do no more than delay any necessary reduction of their real pay to its market level, which is equal to the marginal productivity (in so far as that can be measured), because those workers who try to maintain it above that level will price themselves out of work. The money wages will then rise only in line with productivity, once unions realise that the money supply will rise no faster, and thus pitch their demands in the light of that expectation. A less sophisticated form of the argument is that union power will be brought into line by unemployment, so that the stronger the union power, the sterner deflation will have to be.

Three years after this Government came to power, inflation was little lower than at the outset. The price of oil in 1979–80 did not help; but the delay in reducing inflation, despite the severity of the deflation shown by the sharp falls of production, investment and employment, indicates the presence in the economy of inconvenient facts of which the monetarists have not taken sufficient account.

Just as firms' sales and profits increase when there is a rise in general demand, so they fall when demand is deflated. In perfect markets, not only prices but also pay would quickly fall too, so that profits would rise again and investment and economic development continue. Even in imperfect markets, with perfect understanding by firms and workers of their common interest in development and perfect co-operation between them, pay would be reduced to leave room for investment from which all would benefit. But in the imperfect markets that prevail in the modern economy, profits fall while pay does not. On the contrary, the imbalance of bargaining power remains and the workers continue to obtain increases of pay, squeezing profits still further. It is true that overtime payments fall and the rate of basic pay increases declines, because the firms have less capacity to finance them. When a firm is making losses that endanger its existence, most employees will refrain from pressing for rises that would push it over the edge, particularly when the deflation has made new jobs hard to find; and the high unemployment will reduce the bargaining power of many other workers who are not securely placed. But none of this prevents the pressure of the deflation from squeezing profits rather than pay. The bargaining power of most workers, let alone those in the more powerful positions, is still strong enough to ensure that; and, as we shall see later, the imperfection of many product markets gives less scope for price rises in these circumstances than the imperfection of labour markets gives for increases of pay. It follows that the first impact of the deflation is on profits, investment and economic development rather than on pay.

The lack of new investment implies a lack of new workplaces for those who are entering the labour market from school, redundancy or bankrupt firms. Thus unemployment rises – not only because the workers getting pay rises are pricing themselves out of their own jobs but because their rises combined with the deflation are squeezing the profits which should generate the investment to provide jobs for others. It can be said that indirectly, by obtaining pay rises instead of accepting pay cuts which would maintain profits despite the deflation, these workers are pricing other people out of jobs. But it can equally be said that it is the deflationary policy which is depriving people of jobs and the economy of development, *if* there is a policy that could bring down inflation without causing these deprivations.

Where there is scope for higher productivity with existing equipment, the push for higher pay in firms making low profits may bring about the improvement in productivity, because managers and workers will realise that this is the only way in which the higher pay can be financed. But so long as deflation is inhibiting the creation of new jobs elsewhere, the benefit of this goes only to the workers concerned, at the expense of those who are consequently unemployed (because the firm has reduced the number of employees through normal wastage or redundancy) and without net gain for the economy as a whole. Despite the hardship this creates meanwhile, it does provide scope for the future growth of the economy, provided that the new jobs are eventually created. But we have to ask whether the new jobs will indeed be created as a result of the policy, and if so, whether there is a way to bring down inflation and improve productivity without inducing so much unemployment and so little investment for several years.

Higher pay with lower numbers employed was also the result of the attempt to contain public sector pay by cash limits. In the first year of the present Government, departments were able to finance pay increases of over 20 per cent, despite the much lower increase of their cash limits, by refraining from recruiting new staff and by cutting capital expenditure – thus again shifting the impact of the monetary restriction to employment and investment instead of pay. How far this resulted in higher productivity in the public sector is another question; but it certainly demonstrated again the power of employees to deflect the impact of general monetary or financial measures from the intended target of their pay and on to employment and investment instead.

The force of the impact on profits and employment and the

stubbornness of pay may have surprised many monetarists. If so, they had probably underestimated the strength of workers' bargaining power, believing it to be based more on irrational behaviour in markets near enough to the perfect model than on behaviour that is fairly rational in imperfect markets from the perspective of the individual's or the group's interest, though not in the collective interest of the society as a whole. But many monetarists did warn that the medicine would be painful: the distortions caused by years of inflation and incomes policy would take time to remove. Once the proper control of money had induced in unions the expectation of domestic price stability, however, their demands should be trimmed to what stable prices could accommodate, i.e. roughly the growth of productivity; and in so far as they still pressed for more and got it, workers would price themselves out of jobs again until unemployment brought them back into line.

Strangely enough in adherents to a doctrine that lays so much stress on free response to market forces, this implicitly assumes collective restraint on the part of workers and their organisations. For the dispersal of bargaining power among many groups, whether formal or informal, will remain. Market forces will enable those with greater power to get rises beyond the growth of productivity, for any of the various reasons already given. Others must then either accept a reduction in their real incomes because the leaders in pay push have increased their share of the available money more than they have increased their share in production, or in turn use their bargaining power to catch up. Again for the reasons given, this bargaining power will remain substantial for many workers, so that they can eat into any profits their firms may be earning and induce higher prices in their products where these are sold into strong or imperfect markets.

Because the structure of production will still place so many workers in labour markets in which they have this power, market forces will encourage its use as soon as enough firms begin to return to adequate profitability. If, therefore, the deflationary policy brings inflation down to a level regarded as acceptable, and the policy-makers relax it so as to restore profits and industrial investment, pay push will begin to eat into the profits again and to press prices upwards whenever the markets for the products are strong enough to allow it. This does not require a return to full employment, although if full employment were ever reached within this policy context it would spread the pay push more rapidly throughout the economy. Only a return to normal profitability in large parts of industry is required to start up the cycle of pay push again.

Monetarists are right to point out that the whole economy and society would benefit if all workers refrained from using their power in this way, and instead took the officially planned rate of growth of the money supply (if indeed one could believe in such a figure) as the criterion for their pay demands. But they are wrong to suppose that workers accepting this view can discipline those who do not. Those who stick to the official criterion can be sure that others will exceed it because bargaining power is so widely held and many of those who hold it will, for the variety of reasons given, use it to force up their pay. At best a minority, but very likely before long the majority, will have raised their incomes at the expense of those who exercised restraint (or in terms of the monetarists' concept, will have pre-empted a share of the limited money supply that leaves too little for those exercising restraint even to maintain their real incomes, let alone increase them in line with their own contribution to higher productivity). Thus it is not expectations about the rate of growth of the money supply that are relevant to each of the thousands of groups with bargaining power, but expectations about the rate of increase of pay of the other such groups. Restraint which causes you to fall behind the average rate of increase becomes a quixotic act, quickly punished by a drop in living standards, and contributing little to the monetarists' worthy aim of keeping inflation down and allowing the economy to develop, because the fate of that is determined by the average.

If all the bargaining power were controlled by one well disciplined trade union group, or if the standard for the use of bargaining power were set by one powerful group which the others follow, it should be possible to persuade that group that its own members will benefit, along with the rest of society, if the average pay rise is confined to the average growth of productivity. The national association of Swedish trade unions (the LO) for a considerable period kept the bargaining power of the majority of trade unionists in Sweden under some such control, and Germany's biggest union, the IG Metall, has played an effective role as a responsible oligopolistic price leader in the German labour market, setting a standard for each wage round, not too far above the likely growth in the economy, which is not only enforced on its own members but also followed by the other unions. But in Britain workers' power is not arranged in the form of a monopoly or oligopoly. It is distributed among thousands of groups, large and small, each of which has to do the best it can in its own imperfect market. The monetarist medicine might work if the markets were either much less or much more imperfect. But ironically, given the imperfections that are embedded in the structure of labour markets in the modern economy, the market forces that the monetarists invoke, unrestrained by anything except a general monetary control, include the power to press to obtain rises in pay to the point where profits and hence investment remain low, jobs for school-leavers and the unemployed fail to be created and the economy fails to develop. This is likely to apply not only while inflation is being reduced but also when it is low and is being kept low by monetary policy. The result of holding down inflation by monetary control without any other policy to counter the push from pay will therefore be permanent deflation, stagnation and high unemployment; and this is due not to a freak of contemporary behaviour but to free competition among many groups in a labour market whose structure gives each of them decisive bargaining power.

Even if this dismal prospect does not form part of the monetarists' expectations, there has been no lack of proposals to redress the balance of bargaining power, and the present government is not the first to wish to put some of them into effect. One aim of industrial relations legislation has been to prevent strikers from picketing in order to discourage work at other establishments not directly involved in the dispute. In some other countries workers providing certain essential services are not allowed to strike. Such measures can narrow the area in which strikers inflict economic or social costs. But they do little to redress the balance of power where its effects are crucial to industrial development: in the industrial establishment itself.

Another element in the balance of bargaining power which has attracted attention is the welfare benefits obtained by strikers and their families. If these were reduced or removed, some strikes would certainly be discouraged. But the effect on those with the stronger bargaining power would not be great. They usually belong to unions which can afford significant strike pay (and which would be able to increase subscriptions and build up their funds if the welfare benefits were reduced); but more important, the cost they can impose on their firms is so great, and the cost to the firm of the rises they want so small in comparison, that the strike will still seem a sound business proposition for them. They are likely to believe that they will get enough to compensate them for the money lost while on strike and for any hardship they may incur; and given the various resources in addition to strike pay that most will be able to command, the hardship should not be severe.

This brings us to a major difficulty confronting many proposals to redress the balance of bargaining power. This power is not only dispersed among a myriad of groups in the economy, but it is very unevenly distributed among them. There is a range from those whose power to impose costs on the whole economy as well as their own organisation is enormous, through those who can inflict a heavy cost by the standards of their firm if not of the economy as a whole, down to those who could be replaced by other workers tomorrow and have no power whatever. General measures such as the reduction of welfare benefits would increase the numbers of the weak who are at the mercy of their employers and would have little influence on those who have disproportionate bargaining power. There would be, somewhere in the middle, an indeterminate number for whom a more even balance of power might result. But this seems a modest result for measures that would have some of the effect of a bombardment in the class war.

A determined use of their own resources of bargaining potential by employers who are confronted with workers with disproportionate power can do something to redress the balance. The equilibrium in the German engineering industry which has had such a benign influence on the German economy has depended not only on the strength and responsibility of IG Metall but also on a strong employers' association, capable for example of using collective lock-outs as a bargaining instrument. But if British employers were better organised for effective united action, or even if they were to make more determined use of each firm's bargaining power, most of them would still be faced with a number of groups which act more or less autonomously, either because they belong to different unions or because, even though they belong to one union, they do not accept much control by it; and the stubborn fact would remain that many of these groups have a great deal of power.

While this power rests on the structure of production, it usually also depends on the unwillingness of others to do the work of those on strike, or to allow it to be done by anyone else. Although the importance of specialised skills in the modern economy continues to increase, it must still be the exception that other workers cannot be found with the skills to do the job. If any single change would be potent in redressing disproportionate workers' power, it would surely be the possibility that the strikers' work would be done, to the extent that the work of others who depend on it could continue. But while many will doubtless agree that disproportionate power should be redressed, and the majority of workers may wish to see a curb on the activities of small groups who are reducing the majority's pay or endangering the viability of their firm, there will need to be an overwhelming conviction that the power is disproportionate and the activities mischievous before the inbred objections to blackleg labour are allayed. Hindrance of blackleg labour has been one of the principal tactics of manual workers in their struggle to redress the disproportionate power of the employers which Adam Smith described, and they will need to be very sure that the power of employers will not be used to their disadvantage before they agree not to hinder blacklegs when this stands a chance of success. Thus we find once more that behaviour and institutions determine the working of imperfect markets. Inconvenient though it may be, particularly for the many economists who wish to exclude such matters from the discipline, the fact remains that disproportionate power will prevent monetarist, incomes or full employment policies from curing our stagflation until there is a consensus, shared by the big majority of workers and their representatives and acceptable to managers, as to what is a fair cause for the withdrawal of labour and what are fair terms on which work which is the subject of dispute should be undertaken. With bargaining power so great, so various and so dispersed, no general measures to redress its balance can be a substitute for that.

Social or industrial contract?

The £6 a week limit on pay rises that succeeded in reducing inflation by two-thirds between 1975 and 1977 was accompanied by social and employment legislation in an arrangement called the social contract, implying that the social measures were enacted to compensate the workers for exercising pay restraint. Although it sounds plausible and was for this period successful, the bargain was not based on faultless logic. The big majority of workers would have suffered much from a continued rise of inflation and still more from its reversal through deflation without incomes policy. There should be no need to be compensated for doing something that is so clearly in your own interest. Those who could be said, in some sense, to suffer from restraint were the workers' representatives for whom bargaining about pay is a way of life. When such bargaining is regarded, for a time, as against the public interest, they may wish to be compensated for being prevented from doing it. Thus the social contract may be seen as a national agreement which enabled the government to induce workers' representatives to suspend the performance of that function, in return for measures that some of the most powerful representatives were keen to see enacted.

If the foregoing argument in this chapter is right, arrangements will continue to be needed to induce those workers who have considerable bargaining power to refrain from using it to secure pay increases which cause inflation or depress employment and development. Even if social contracts could work again, there would be a limit when all the legislation that the union leaders wanted and was acceptable to the government of the day had been enacted. But what would happen if the public reacted against these laws and elected a government which repealed them? Would the public have to pay for that with accelerating inflation, followed by severe deflation? And what if an equilibrium were reached in which the union leaders had secured all the legislation they wanted and to which the public did not object? For so long as the modern economy is with us, and whatever the state of social legislation, the power that gives rise to pay push will continue to generate stagflation if it is not harnessed to more constructive ends.

Uncontrolled pay push is against the interests of workers as well as the general interest because it stunts the healthy development of the economy. Either it is accompanied by an equal price push in a spiral to which there is no foreseeable limit and which will increasingly distort the distribution of resources within the economy, hurting the weak and making competition in world markets impossible; or it is checked by deflation, with the accompanying damage to investment and employment. It is in the interest both of workers and of society as a whole that growth of pay leaves room for investment without causing too much price inflation; for the investment is the means whereby real incomes can be increased, working conditions improved, new jobs created and the wealth of the country as a whole enhanced. If pay presses too hard against prices, none of this will be possible. The worker's interest in restraint over the use of his bargaining power comprises, then, his share in tomorrow's development of production that will be impossible if he presses too hard for higher pay today. Here, surely, is the logical basis for agreement about the use of bargaining power. Instead of a single social contract between central government and some of the unions' national leaders, this would imply a series of industrial or development programmes or contracts within firms, overarched by a national understanding or agreement. Under the development programmes of firms, workers would accept pay at rates that would, given stable prices, leave room for adequate profits, while the firms would undertake programmes of investment and development commensurate with the profits, leading to higher production reflected in correspondingly higher pay. Under the national agreement, leaderships of unions and employers' associations would facilitate the acceptance of development programmes or contracts within their spheres of influence, while governments would take measures to encourage investment, including a check that the development programmes and contracts were based on sufficiently stable prices, so that there was no need for deflation which would depress employment and development.

We develop these ideas in chapter 9. It might seem ideal if the harder version of what is proposed, that is the use of contracts for development within firms, could be paralleled by a strong national contract between unions, employers and government (rather than just a general understanding). Such a thing is possible in countries where unions and employers each have strong national organisations which can commit their members to a bargain and ensure respect for it. But the CBI and the TUC do not have that kind of strength, and, so long as this is the case, the national parallel for the firm's development contracts cannot be more than an understanding whereby the CBI and the TUC use their best endeavours to secure their members' compliance with a policy agreed between them and with the government. To achieve even this would be hard enough: it would arouse false expectations to give such an understanding or agreement the name of 'contract'.

For British experience shows that ensuring respect for pay agreements by the various groups with strong bargaining power is not at all an easy task. Firms, unions and governments have, at different times, had varying degrees of influence in this. The range of possibilities is well demonstrated by three of the industrial countries that have been among the most successful in containing pay push: Germany, Japan and Austria. In Germany, the unions play a more important role than in most other countries. The unions' policies for the pay negotiations are formed after thorough discussions among workers throughout the industry that each union represents, and the groups with potential bargaining power have therefore participated in a process which aggregates their various interests into a policy for the workers in the industry as a whole. Once the agreement, which the union has negotiated on the basis of that policy, is concluded with the employers, the union assumes an important share of the responsibility for ensuring that the agreement is kept by all its members, whether or not they are in positions that could afford them autonomous bargaining power. If members do not accept union discipline, they may risk expulsion. In Japan, the big firms are by far the most important in determining the rate of growth of pay. After the preparations and discussions that precede the annual pay round in the spring, when the likely general rate of pay increase has emerged, specific agreements are made between each large firm and a single union, which thus aggregates the various elements of bargaining power within the firm; and the groups within the firm evidently find it in their interest to respect the agreement. In Austria, a tripartite system for fixing pay and prices ensures that employers and unions as well as the public authorities play their part in pay and price determination; and these tripartite decisions therefore have the backing of employers and unions, although the public authorities have the power to enforce them if necessary. In each of the three countries, the pay agreements are widely respected and usually leave room for profits that result in adequate investment and development, without pushing up prices in an inflationary way. While there may not be explicit development contracts, the workers' experience is that profits do in fact result in investment to improve productive capacity, and the restraint in use of bargaining power depends implicitly on their confidence that profits will be used in this way.

The national unions in Britain will not be able to ensure that their members respect agreements as the German unions do, unless the centre secures more control over the shop floor than it shows any signs of doing in most unions at present. The aggregation of bargaining power of all the groups that possess it within an industry is not in any event possible except in the few British unions that are coterminous with an industry. Nor is it easy to see the largest unions recognising one of their number as an oligopolistic price leader, which could set the broad level for settlements reached by other unions, as the IG Metall does in Germany. The union leaderships clearly have an important role. Apart from anything else, they as well as shop floor groups among their members have substantial bargaining power. But many changes would be required before their role in securing agreements at levels not likely to cause stagflation and in ensuring that their members respect the agreements could become as important as that of the German unions.

The larger firms do already play a big part in pay negotiations in British industry. The problem here is that the tradition of relationships between employers and employees in Britain does not conduce to a ready acceptance by workers of managers' views about suitable be-haviour, or to a confidence on the part of workers that profits will lead to the development of their firm in a way that will benefit them suf-ficiently. Nor is negotiation of agreements and respect for them helped by the number of unions represented in most industrial establishments, where multi-unionism is normal. Yet many of the firms do negotiate agreements that are not particularly inflationary and do secure respect for them despite the multi-unionism. The question that arises here is whether the prospects for reasonable agreements and of respect for them would not be enhanced if the agreements could be seen as an aspect of the firm's development programme from which all groups in the firm believe they will benefit and to which they therefore feel a commitment. Some such feeling seems to have emerged in some firms as a result of their parlous state in the current recession. It needs to crystallise and become permanent if stagflation is not to be continually recurrent; and this is likely to require not only a major effort by managers to expound the benefits to all concerned of securing high profits and investing them in the firm's development, but also stronger arrangements for employees' participation, which we consider further in chapters 5 and 9.

The government plays little part in the pay agreements in Germany and Japan; and in Britain the association of incomes policies with sub-sequent pay explosions and lost elections has made a government role in pay policy unpopular among politicians and suspect among economists. Yet given the fragmentation of union organisation and bargaining power and the uneasy relationships between employees and employers in much of industry, together with the inflationary reflexes that experience since the 1970s has instilled, it is hard to envisage an effective limitation of the use of bargaining power without some intervention by the government. The Austrian example shows that this can be effective in a remarkably efficient as well as non-inflationary market economy. But Britain, lacking the Austrians' years of successful experience of pay and price controls, is less well-placed to organise them effectively. It would seem wise, in these circumstances, to lay as much stress as possible on development contracts within firms, agreed between employers and the workers' organisations, with the public authorities setting only a framework to ensure price stability and to encourage development contracts that make adequate provision for investment, concentrating upon those fields in which bargaining power and hence pay push are strongest.

PRICES AND PROFITS

We have seen how the structure of the modern economy gives organised groups the power to push up their pay faster than productivity; and how such pay push must cause either inflation of prices or reduction of profits, investment and employment, or a combination of both. Both have been combined with a vengeance in the 1970s, with inflation averaging around 10 per cent a year in countries of the Organisation for Economic Co-operation and Development (OECD) during much of the decade, and unemployment rising towards that percentage by the end of it. Yet during the 1950s and 1960s the possibility of such disequilibrium seemed hardly worth considering. Prices rose as fast as the fairly modest rate of growth of wages less productivity; profits, investment, growth and employment were maintained. How can this be explained?

The power of oligopolistic firms to fix prices at profitable levels was vividly depicted by Galbraith.[4] These firms, which had become the leading force in the western economies, were able to escape the rigours of perfect competition by differentiating their products and by conventions of behaviour in pricing and production to which the few major competitors in each product group adhered. This enabled the firms to cover the high fixed costs that are inherent in the modern economy. It also explained, in Galbraith's view, the emergence of countervailing

[4] J. K. Galbraith, *The New Industrial State*, (Hamish Hamilton, London, 1967), p. 179 ff.

power among groups such as workers and consumers, who had to protect themselves against the dominant power of the oligopolies.

What Galbraith did not explain was why the power should be evenly balanced: why the equilibrium should not be upset in favour of one or other group. Although he analysed in some detail the sources of the big firms' power, he hardly attempted any equivalent analysis of the power of workers and of its relationship with the structure of the economy. But in treating the market power of firms as a major element in the successful working of the modern economy he was more shrewd and perceptive than most other economists. The subject of imperfect competition had been largely neglected since the 1930s; and even then, although considerable intellectual effort went into the development of theory, its practical value had been vitiated by a failure to appreciate the role of investment in economic development and the potential, which Galbraith brought out, of imperfect competition in generating investment.[5] Thus most economists failed to make any serious study of the market power of either firms or workers; and there was virtually no interest in the balance of power between the two. The profession was ill-prepared to consider what may well have been the most important element in the economic failures of western countries in the 1970s.

A crucial aspect of the stagflation has been the low level of profits in western economies. The problem in the United Kingdom is illustrated by diagram 2.5 and by the figures given on p. 26. There have been attempts to explain this in terms of a shortage of labour in relation to capital. But with unemployment pushing up towards 10 per cent in the OECD countries, this hardly seems plausible, even when shortages of particular skills are taken into account; and, having examined the workings of supply and demand in the labour market, we may wonder how useful explanations that rest on implicit assumptions of perfect markets are likely to be. It seems sensible to consider how prices, as well as pay, are affected by imperfections inherent in the modern economy, and how this affects profits which depend largely on the difference between the two.

Weak demand and high fixed costs lead to weak prices

While imperfect markets are inconvenient facts of the modern economy that must not be ignored, it is equally foolish to ignore the fact that they remain markets in which the basic forces are supply and demand; and the weakness of prices compared with pay in the 1970s

[5] In Joan Robinson, *op. cit.*, only one paragraph was devoted to the case where capital accumulation takes place, which will 'tend to increase the real wages of labour progressively through time' (p. 323).

has been associated with weakness in the demand for products. A fall in demand for a firm's products can be caused by a weakness of total demand in the economy, by a decline in demand for the firm's products as a proportion of total demand, or by encroachment of competitors in the markets for the products. Many firms in western countries have suffered in the 1970s on all three counts.

The OPEC surpluses that followed the oil price push in 1973 and 1979 removed equivalent demand from the oil importers without corresponding increases in demand from the oil exporters. But the amounts were small percentages of the gross product of the advanced industrial countries, which would have recovered quite quickly from their recessions had the oil price push not been converted into pay push, and had the western governments been able to check the pay push by means other than deflation. Some deflation was, indeed, applied after the earlier bout of pay push that was started by the disturbances in France in 1968 and followed in a number of other countries; but the main cause of weak total demand in western economies in recent years has been the deflationary policy used to counter the pay-push inflation that followed the oil price shocks. Since deflation, for reasons that we have considered earlier, is so slow and inefficient a means of controlling pay push, and since further oil price shocks may be expected when demand does revive strongly, this weak general demand can be expected to prevail for most of the time until we have developed more efficient ways of controlling the growth of pay.

Within the total of gross domestic product, there will naturally be some products for which the share of total demand is growing fast, some for which it is fairly static, and some for which the share or the absolute level of demand is declining. Again naturally, the latter tend to include groups of products which were developed some time ago and demand for which has reached the point of saturation. In the 1950s and 1960s, food and textiles were the principal examples. As a result of the successful growth of the advanced industrial economies in those years, however, other product-groups reached during the 1970s the stage of maturity and in some countries of saturation. Among consumer goods, cars are outstanding among the consumer durables to which this appears to have applied; steel and heavy chemicals are among the industrial materials; and ships have been the most prominent of a range of capital goods that may be suffering from secular decline (partly as a consequence of more effective utilisation) as well as from the recession which, as we have seen, is likely to remain endemic until more appropriate methods of economic management have been developed. Thus a number of the products that had been leaders of postwar economic growth have encountered a prolonged, and in some cases perhaps permanent, weakness in demand. Adjustment to this is particularly hard when general demand is weak, so that the sectors which enjoy stronger demand lack the pulling power and the ability to absorb unemployed resources that growth sectors previously had; moreover, the sectors troubled by maturity, saturation or cyclical weakness of demand for their products comprise no longer a small number of old industries but large tracts of what has hitherto been the heartland of the modern economy.

Demand for the products of such sectors of industry in Western Europe and North America has been further reduced by the inroads of competition from Japan and the newly industrialising countries (NICs). For although Japan has now penetrated world markets with products in some of the most advanced sectors, and the NICs are still heavily engaged in old industries such as textiles and footwear, both Japan and the NICs have been successful in those mainstream postwar industries for which demand in western countries has reached maturity. Nor is this surprising, because production techniques have also reached maturity and have therefore become easier for new producers to adopt. Exports from the NICs have expanded rapidly in the 1970s, to comprise not far short of one-tenth of world trade in manufactures, a proportion equivalent to that of Japan. The two combined have therefore exerted a further heavy pressure on those European and American industries which were already faced with weak demand for their products. Nor should we take too much comfort from the fact that the majority of jobs in the modern economy are provided in services rather than in manufacturing; for manufacturing industry is still central to our economic development. If much of that industry languishes, so will the economy as a whole.

On a conventional view of cost structures, which is deeply embedded in our habits of economic thought, weak demand for a number of product groups will not do the economy any lasting damage, and should indeed be turned to good account; for the marginal, less efficient production will be eliminated, leaving the more efficient elements of those sectors and of the economy as a whole to expand and put to better use the resources thus liberated. But in large parts of the economy this conventional view does not reflect reality. Where demand is weak and fixed costs are high, the more efficient as well as the less efficient firms can remain for long periods without enough profits to generate new development.

The proportion of fixed to total costs has been increasing since the industrial revolution began and is continuing to do so. A vital part of these costs relates to a firm's investment. In order to develop its ability to produce and sell its present range of products, the firm has had to invest not only in plant and equipment but also, if it is large, in research, development and the training of people with the necessary skills. Part of these costs are likely to be reflected in debt on which payments of interest and principal must be made, as a fixed cost that does not vary with the volume of current production. Part will represent the firm's equity and reinvested profits, on which fixed payments do not have to be made; but the firm's future development will be threatened if it does not earn an adequate return on these resources. At the same time the firm, if it is to remain viable, must be spending enough on training, research and development, and on plant and equipment, in order to be able to make and sell enough competitive products in the future. These costs are not fixed in the sense that they must necessarily be incurred in order to remain in business this year or next. The lead times for establishing new plant or developing new products in modern industries may be several years; and the gestation period for the more basic research and development can be measured in decades. So a reduction of such expenditure to very low levels may not affect the firm's competitiveness in the short run; and a more modest squeeze on development expenditure would undermine its strength only on a long time scale. But the costs of development must, within limits that depend on judgement rather than scientific certainty, be met if a firm is to maintain its business in the future. They are therefore, from the point of view of the firm, costs that are fixed by an intention to remain in business, although they can be postponed or abandoned if the will or the means to fulfil that intention are lacking.

At the same time as the costs of a firm's development have become an increasingly important part of its total costs, a large part of its employment costs, which used to respond fairly closely to fluctuations in the firm's production, have increasingly adopted the characteristics of fixed costs. Managers, specialists and office staff are not hired and fired with every shift in output; and the same has come to apply to many skilled workers and other workers too. This is partly because the volume of much of the work is not proportionate to the volume of production. Partly it is because the costs of hiring and training people with the necessary skills have grown with the development of the economy; and when skill shortages occur, as they do with every upturn in the British economy, there are severe penalties, in terms of lost production and market shares, of being caught without enough skilled workers. Partly it is due to the security of employment and the cost of redundancy payments required by law, or by custom backed by workers' bargaining power. Of course the costs of employment are not permanently and immutably fixed; the number of redundancies in recent years and the slimming achieved through employees leaving for other reasons are enough evidence of that. But as Okun has pointed out,[6] contracts for a period, explicit or implicit, have become more typical than instant response to market forces in the contemporary labour market; and the same can be said of some of the supply of bought-in components and industrial materials. The balance has shifted from a ready reduction of employment costs in response to lower demand, to a large element of fixity in such costs. That element varies widely, of course, according to the varying circumstances of different employees and the length of time ahead. But the contemporary firm has to regard a substantial part of its employment costs as fixed at least for the shorter term.

Firms tend, not only to have heavy fixed costs and to operate in imperfectly competitive situations, but also to operate at most times some way below their full capacity. The larger the fixed costs, the greater the tendency of average costs to fall as output rises; and this tendency is not likely to be overcome by 'diminishing returns', because there is available capacity. Typically, marginal cost will be fairly constant, not rising sharply. If, in these circumstances, a firm tries to react to a fall in demand by cutting its production, it will tend over a considerable range to reduce its profits because of its higher average costs. Therefore it will be tempted to try the opposite course: to cut prices and hope to take markets from its rivals, thereby allowing an increase in production which will help to carry the fixed costs. Thus shipyards around the world have, with government help, cut prices to ridiculous levels, because the alternative of carrying the fixed costs with little or no business looks even worse. The case for price-cutting will be strong in sectors such as steel or heavy chemicals, where the products are homogeneous so that consumers' response to small price differences is relatively great; but the relationships between cost patterns and demand elasticities in many other sectors also seem to be such that firms are under strong economic pressure, when demand is weak, to maintain production by initiating or meeting price competition.

The purpose of oligopolistic price and production conventions has, of course, been to control this pressure and thus maintain prices at levels that leave room for profits and development. Even in the 1950s and 1960s, when the system worked with such beneficial results, the conventions were broken from time to time. New, aggressive entrants to the market would cut prices and expand production at the existing oligopolists' expense; established firms might try to regain market share they had lost as a result of what they saw as unconventional en-

---

[6] Arthur M. Okun, *Prices and Quantities : A Macroeconomic Analysis,* (Blackwell, Oxford, 1981), chapters 2–4.

croachment in the past; firms with a philosophy of volume and market share would react to temporary over-capacity by cutting prices more readily than firms with a philosophy of stable prices and profit margins. Such differences of attitude often correspond to differences of circumstance as well as of business culture. Those with more saleable products, or with lower costs due to cheaper labour, newer equipment or government help, are the more likely to be aggressive. But until the 1970s, these differences of attitude and circumstance were accommodated by the system. Most of the competition was among European or American firms, and the range of differences in attitudes and economic circumstances was not enormous, at least by the time that postwar recovery was over and trade rivalry within the area became intense. The steady growth of markets enabled convention-breakers to gain without forcing the conventional oligopolists to cut the volume of their production. The more efficient firms were able to improve their position steadily over the longer run without pressing their competitors to the point of a price war that would undermine the price structure on which even the efficient depended to finance their development costs.

These conditions evaporated in the 1970s. Deflation together with the maturity of many products removed the growth of demand that had smoothed such turbulence as is to be found even in well-ordered oligopolistic markets; and into these weak markets came swiftly intensifying competition from Japan and the NICs, bringing a wide diversity of circumstances and attitudes. Labour is much cheaper and more pliant in the NICs and more zealously loyal to the companies in Japan. Plant and equipment tend to be newer and better, thanks to the higher rates of growth and investment. Corporate attitudes and culture are very different; and even where this might not be an obstacle to the sharing of oligopolistic conventions, a foundation of shared experience is bound to be absent at least for a time. All these factors led to sharper price cutting and market encroachment than had been experienced in the preceding golden age of western oligopoly. The weaker firms in Western Europe and North America were forced to meet the price competition wherever this would help them to maintain sales and pay the unpostponable fixed costs which they were hard put to cover. The stronger firms could not stand aside, and had to accept price levels that implied a reduction in their postponable development expenditure. The process was to some extent masked by inflation, because a price squeeze could take the form of price increases below the general inflation rate, rather than absolute price cuts. But the immediate crisis for the weaker firms and the erosion of the stronger firms' capacity to finance future development has been none the less real for that. The oligopolistic system which had appeared so stable can now be seen to have constituted an unstable equilibrium that enabled the high fixed costs to be covered only as a result of the favourable conditions of fast economic growth and homogeneity among the oligopolists. With both these conditions removed, the equilibrium is broken and prices are not maintained at levels that provide for development. The benign circle of high growth, high profits, high investment and hence high growth is replaced by a vicious circle of low growth, low profits, low investment and hence low growth. The question to which we have to address ourselves is how this vicious circle can be broken.

Profits squeezed between weak prices and strong pay

There are two prevalent views of this vicious circle of poor economic performance. One is that we must await the upturn after a long recession, when profits, investment and growth can be expected to recover; the other is that low growth and high unemployment are part of a new economic order from which there is no escape. If our argument so far is correct, both these views are mistaken, for the poor performance of most western countries results neither from a conventional trade cycle nor from ineluctable trends in technology or consumer behaviour, but from adverse trends in pay and prices which, though they stem from the structure of the modern economy, can be corrected by perfectly feasible changes of policy and behaviour.

We have seen how specialisation, interdependence and capital-intensity have given numerous groups of workers the bargaining power to push up their pay, so that equilibrium of pay and prices, and hence employment and growth, depend on effective means of controlling this power. In the absence of such a means, any turbulence in the labour market is only too likely to upset the equilibrium, leading, as it has in almost all western countries, to prolonged stagflation. Workers' representatives have both the power to disrupt the stability of pay and a variety of motives for doing so, just as oligopolists have the power and a variety of motives for disrupting prices. The difference is that the competition among workers' representatives takes the form of pushing for higher pay whereas that of oligopolists takes the form of depressing prices. In so far as the oligopolists try to use their market power to maintain or raise prices in the face of weak demand, moreover, that power is usually less than the power of workers to raise their pay. For much of the labour in modern industry is needed at once if a firm's complex system of production is to continue and thus avoid heavy loss, whereas the purchase of most products can wait without causing significant loss to the purchaser; and the market for products is generally wider than that for labour, making price-cutting harder than pay-cutting to control. In particular, the labour market is usually, at the widest, national, whereas the product market is now normally international, for reasons that we will later see are intrinsic to the modern economy. Thus the ability of the oligopolist to administer his prices has diminished with the widening internationalisation of the market for his products.

It is understandable that those who represent the views of employers should not be pleased if the market power of workers is shown to be greater than the market power of firms. But it is a paradox that such a conclusion is more likely to be greeted with cries of protest than to be welcomed by many of those who represent workers' views or adhere to theories that purport to reflect workers' interests. For if workers' market power indeed exceeds that of employers, this will have to be reflected in the way in which workers participate in arrangements for controlling power in the economy. Some people will doubtless find it vexatious that this basic aspiration of the labour movement may be fulfilled in ways that their theories have not led them to foresee. But if a change in the balance of power rests on changes in the structure of the economy, it is likely to have lasting consequences within our market economies, whatever the devotees of certain theories may expect.

There should be little doubt that both the weakness of prices and the strength of the push from pay will be long-lasting unless policies and behaviour are changed. Most firms can survive for a long time even if prices are such that profits are low because, as we have seen, development expenditure can meanwhile be reduced.[7] The reduction of capacity through the bankruptcy of major firms is therefore likely to be a long-drawn-out process. Even if a firm that accounts for a significant share of production is very hard pressed, the external costs of its bankruptcy, which would have to be met by creditors or the government or society, are such that assistance from banks and government is often forthcoming. Since bankruptcy is likely to cause banks to lose part of the money they have lent, it is to their advantage to let the firm postpone payments of interest or principal, and even to increase their lending so long as there is a reasonable chance that the firm will recover its ability to pay, either through its own efforts to cut costs and improve sales, or after a cyclical upturn in demand, or because the government comes to its help. So long, again, as there is a good enough prospect that the firm will become viable again, the government has an interest in helping, because of the costs that the public purse as well as the economy and society will have to bear if the firm folds up without the

---

[7] One is reminded of Marshall's description of the growth and decline of firms, as with the trees of a forest : 'And as with the growth of trees, so was it with the growth of businesses as a general rule before the great recent development of vast joint-stock companies, which often stagnate, but do not readily die'. Alfred Marshall, *Principles of Economics,* Book IV, ch. XII, § 1.

redeployment of its workers and other resources into productive use. Government will lose both central and local taxes and social security contributions. There will also be social security and welfare payments for the unemployed, the cost of labour market services and job creation, and the greater burden on health, welfare and other services that goes with higher unemployment. There will be the economic and social costs to the unemployed and to others in what will be a less prosperous economy. All these are costs which it is rational to try to avoid, even at the expense of tax remissions and subsidies, or by providing some protection against imports; and all western governments do take such steps in order to avoid the costs. Where help is given by the government of one country, moreover, it reduces the room for manoeuvre of others.

Major bankruptcies cannot, therefore, be expected to make any speedy contribution to the reduction of productive capacity in a sector, which would enable the remaining capacity to be more fully used and the development and other fixed costs thus more readily covered. Capacity can, at a stiff price in redundancy payments as well as external costs, be reduced by means of plant closures within firms; and much capacity has been taken out of service in this way in Britain and other western countries in the last few years. This has doubtless strengthened the finances of firms that have got rid of their weaker elements. But we have to ask whether profits in these firms will be restored in this way to levels high enough to ensure their healthy future development, and whether profits more generally will be high enough to provide for sufficient investment and hence employment in the economy as a whole.

Capacity use and profits in the sectors where plants have been closed will be restored to levels that allow long-term viability only if the relationship between the sector's capacity and the demand for its products becomes and remains sufficiently favourable. But demand will be restricted so long as macroeconomic policies remain deflationary; and they are likely to be deflationary, on and off but more on than off, for as long as the means of controlling pay push remain inadequate, for we have seen that the workers' bargaining power which is the basis of pay push is a function of the structure of the modern economy. This restricted demand is, moreover, likely to be met increasingly by the NICs as well as Japan, because the advantage of NICs in terms of cheaper labour, and of newer equipment (thanks to faster growth), is likely to last for decades or even, given that there is a long line of countries queuing up to become NICs, for centuries; nor is any end in sight to the competitive power of Japan, whose uniquely appropriate industrial culture does not seem now to depend for its competitive strength on any additional advantage from low wages. Thus in the sectors affected by competition from Japan and the NICs, the reduction of capacity is not in itself enough. To restore capacity use to truly profitable rates, capacity has to be reduced faster than the resulting advantage is eroded by competition from these sources; and it must continue to be reduced at such a rate. But there are powerful resistances to capacity reduction, which are entirely rational from the points of view of the resisting firms, workers, local authorities and central treasuries. The costs to central and local government when firms go bankrupt have already been mentioned, and the costs of plant closures are similar. The workers naturally do not want to lose their jobs, though some will accept voluntary redundancy. For the firm, the plant is worth keeping so long as it covers its variable costs; and even when it does not, the firm will be reluctant to incur the heavy costs of closure and to lose any hope of future return on its investment, so long as there is a hope that other firms will reduce capacity enough to cause buyers to transfer their purchases to the plant in question and thus render it viable again. While there is a chance of this, a firm will not be in a hurry to shut its own plant down. Given these resistances, it seems unlikely that capacity reduction will, without policy changes that take account of the inconvenient facts we have been discussing, be undertaken at a pace that keeps capacity use at levels that are sufficiently profitable; and if profits in large parts of industry are consequently low, it is unlikely that the economy will generate the investment and employment that such a rate of capacity reduction would necessitate. Thus the balance between supply and demand is not self-regulating in a way that allows for either the short-term health or the long-term development of the economy. Evidently, we must seek methods of bringing them into a more productive balance.

Possible remedies

The Japanese have been more successful than Europeans or Americans in maintaining the financial strength of their firms as a basis for continued employment and growth. Because Japan is a mystery to most of us and Japanese society and culture seem so well adapted to the needs of the modern economy, there is a tendency to attribute the whole of Japanese success to social and cultural patterns which cannot be transferred, and to ignore the possibility of learning from Japanese policy. But this is to underestimate the rationality of Japanese policy and its appropriateness to the problems which face any advanced industrial economy, and hence the extent to which we can learn from Japanese ideas just as they have in the past learnt so much from us. Their policies for maintaining prices and profits in sectors that face weak demand provide one good example. Later we shall consider the necessary complement, in the form of policies to promote industrial development in other, less troubled parts of the economy.

When a sector containing large production units with high fixed costs has been hit by weak demand that is thought to be cyclical and expected to recover in a year or two, the Japanese government has been ready to authorise a recession cartel, whereby prices and hence profits are protected by production and import quotas and the licensing of investment in new capacity. This has prevented the erosion of the financial structure of firms in the sector and hence enabled them to continue their development unimpaired after the anticipated recovery of demand, when the recession cartel is of course wound up. But what if the weak demand for the sector's products is not just cyclical and short-term, but is expected to last a long time, or against expectations in fact does so?

The sector is then confronted by a need to reduce its capacity for production of the goods for which demand is weak. A laissez-faire policy would leave the reduction to be effected by bankruptcy and plant closure. But, as we have seen, this is likely to take a long time, during which the financial and eventually technological strength of efficient as well as higher-cost firms will be sapped by prices that do not allow them to cover adequate development costs. Prices therefore have to be maintained if the efficient firms are to be able to develop. But the formula of the recession cartel would, since excessive over-capacity is likely to be long-lasting, restrict competition for too long a time, prolong the survival of uncompetitive plant even longer than a laissez-faire policy would do, and stand in the way of the very development of the more efficient firms that the price maintenance is supposed to encourage. The Japanese have therefore evolved the policy of the rationalisation cartel, in which price support through production quotas, investment licensing and import protection is conditional on a sufficient reduction of capacity and on the use of profits for new development.

The details of capacity reduction are usually agreed by the government and the firms in the sector, after the pattern of co-operation between government and industry that is so well developed in Japan. But the industry may be reluctant to cut capacity enough; and the firms that should, by economic logic, cut the most are likely to resist. The government has both carrots and sticks to deal with such difficulties. The carrots include various ways of helping to buy out the higher-cost plant, often, as in the case of the rationalisation of Japanese shipbuilding, by means of low-interest loans; there are also incentives for new development, which might not be forthcoming if a firm makes too many difficulties over capacity reduction. The sticks could include the withdrawing of any of a range of incentives and advantages that the government can offer to firms, and eventually of the protection and other elements that are essential for price maintenance.

Capacity reduction is the negative part of a programme for rationalisation. The positive part is the use of the resources that the programme provides, through price levels which leave room for profits and perhaps through subsidies or tax incentives or government-guaranteed loans, to improve the firms' competitiveness and promote their future development. Within the troubled sectors the firms may move up-market to concentrate on higher quality goods where demand may be stronger and the competition from the NICs less sharp, or they may be able to regain their competitiveness by investing in improved and more capital-intensive production processes; or the firms may expand in other, growth sectors in which they have a good prospect of applying their skills and other resources successfully. The reduction of capacity will not solve the sector's problems for long, let alone the problems of the economy in which employment and incomes in the future depend on present development efforts, unless it is accompanied by investment along such lines; nor will the support of prices and profits have any justification for the consumer unless the profits are used to provide him with something better in future.

The selection of capacity to be cut and the choice of investments for industrial development depend on commercial judgements which governments, in Britain and many other countries, are ill-equipped to make. The skills and experience may be expected, rather, to be found in managers of industrial firms and of financial institutions that specialise in industrial investment, which will be further considered later and which we will call industrial banks. The difficulty is that, because a laissez-faire policy has such bad results, governments have to be involved in deciding on subsidies, protection and other measures of support. If they are unable to judge the merits of schemes for capacity reduction and industrial development, they will find themselves backing losers and propping up high-cost capacity indefinitely. Yet a strong democratic political process, at least as it has worked in Britain, seems ill-matched with the technical and long-term character of decisions about industrial strategies. Evidently, governments will have to rely heavily on the judgements of industrial bankers as well as on proposals emanating from the industries themselves. But the governments are responsible for public money and for the social and economic effects of measures such as protection, so they need a capacity at least to evaluate the judgements of the experts; and for this they probably need enough civil servants with appropriate skills and experience, as well as public-sector industrial banks, operating, like the British Technology Group, on business lines separately from the civil service. The combination of experts from both the private and the public sectors is the pattern for deciding on these matters in Japan, and it seems necessary where a combination of private initiative and public policy is required.

Most western countries are backward in comparison with Japan in their ability to pursue sensible public policies of this kind. The terminology even impedes our thinking about the subject. The word cartel is not respectable but there is no other word that clearly describes the types of arrangement the Japanese make for industries suffering from over-capacity. The need for such arrangements has indeed been recognised in Western Europe. The European Community has what amounts to a recession cartel for steel; the producers of synthetic fibres approached the Commission of the EC with a proposal for a rationalisation cartel, which the Commission did not see its way to authorise under the Community's competition rules, although the firms have in fact implemented much of what they proposed; and the Commission has been trying to get the member governments to accept a programme of reduction in shipbuilding capacity, on which however the governments have not been able to agree. The lack of understanding among Europeans as to how such rationalisation cartels can best work is one serious obstacle to their successful application; another is the lack, at the Community level, of strong enough instruments, institutions and habits of working together, which are needed if such arrangements are to be made for the Community as a whole and thus reflect the size of the relevant market. For each of the single States of Western Europe is too small to deal on its own with the problem of over-capacity, since none can escape the effects of over-capacity in other member countries without retreating into an autarky that is incompatible with much of modern industrial technology. Thus in Western Europe we have to acquire the ability not only to apply these new forms of industrial policy as the Japanese have done, but also to apply them in an integrated way, if we are to restore such sectors as steel and shipbuilding to better health and keep them healthy in future.

As this is a difficult task and the learning process is not likely to be quick, it is well that such treatment is required only for a minority of industrial sectors, which contain large-scale units of production and have encountered weak demand for their products, usually associated not only with a weakness of consumer demand but also with growing competition from Japan and the NICs. Other sectors hit by weak demand and growing competition, but less dominated by large oligopolistic firms, may likewise need some protection or other support if their capacity to finance development is not to be whittled away; but there is not such a compelling need for the associated programmes of restructuring and adjustment assistance to be organised at the Community level. Some European governments are capable of effective action in this respect. The German textile industry, for example, devised a programme for conversion to capital-intensive production of industrial textiles, which was carried through with the help of low-interest loans from the government, and Germany consequently became the world's biggest exporter of textiles. The similarity with Japanese policies for such troubled sectors is striking.

In the conditions we have earlier described, it seems likely that many sectors will need some protection and support, as they do at present, and that this can be turned to the long-run benefit of the economy only if governments require, in return, the removal of capacity that can never compete and the investment in viable development of the profits that result from protection and support. If this is done, the consequence of protection will not be the sclerosis of whole industries and economies, but the renewal of competitiveness in sectors that have been purged of their inefficient or excess capacity. The protection becomes, not a way of perpetuating inefficiency and stagnation, still less of subsidising the weak firms of one country so that they undermine stronger firms in another, but a lever for securing necessary industrial change. As such, it is not likely to succeed unless it is seen as but one element in a national development of individual firms that alone can offer greater prosperity and full employment over the longer term; and a complementary element in such a programme would be a strengthening of competition policy, as we propose in chapter 9. In this perspective, recourse to protection and to rationalisation cartels is a temporary measure, while production is developed to a more sophisticated level, with products that can be internationally competitive because they are differentiated from the simpler and cheaper output of the NICs. If the policy succeeds, it leads to an open economy, which can maintain its strength through competitive participation in the international division of labour.

Such policies require an understanding between industry and government, which includes bargains to trade firms' capacity reduction and new development against the government's protection and support. But the policies can hardly succeed unless there is also a bargain with labour, to ensure that pay push does not pre-empt the resources which derive from the protection and support. For just as the development of the economy has been frustrated by the conditions that have obtained in recent years, so it will equally be impeded if any margin for profit which protection or subsidies may provide is immediately sucked into an inflation of pay at the expense of investment. Japan in particular and, to a lesser but still substantial extent,

Germany avoid this because levels of pay and investment are determined in what we have called an implicit development contract. When governments contribute to restructuring and new development in the ways we have discussed, they too become parties to such contracts; and their contribution will be in vain if the firms and workers do not agree to keep investment high and pay inflation low. Nor will many sectors escape the need for official support and intervention unless their firms and workers can deal with the linked issues of pay and investment in this way. None of this is likely to happen without a widespread understanding of the process of development and its benefits for all concerned. We therefore turn now to consider the attitudes to this development and the process by which it can be achieved.

5   Some Conditions of Development

Our examination of pay, prices and profits has concentrated on certain aspects of the structure of the modern economy which may explain much of the miserable combination of high inflation and unemployment from which western countries have been suffering for most of the past decade. We have also seen how Japanese industrial policy has helped to maintain the stability of price structures and hence the financial strength of firms and their capacity to develop; and how the systems of industrial relations in Japan, Germany and Austria have helped these countries to control pay push and thus maintain profits and investment better than elsewhere. But it is important to understand more fully why some countries have been more successful than others in developing their economies: why, both during the past decade and during the prolonged boom of the two preceding decades, British productivity has grown only half as fast as the average on the Continent, which in turn has grown half as fast as that of Japan – with the Americans more like the British than the rest; and why British industry has been losing ground to its competitors for more than a century. For differing capacities to deal with the adverse pressures on pay and prices and the consequent stagflation of the 1970s seem to have been related to these differing capacities for economic development; and a better understanding of the relationship may help in dealing with both.

We have observed that attitudes and institutions become more important when markets become more imperfect, and hence economic behaviour less closely determined by impersonal market forces. Most economists are reluctant to relate economic performance to attitudes, partly no doubt because they appear less precisely measurable than, say, prices or production. It is almost certain, however, that differences in attitude contributed to the divergences of performance, favourable to Britain from the start of the industrial revolution up to the 1870s, and unfavourable thereafter; and that attitudes, institutions and performance have since interacted in a vicious circle of negative attitudes and low productivity growth. Whatever the historical chain of cause and effect, it is hardly credible to contend that attitudes and institutions do not matter in the imperfect markets of today, or that they should be ignored in devising policies to deal with such problems as market power and externalities (that is, divergences between net benefits to the whole community and those to the originating firm), which loom larger as markets become less perfect.

A review of attitudes and institutions and their effect on development therefore follows. Since the focus of this book is Britain, we shall concentrate on British attitudes, although the relationship with development is of significance for other industrial economies too; and we shall consider the attitudes not just of those who work in industry, but also of those who provide the often unhelpful environment in which industry works.

British attitudes and their effect on development

British attitudes towards the economy have been heavily influenced by two episodes in the history of the past two centuries: the industrial revolution and the empire.

The industrial revolution confirmed and continued the existence in Britain of two nations, the Privileged and the People, of which Disraeli wrote and who comprised the society in which Marx and Engels developed their theory of incompatibility between bourgeoisie and proletariat. Ironically, although this theory attracted more support in many other industrial countries, including Germany and Japan, it was those countries that went on to demonstrate most convincingly the success of an economy based on co-operation between the social partners, whereas in Britain, where the theory was until recently largely ignored, lack of mutual comprehension between the so-called middle and working classes, and antagonism between what we persist in calling the 'two sides of industry', have to this day remained a serious problem for our society and economy. Many workers in industry, whose habits of collective behaviour still reflect the harsh impact of the industrial revolution, have remained suspicious of managers and of middle class people more generally, hostile to profits and ambivalent or resentful towards the companies in which they work. Much of the middle class remains deficient in knowledge and understanding of the point of view of manual workers, as it has been shaped by British social and industrial history. The mobility between the classes has not sufficed to eliminate the differences of attitude. But, though starting from different premises, both have shared a widespread belief that economic development is an autonomous force which does not require any conscious adaptation of behaviour and institutions (at least of one's own behaviour and the institutions to which one belongs) in order to secure it; and against this background, collective class attitudes and institutions have failed to respond to changes in the economy that have made them counter-productive and changes in society that have made them out of date.

During the period in which the country's relative economic decline started and became endemic, Britain ruled an empire that contained a quarter of the world's population. The scale was such that a high proportion of the ablest among the middle class were concerned with the administration and security of the empire, and with the diplomacy, finance and trade to which this position of imperial power gave rise. The focus of politics and the structure of education were directed towards the empire and related needs. Ironically, although it was the industrial revolution that had given Britain the economic power to establish and sustain the empire, this concentration of attention and human resources on it may well have drained industry of the talent required to maintain the technological and industrial lead. Adjustment to the ending of the empire was fairly smooth, even if a legacy of financial, strategic and political burdens lasted for a number of years. But the aspirations of the middle class did not rapidly crystallise around new objectives such as economic or industrial success. In order to reverse the relative economic decline, the flow of ability and enthusiasm into industrial management would need to be greater than that of other countries which do not have such a backlog of weaknesses to remove. But over many years the flow into business has been both inadequate and unevenly distributed: the financial sector has attracted talent, but manufacturing in particular has failed to get anything like its requirements of high ability.

These general attitudes of the middle class and of the manual workers are a constraint on the development of the British economy; and they are reflected in the behaviour of particular groups, such as politicians, civil servants, educators, intellectuals and financiers, as well as managers and other employees in industrial firms, who directly or indirectly influence economic performance.

Having been more concerned on the right with the affairs of empire and of military power, and on the left with the social legacy of the industrial revolution, British politicians have been too readily guided by the nineteenth century ideologies of laissez-faire liberalism or centrally-directive socialism, and too little inclined to get to grips with the realities of the modern economy and the appropriate role in it of public policy. Increasingly during the last decade, politics has become polarised between these two ideologies, which may appear to reflect class interests but in fact represent almost nobody's interest because they are unable to deal with our economic problems and hence to deliver the goods they promise. By the time they are filtered through the process of government, the conflicting ideologies have been diluted into policies that are sometimes fairly similar but sometimes quite sharply divergent. The divergences have caused abrupt swings of policy which in themselves damage the economy because they disrupt the plans of industry, whose time scale depends on lead-times for investments and payback periods that stretch far beyond the electoral cycle. No industrial or pay policy can work if the institutions through which it is to be implemented are frequently uprooted by incoming governments, as they have been in Britain. Nor is the economy likely to prosper if politics focuses on the question of private or public ownership, with the consequence of frequent shifts between the two, rather than on the health of enterprises, which even when related is a somewhat different question. Nor will either private or public enterprise thrive when alternating governments are hostile to each in turn. Even where sharp shifts of policy have been avoided, the irrelevance of the ideologies which appeal to so many political activists has distracted governments from consistently developing policies such as have made for success in other industrial countries.

Alongside the sharpening of ideological conflict, there has been a growth of awareness of the damage done to the economy by excessive adversary politics and of the need for politicians to get closer to industrial problems. But the distance between politics and the realities of economic development may at least partly explain the failure of public policy to do more to help reverse Britain's relative economic decline during the past century; and adversary politics has surely undermined our capacity to cope with the difficulties of the past decade. The addiction of many politicians to inappropriate ideology is, moreover, a constraint on the steady pursuit of policies to deal with such crucial issues as the control of pay push, the promotion of development in both the private and the public sector, participation in the wide international market in which modern industry must operate, and the fostering of attitudes in education and in the civil service which encourage economic development instead of hampering it.

British civil servants, like politicians, have to work against the grain of their traditions if they are to play a useful part in the development of the economy. The civil service has been evolving from a background in which the diplomacy and finance relating to the imperial system counted for more than the health of industry, and in which the relationship between government and industry had never escaped from its negative origins in the principle of laissez-faire, and achieved the constructive and positive nature which can be seen for example in Japan. Traditionally, detailed knowledge of industry was not called for and contacts with industrialists were shunned; and efforts to change this have been sporadic and not yet really successful. Thus it was not surprising that, when the policies of left-wing governments or the pressure of the modern economy required civil servants to intervene in industry, the pace and style of their action was often found by industrialists to be less than helpful; or that the growth of public policy in fields such as housing, land-use planning, education and research should have taken so little account of industrial needs as to appear to amount in practice to a systematic anti-industrial policy. The present generation of civil servants have become more aware of industrial problems and better able to handle their relationship with industry; but the capacity of the civil service to assess and deal with industrial needs remains a constraint on the usefulness of British industrial policy. The learning process is a long one; it has to work against the grain of the admirably strong corporate spirit of public service among civil servants, which unfortunately acts as a preservative of ways of working that are hard to adapt to industrial needs; it is obstructed by the tradition that administrators in the civil service are all-purpose amateurs, frequently changing from one job to another; and it is frequently interrupted by the politicians' reversals of each other's policies.

Like the civil servants, British educators designed a system to meet the needs of an imperial power, with the most prestigious schools and colleges catering for administration, diplomacy, the services, the church and the law, while the skills required for industry took second place. Despite efforts to redress the balance, the system remains biassed against the increasingly complex industrial needs. Engineering is still one of the less-regarded subjects. The bias of secondary education tends to be academic. Schools contribute less to preparing young people for their future at work than in more successful industrial countries. There is still a reluctance to recognise that a broad preparation for life has to include the development of a capacity to perform well in the modern economy, if the life is to be a satisfactory one. The bias in the system seems to be supported by the attitudes of many teachers who are uninterested in the needs of the economy or even hostile to them. Not surprisingly, the system fails to produce the abundance of excellent engineers, highly skilled workers and others eager to work in modern industry, without whom a strong economic performance is not feasible.

Nor has this historic mistreatment of British industry by politics, the civil service and education run counter to the current of the country's intellectual life. Most intellectuals have ignored or disliked industry. The subject of technological development has been alien to them. They have had no feel for the springs of employment and prosperity. Acting as cheer-leaders for economic success is not, they may well feel, their job. But there is a danger for the society when intellectuals not only have no interest in something that is of great concern to most other people, but also foster attitudes that hamper the achievement of what most people quite legitimately want.

Among intellectuals, economists of all people could hardly justify a lack of interest in economic success.[1] In principle, such an interest is usually a reason why they work in the subject. But the main focus of attention in the profession has in recent years been on themes which, if the argument of this book is justified, contribute little to industrial development with stable prices in the contemporary economy. The big macroeconomic models, whether applied for the purpose of monetary control or of Keynesian demand management, do not show how pay push is to be controlled or how, in the absence of such control, economic development is to be promoted. The assumption must be that, if money or demand is managed in line with the outcomes of the models, pay push and economic development will either look after themselves or somebody else will look after them. But we argue, and the state of the economy supports us, that they will not look after themselves, whatever macroeconomic devices of monetary control or demand management are applied; and we are concerned that too few of the most able economists are working on such issues as technological development or pay determination. Industrial, labour and business studies have too little prestige in the profession. Not a few economists have never been inside a factory or discussed their subject with an engineer or banker. One reason for the diversion of attention away from fundamentals may be the force and elegance of the marginal concept which has, for nearly a century, made equilibrium analysis so attractive and hence perhaps allowed a static view of the economy to loom too large in British economic thought. The new power of computer-based statistical analysis has also distracted attention from close observation of firms, shop floors and negotiating tables, where one might expect to identify some of the forces that make for price stability or economic development, even if this would require the use of case study and survey methods of research that are more widely used by other social scientists whose disciplines economists tend to disparage. More generally, economists could hardly avoid being influenced by the prevailing anti-industrial climate of British intellectual life. But whatever the reasons, the lack of attention to those branches of the subject that could probably throw most light on the causes of stagflation, and hence on its cure, is at the least regrettable, the more so since there are many able and energetic economists whose work

---

[1] 'Political Economy or Economics is a study of mankind in the ordinary business of life; it examines that part of individual and social action which is most closely connected with the attainment and with the use of the material requisites of wellbeing'. (Alfred Marshall, *op. cit.*, I, I, § 1.)

could do much to point towards practical solutions to our critical problems.

Although more directly involved in industrial affairs, those who work in the financial institutions have also been constrained by a tradition that has diverted their attention from the issue of industrial development. Whereas in many other countries banks were established in order to promote industry (in some cases, ironically enough, responding to British industry's early technological challenge), in Britain industry had developed under its own momentum, and banks were concerned rather with personal accounts and with the finance of trade and of public borrowing. Involvement of the commercial banks in lending to industry has evolved from the short-term financing of stocks to what are in practice, and increasingly in principle, longer-term loans; and the pension funds and insurance companies, which now dominate the British capital market, have very large investments in those British industrial shares which they accept as meeting their need for security. But the traditions of both the banks and the other major financial institutions have pointed them in directions other than the financial needs for industry's long-term development; and despite their growing awareness of the problem and a number of things they have done to meet it, the attitudes of the financial community seem still to be a constraint on industrial development in Britain as compared with most of the main competing industrial countries.

So far we have looked at the attitudes and institutions of a number of groups in the environment in which industry works. It may be objected that the judgements are subjective or unfair or that conclusive evidence has not been provided or is unobtainable. But we have chosen to risk the objections because we are convinced that such attitudes constitute an important constraint on the health and strength of Britain's economy, so that an analysis of Britain's economic problems is incomplete and may be no help towards solving them if the attitudes are not discussed. We have, moreover, looked first at the groups that are not directly involved in industry, because discussion of attitudes tends to focus too readily on those that are, and particularly on the manual workers and trade unions, without placing them in the context of a culture in which counter-productive attitudes have been only too normal. But it would be wrong to go to the other extreme and exonerate those who work in industry, including the manual workers, from the suspicion of counter-productive attitudes.

The source of workers' bargaining power has been identified above, in the specialisation, interdependence, capital-intensity and skill-intensity of the modern economy. Because the double digit inflation of the past decade is a new condition for Britain, the focus of our analysis was on the translation of bargaining power into pay-push inflation, and on the deflationary policies to which this has led. But while the consequent erosion of profits and hence investment may go far to explain the economic stagnation in Britain and many other countries during this recent period, it can hardly explain the inferior British performance of the past century. Among other causes, however, it seems likely that the workers' attitudes which we have just noted, made increasingly effective through the growth of bargaining power as both economic structure and workers' organisations have evolved, have acted more directly as a brake on industrial development. Industrial development implies change and hence uncertainty; and to British manual workers uncertainty has been associated with a collective memory of the pains of laissez-faire and unemployment. They have resisted changes by means such as demarcation, reluctance to use new machines, limits on the number of apprentices and refusal to accept skilled workers trained in other ways; and in various sectors of industry there has been a deep-rooted tradition of ca'canny, which spreads out the work so as to postpone the day of the next redundancies, as well as depriving the employer of what was held to be an unjustified profit. Nor are such practices a special fault of manual workers, for versions of them are often employed by middle class and professional groups. It may be easy enough now to see that such behaviour has imposed a severe constraint on the rise of British living standards and, in a changing and internationalising economy, will in fact have destroyed far more jobs than it has protected. But that is not how it has looked to countless workers organised in a multitude of groups, large and small, formal and informal, in most parts of the British economy; for over the time-span in terms of which most workers usually judge, the restrictive behaviour may well have brought results that seem quite satisfactory, such as protection from early dismissal and a greater sense of control over the working environment. In the use of the groups' organised strength, strikes have been only the tip of the iceberg. More pervasive and more of a drag on development has been the unspectacular, day-to-day resistance on the part of people who have to be persuaded if changes are to be made effective.

Partly because this subject is not readily amenable to quantitative analysis, partly perhaps because it has not proved attractive to economists, we have no figure to attach to the effect of this on the growth of productivity and real incomes, or on the availability of jobs, or on the loss of competitiveness due to the late appearance of our new products on export markets or the failure to introduce cost-reducing processes as fast as competitors. But our guess is that it may explain a major part of Britain's poor performance. If that is so, we have to ask why British people have made this contribution to bringing their living standard from ranking among the highest down to one of the lowest among the industrialised countries. Is there a genuine difference of interest between the groups that act in this way and the society as a whole? Do the groups fail to understand the consequences of their actions on themselves as well as on others? Do their representatives underestimate the workers' capacity for such understanding? Do people, perhaps, deliberately choose to slow the pace of change because they prefer more stability to higher living standards?

The idea that higher real incomes and hence the development of British industry are a low priority emanates usually from people whose incomes are above average, whose education enables them to enjoy cultural as much as industrial products, and who nevertheless endow themselves adequately with the products of industrial development. There may well be differences of national culture in reactions to change and in the trade-offs that people make between higher consumption and a quiet life. But it is hard to credit that the British have really wanted their real incomes to grow only half as fast as those of their neighbours, or that their neighbours are so weak-minded that they have been persuaded by advertisers to consume more, when they really wanted to consume as little as the British. When we also take into account that modern industrial development leads to cleaner, lighter, more pleasant work and shorter hours as well as higher real incomes, the notion that British workers do not want the fruits of development, such as have been reaped elsewhere in Western Europe, North America and Japan, must surely be ruled out.

Nor can the relationship between the interests of particular groups and of the society as a whole differ so greatly in Britain and in these other countries. Of course the interests of groups can diverge from those of the society: some can use their monopoly power to extract money from others or to obstruct their progress; and workers who are made redundant when production is modernised, and the wealth of the society as a whole consequently increased, may themselves be unemployed for a long time. It is understandable if those workers resist redundancy; and human nature, as well as markets, being imperfect it is not unusual that monopolists exact a monopoly rent. If there is a difference between the effect of group behaviour on economic development in Britain and in other countries it is not, surely, because the potential for groups to gain at society's expense or to lose while society benefits is intrinsically greater in the British economy, but because in other countries these divergences of interest are resolved with less damage to economic performance. Nor, in some countries at least, is this done at the expense of groups of workers whose particular interests are threatened by change in markets or technological progress; for the manpower policies of the governments in Germany and Sweden and of the larger firms in Japan have been rather successful in giving workers confidence that they will be sufficiently compensated, usually by new employment but at least by access to training and by a high rate of unemployment pay, if they do lose their jobs. When set against a complementary expectation that workers will usually gain from economic development, this has made for a different attitude towards industrial change from that which has prevailed in Britain – even with the greater readiness to accept redundancies that has been associated with high redundancy payments.

There may well be many occasions when British workers reject changes of a kind that would be accepted elsewhere, just because they are collectively more determined to resist the imposition of hardship. Conversely, there is no doubt something in the claim that very high unemployment and the closing down of many plants have recently induced a keener awareness of the reality that jobs depend on efficiency. But without an equal awareness of the *benefits* that derive from industrial development and a confidence that those involved in the attendant changes will get a sufficient share of the gains or be adequately compensated for loss, any such realism will hardly survive beyond the period of the deep recession and high unemployment. It is on the contrary more likely to be replaced by yet stronger determination to resist changes that may affect the existing employment pattern. The only solid and durable basis for workers' co-operation in industrial development in a democratic society is the confidence that they will gain from it; and this brings us to the managers of firms, who, together with those responsible for public manpower policies, have to persuade workers that this is so.

The relations of British managers with manual workers have been prejudiced by the division of the country into Disraeli's two nations. Senior managers of British companies with factories abroad say that British managers perform better with foreign workers; conversely it has been shown that British workers have performed better in the subsidiaries of foreign companies, where there are usually foreign managers. This supports the view that the nature of the British class relationship has been an obstacle to communication and mutual trust. It is the task of managers to overcome obstacles to efficiency; and the tougher the obstacles, the higher the quality of management that is needed. We noted earlier that the cast of British education and culture had not been as favourable as in more successful industrial countries to the recruitment of the most able people into industrial management; and this could not fail to impede the process of adaptation to the needs

of modern industry, which include the ability not only to plan developments that are well-founded in technological and marketing as well as
financial terms, but also to persuade employees to co-operate in the development plans. There are grounds to think that the quality of industrial management has improved in recent years; but evidently, by
the hard test of industrial success, it has not yet improved enough.

Many managers feel that they work in a hostile environment, in
which the attitudes of all the other groups we have discussed – politicians, civil servants, educators and intellectuals as well as workers –
combine to stand in the way of success. But managers have the primary
responsibility for industrial efficiency, and if that is impeded by other
groups, the managers need to be able to persuade those other groups to
act differently. To do this, they need not only a high degree of
competence in the technical aspects of their jobs, but also an understanding of the process of industrial development and the capacity to
show how these other groups can benefit from it. Closest to home, and
most important, they have to be able to demonstrate this to the workers
in their own firms.

Changing attitudes through development programmes and contracts

Pay push and resistance to development undermine the ability of a firm
or an economy to provide higher real incomes and eventually even to
sustain employment. Thus behaviour which, given the structure of the
modern economy and the context of British history and institutions, is
understandable and even natural, is evidently against the interests of
the big majority of people. It is not enough to ask whether attitudes to
work and pay have really deteriorated, for that question misses two
fundamental points: for a century already, British economic performance has been inadequate, and attitudes to economic development
have probably played a part in this; and with the growing imperfection
of markets which is largely a function of the economic structure,
behaviour that was previously more likely to be controlled by impersonal market forces now instead increasingly controls the markets,
so that it becomes necessary to find new ways to encourage behaviour
that is appropriate to good performance.

The kernel of this issue of economic development is the behaviour of
managers and other workers in their firms. For it is from the firm, not
the government, that the most effective impetus for development can
come. Central planners lack the detailed knowledge of technologies
and markets on which plans for developing efficient production to meet
future consumer needs have to be based. Nor, as the Soviet experience
since Stalin shows, can those who work in firms normally be ade-

quately motivated by the central planners' instructions. We shall go on to outline the essential part that public policy has to play in the promotion of development with stable prices. But first we have to consider how stronger initiatives for successful development can be generated within the firms.

For successful development, firms need both an appropriate industrial strategy and the resources to finance it, which can come either from achieved profits or from a prospect of profits that is convincing enough to justify the provision of external finance. The co-operation of the managers and other workers is necessary if these two conditions are to be met.

To initiate the strategy is the responsibility of managers. In the large firms that account for the bulk of manufacturing production (in Britain four hundred of them produce nearly two-thirds of it), a complex mass of knowledge about markets, technologies and human resources is required, and a view of the firm's operations as a whole, which other people do not possess. In smaller firms, it can be observed that a single entrepreneur or a small group of managers usually identify the direction in which the business is to go. In large or small firms, participation of others in the process of determining the strategy can range from informal consultation, through formal consultation to co-determination or a co-operative; but the strategy is generally devised by managers or entrepreneurs. Without such a strategy, successful development over the medium and longer term is not likely to take place. Nor will the development materialise unless research, investment, production and sales policies are financed and implemented; and it is a mistake to suppose that they will be unless the co-operation of others in the firm is secured.

We have seen how workers can, by withdrawing their labour or just by working less co-operatively, impose losses on a firm big enough to induce managers to concede pay rises beyond the growth of productivity or to forego the introduction of new machinery or more efficient methods of work. Such pay rises will reduce the firm's profits unless prices are raised as fast, which ceases to be possible when macroeconomic policy tries to check the resulting inflation or when competition from less inflationary producers is met; and resistance to new technology can also impede a firm's development. Thus the workers have the power to prevent the firm's strategy from being financed by denying the firm the profits on which, in any efficient economic system, the finance of investment must be based; and even when finance is assured, they can prevent the new developments from taking place, or at least delay their introduction until the lion's share of the market, and hence the recovery of development costs, has been pre-empted by the competitors. If one country contains more firms in which this happens than other countries, its industries will become less and less competitive and its economy will be steadily weakened. If, on the contrary, workers at all levels apply their energy and intelligence to improve their firm's efficiency and the quality of its products, they can greatly strengthen its development and hence their own prospects for job security and prosperity.

Many people in a firm are, then, in a position either to promote the firm's development or to hamper and delay or even prevent it altogether. Just as there is an overkill of bargaining power in the economy which makes the control of pay push such a complex and thorny problem, so power over the firm's development is widely distributed within the firm, among not only managers but many other groups of workers as well. When power is distributed so that many groups can harm a general interest, that interest can be upheld only by adopting appropriate institutions, rules, procedures or habits of behaviour. In this sense, the problem of the modern firm is one of the constitutional order within it. The tradition in many parts of British industry is one of trench warfare between the 'two sides'; and this has been aggravated by the context of our society and polity, with its class division, supported by ideological and political conflict and a belief that one of the two nineteenth century ideologies or classes will secure lasting dominance. Instead, our firms and economy, if they are to function properly, need a peace settlement which recognises the wide diffusion of power and the mutual interest in the successful development both of firms and of the country as a whole. Managers, workers, shareholders, other financial sources, and purchasers of the product all have power, and their conflicting interests need to be resolved and replaced by a recognition of a mutual interest and common obligation.

Why should workers agree to leave room for profits, if this requires restraint in pay demands, and to accept changes in methods of work, if familiar practices are upset, and possibly some jobs lost? Recently, many pay demands have been restrained and changes accepted because firms have faced bankruptcy and the loss of all jobs in them. But this motive cannot persist when profits are good enough for healthy development. Pay restraint and acceptance of changes must then depend on a confidence that workers will gain enough from the development and a realisation that they will lose if it does not take place. Why should managers endure the hassle of resisting pay demands and exert themselves to devise and implement a development strategy, when this requires so much work and the persuasion of so many sceptical or even hostile groups, instead of a quiet life? Recently many have done it in fighting for their firms' survival. In better circumstances, their own and their firm's success is the normal motive; but in too many British firms, managers have for a long time set their sights too low, partly no doubt through lack of the imagination needed to devise ambitious strategies and development plans, but partly also because of lack of confidence that the other groups that comprise the working and economic environment will enable the plans to be carried out. Prominent among these groups are the other employees in the firm. But there are also the sources of outside finance, by now, in Britain, mainly professionally-managed institutions such as banks, life insurance companies and pension funds, which have to be satisfied that the development plans for which they are to put up the money are likely to show an adequate financial return.

It is not enough just to hope that attitudes will change so that firms can develop to the point where we have a healthy and fully employed economy. Attitudes are related to institutions and procedures; and our institutions and procedures have not provided a framework in which managers have been sufficiently ambitious in devising and implementing development plans or workers confident enough that they will benefit from the firm's development. Arrangements are evidently needed that make a firm's employees confident enough of this so that they use their power to promote the firm's development rather than to obstruct it, and the managers confident enough of workers' cooperation to raise their sights and embark whole-heartedly on ambitious development plans.

The core of such an arrangement has to be the company's development programme, an idea introduced on p. 60 above. It would show the expected growth of added value and of competitive strength, the investment and hence financing requirements and the implications for manpower and methods of work. The growth of added value, through sales of efficiently produced goods and services that customers want to buy, and the security of employment that derives from competitive strength are principal ends; investment and efficient working practices are means. This provides the basis for an agreement, or contract, which commits the firm to try to undertake the programme and to provide the employees with benefits commensurate with its success as this is achieved, in particular through higher incomes and greater job security, and the employees to use their bargaining power in ways that enable the necessary profit targets to be met and appropriate working practices, including manning levels, to be achieved.

It may seem to a Japanese worker that his firm's prosperity is so obviously in his own interest that his co-operation in adjusting work methods and leaving room for profits is forthcoming almost without question. The firm has in the past used the profits to invest in development, the working efficiency has made the development successful, and this has provided the workers with both rapid gains in living standards and security of employment. We suggested earlier that this is implicitly a development contract between the firm and the employees, whereby the firm gets profits and co-operation in work, and the employees get higher real incomes and security of employment. If the employees did not co-operate, the firm could not provide these benefits; and if the firm did not use its profits for development and thus benefit the employees, their co-operation would surely be in doubt. Where an implicit contract such as this exists, it is probably not necessary to make it explicit. But in Britain the workers do not so readily believe that their firm's prosperity will result in equivalent benefit for themselves. If the vicious circle of low co-operation and slow development is to be broken, the gains from development need to be made more explicit, in terms not only of the firm's prosperity in general but also of the benefits for the employees in particular. Such programmes and contracts would have to be firm enough to retain the confidence of employees and sources of finance, while at the same time being adaptable, as we suggest in chapter 9, to unexpected circumstances.

One of the arguments used in favour of State socialism was that the workers in nationalised industries would give their best because, with the enterprise owned by the public in general, the work generates public good not private profit. But the public in general has proved too abstract a concept, and altruism by itself an insufficient motive, for workers in State enterprises to be more willing than those in private companies to co-operate in development without being assured that there is a specific benefit in it for themselves. On the side of private enterprise, it can now be argued that the bigger companies are largely owned by pension funds and life insurance companies, so that dividends benefit the general public, not just a few rich people. There is a growing degree of truth in this argument, even if these financial institutions still benefit the middle classes and the more skilled manual workers more than those lower down the occupational ladder. But it still seems to be too general a proposition to overcome the particularist patterns of behaviour that get in the way of development.

The sale of the National Freight Corporation by the State to the Corporation's employees demonstrates one method of making the workers' interest in the firm's success explicit – a method somewhat similar to that of a producer's co-operative, of which there are a number of examples. More modestly, many British companies have schemes for share ownership or profit sharing by employees which fall far short of full ownership of the firm. Directly aimed at the workers' interest in the development of productivity are schemes for a share in the growth of added value, and plant or company bonuses related to performance. There is a great variety of such schemes. What is essential for our argument is that the employees should clearly see how they will gain from the growth of added value in their firm, as well as how the firm's development plan is designed to cause the added value to grow.

Those who are engaged in the uphill task of industrial management in Britain may respond that this is easier said than done. There are of course many difficulties. Having experienced our record of industrial progress rather than those of our continental neighbours, let alone the Japanese, British workers may find it hard to visualise or believe in the resources that would become available if our performance was to come closer to what is technically possible. Groups who see a direct interest in defending an established position or in safeguarding their jobs may not allow the expected, but still uncertain, future benefits for the firm as a whole to outweigh an immediate chance of gain or threat to their welfare. Those who are themselves willing to give the firm's general interest the benefit of any such doubt may find that their productive behaviour is undermined by those who are not. Generally, the habits of a working life will be hard to break. For all these reasons, the benefits of successful development, and the resulting gains to the employees, need to be a constant point of reference in dealing with questions of pay and patterns of work. The ability of managers to communicate this point is clearly important; but except in small companies, it is not likely to be enough without procedures and institutions that encourage consensus on the firm's development policies and agreement on their application. Here again, there is a variety of possible arrangements. Works councils with statutory rights, as in Germany, to ensure that they are not just talking shops, deserve particular mention, as does the German form of co-determination; and in chapter 9 we recommend the adoption of a German-type system in Britain. Employee ownership of shares offers another approach to co-determination, which becomes more radical than the German system if the proportion of shares owned by employees becomes large. Likewise to the point are proposals for the replacement of multi-unionism by representation by a single union of all union members in a particular firm or establishment. Many of the difficulties in securing agreement on the changes involved in industrial development arise from differences of interest among different groups of employees within the establishment or firm; and these are more likely to be resolved fairly in a way that enables the changes to be implemented efficiently if the workers' interests are represented by a single union, which is therefore more impartial about the interests of different groups within the organisation. Such a union can reach an agreement that comes closer to a general interest and is better placed to ensure that the agreement is respected by both its members and the firm.

Agreement between firms and their employees' representatives on policies for development and on the main implications for pay, work practices and security of employment could offer a better basis for industrial progress than exists in most British firms at present. But it would not by itself secure the success of the economy, or even of the individual firm, because many factors in that success are beyond the firm's control. Thus it may be impossible for one firm in a sector to keep pay at a level that leaves room for adequate profits, if the general level of pay in the industry or country is rising too fast or if prices are, as a result of over-capacity in sectors with high fixed costs, too low to finance development costs as well as the pay required to retain the necessary workers. In so far as the problem is confined to levels of pay within the sector, this can be dealt with by agreements that relate to the whole sector. But although this is normal in Germany, in most sectors Britain lacks the strong industrial unions and employers' associations that could render this effective; and the various industrial labour markets are interdependent enough for pay push in other sectors to spill over even into a sector that is itself effective in its development planning. Pay-push inflation has to be dealt with by public policy as well as by the firm. Government organises the manpower service that seeks to provide for any workers who may be displaced in the course of the firm's development. Government decides the macroeconomic policy that can make or break the fortunes of many companies. Without a convincing government development programme, to complement that of the firms, the chances of firms' successful development will be much reduced.

In primitive economies agriculture provides the bulk of employment; in advanced economies, usually 5–10 per cent, though less than 3 per cent in Britain. Changes in markets and technologies cause changes in the numbers employed in different sectors, and in some sectors the numbers are reduced. It is natural for those who work in such sectors to resist the process; but the experience of recent years shows that too much resistance can cause the sector to collapse, with a rate of loss of jobs which is frighteningly high. The German steel industry offers an instructive contrast to the British and the French. The Germans have been steadily reducing the number of steelworkers for more than a decade as they introduced new technology. Natural wastage looked after much of the reduction and those made redundant were not very many at any one time and place, and hence more easily absorbed in the labour market; the firms remained financially stronger and thus better able to maintain their development. The British and French industries did not face the need for this kind of change until their steel companies were making enormous losses; they then rapidly decanted large numbers of workers on to labour markets that could not absorb them, and they are badly placed to finance the development needed to secure the remaining jobs in the future. The Germans have one of the world's most highly developed public policies for manpower; and the availability of training, excellent placement services and meanwhile high unemployment pay makes industrial change that may require redundancies more acceptable. This helps firms to plan their development boldly, without waiting until impending bankruptcy forces the issue, when the investment needed to become competitive is hard or impossible to finance. Evidently, first-rate and well-funded manpower policies make it easier for firms and workers to initiate development in good time.

More controversial and difficult is the role of public policy in pay determination. Yet the individual firm, however well the employees understand the need for profit and the benefits of development, cannot stand aside from general trends in the labour market; and we have seen that monetary policy or global demand management cannot themselves stop pay-push inflation without at the same time stopping economic development. The firms that organise themselves to finance development, with the necessary support from employees, also need support from public policy if pay is to be kept within bounds that allow prices, which must include provision for development costs, to be internationally competitive.

Professor Meade has proposed a form of incomes policy in which those concerned with a collective bargain could appeal to an arbitration body that would be able to impose powerful sanctions, short of compulsion, on those who failed to comply with its award. In determining its award it would be the statutory duty of the arbitral body to lay stress on the promotion of employment in the sector under review; that is to say, it would have to determine whether or not the rate of pay that was in dispute would be likely to impede or to encourage employment in the sector of the economy under examination, taking into account the knowledge that fiscal and monetary policies would be so designed as to cause a predetermined steady rate of growth in the total money demand for labour (of, say, 5 per cent per annum) and having regard to the probable development of rates of pay in other comparable employments.[2]

---

[2] James E. Meade, *Stagflation, Volume 1: Wage-Fixing*, (George Allen and Unwin, London, 1982), p. 109.

In this form the proposal is open to serious criticism. First, the process is not really arbitration, which is a judicial process for the equitable resolution of a difference between two parties *based on the evidence which those parties give*. Here the deciding body, having been instructed on a key issue in its determination, would have to be free to call for such additional evidence as might be required to illuminate that issue. This opens up the possibility of an award which is supported by the evidence of neither party. What is being proposed is a tribunal with compulsory powers to hear disputes referred by one party, and a considerable armoury of penalties to enable it to enforce its will. But in what circumstances would it do other than award what the employers have offered? There is, after all, a general presumption that *in a particular sector* less labour will be used the higher its price. This presumption will be overturned (a) if the dispute relates to the attraction of some key types of worker in short supply, so that a higher wage to attract such workers will increase the employment opportunities of other grades, or (b) if, having regard to the growth in the total money demand for labour, the employer's offer is unrealistically low – that is, he could pay more without loss of markets. But disputes of these kinds are much more likely to be settled without recourse to the tribunal. Consequently the tribunal would be seen (at least in the labour conditions predicted for the rest of this century) as mainly an instrument for frustrating the trade unions.

We do not see this, therefore, as solving the problems of incomes policy – a subject to which we revert in chapter 9. But for the present purpose we can learn from Professor Meade's proposal. The criterion of 'employment promotion' is ill-defined unless one specifies the *period*. British Rail would no doubt employ more porters on its stations if their wages were halved; but few would see this as a genuine strengthening of their long-run ability to compete. Secure and continuing employment opportunities depend on adequate investment and technological advance, often (though not always) leading to an increase in the 'quality' of employment: that is an increase in skill content and an improvement in conditions. It might be suggested, therefore, that any bodies established to help to resolve disputes in collective bargaining should be advised to use the criterion of *development*: that is, to allow firms with adequate development plans to continue to finance them while remaining fully competitive with relevant rivals at home or abroad. It might be thought that such an issue, which bears on 'ability to pay', would automatically be raised by the employers' side in any hearing; but in practice employers frequently fail to deploy evidence on the matter, even though the issue is vital to the firms' survival.

Just as a stock objection to rationalisation cartels is that governments cannot judge the validity of rationalisation plans (although the Japanese and German governments have demonstrated their ability to do so well enough), so it may be objected that tribunals cannot judge how much money should be allowed for development plans. But they must include people who understand how to do this, if they are to play their necessary part in controlling pay push in a way that allows for development that is in the interest of both employees and firms. Since pay is about the most important element in determining the finance available for development, and development in turn determines the real value of pay in any but a short time scale, it should be regarded as extraordinary if tribunals do not usually command this sort of knowledge, rather than that its provision should be required. The number of cases in which complex judgements of this sort would have to be made could anyway be limited by the number of large firms. Thus if pay and prices are set at appropriate levels in the top four hundred firms, which produce two-thirds of manufacturing output, and comparably in the public sector, this would set a general trend for the economy.

In focusing on the ability to finance development, tribunals would be helping to concentrate attention on the fundamental reason why it is in workers' interests that pay push should be controlled: that uncontrolled pay push kills the goose that lays the golden egg. By setting up tribunals with instructions to do this, public policy would make a major part of its contribution to a national development understanding or agreement more relevant to the country's needs than a social contract which trades pay restraint against social measures that may be desirable in themselves but have less logical connection with the need to restrain pay.

Not that social policy is irrelevant to pay determination. However well designed the schemes for distributing the fruits of a firm's development among the employees may be, workers will be liable to suspect that the benefit will be unfairly biassed in favour of the owners of capital, unless they themselves share adequately in the ownership either of their firms or of the business sector as a whole. Capital transfer tax should, in the long run, lead to a more equal ownership of property in Britain; but a change of attitude is needed sooner if Britain's industrial strength is to be restored. Share ownership schemes might be more popular if they attracted tax advantages similar to those of house ownership; and the less the participation in pension and life insurance schemes is skewed in favour of those with higher incomes, the more convincing will be the argument that the ownership of industry has already been socialised by the insurance companies and pension funds. Thus a property ownership policy, defining property in a wide sense, should be an important element in a national development programme. More broadly, social policy in Britain and other West European countries has played a large part in moderating class conflict, and workers' co-operation in a national development understanding that includes an effective pay policy would be hard to sustain if social policy were at the same time seen to be fomenting stife between the classes. Pay policy will not stick, and stagflation will therefore continue, unless the pay policy is widely held both to be necessary for an economic development that benefits the big majority and to be accompanied by a social policy that is believed to be just. Critics of pay policy often assume that justice and self-interest are incompatible concepts. But the world is not so simple. Most systems will not work unless they appeal to both self-interest and a sense of justice; and this applies with particular force to pay, in the imperfect labour markets of the modern economy.

Since the co-operation of both employers' and workers' representatives is necessary if pay policy is to succeed, joint institutions are indicated to advise on its formation and to help in its implementation. Joint bodies are, by the same token, necessary to an effective manpower policy, and do indeed exist in the Manpower Services Commission and in similar bodies in other countries. With respect to development policies, the National Economic Development Council was established to perform this role, which it has continued to do though without ever becoming central to the policy-making process. If government is to play its due part in restoring British economic strength, and in particular in securing the necessary changes of attitude towards the linked issues of development and pay that have been the subject of this chapter, it needs to show a new determination to give development policy a high priority, not only in policy to control pay push, but also in matters such as training, research, development, investment and Britain's relationship with the international economy; and these are the subjects of the next two chapters.

6 Paying the Costs of Development

We have seen how economic development, in most other industrial countries as well as in Britain, has been suppressed during the past decade by pay push and weak prices squeezing profits and hence investment, and how British attitudes towards industry have weakened the British economy for a century before that. Firms' policies and public policies that restored enough space between pay and stable prices to enable development to be financed, combined with a commitment by firms and employees to carry through development programmes, would do much to make the British economy more dynamic. But the development of a modern economy requires not only initiative and efficiency from the firms themselves, within a framework of pay and price trends that allow for adequate profits, but also a major contribution from governments in the form of industrial and manpower policy. The technical reason for this lies in the relationship between the private and social costs and benefits of development. Some of the costs of modern economic development cannot be financed by the individual firm: general education and fundamental research are obvious examples but there are, as we shall argue in this chapter, many more, associated with the high and rising costs of developing the necessary new skills and technologies, and of converting the economy away from inappropriate old ones. If governments do not help to pay the costs which efficient firms cannot finance, the development will not take place.

Conventionally, economists have stressed the private gains and the social costs of industrial development. In Britain this has for a long time been perverse, since it has been clear that resources of the size generated by other countries' more dynamic development would have offered vast scope for social as well as private benefit in Britain, so that our industrial weakness implied equivalent social loss. During the last decade, when almost all advanced industrial countries have stagnated, the social costs of deficient development have become yet more obvious, not only in Britain but also in other industrial countries. The impact on public finance alone has been enormous, with loss of revenue and high expenditure on unemployment pay. Even after unemployment has been reduced, revenue will remain lower than it would have been had normal development continued through the years of stagflation, bringing the national income of which revenue is a function to a higher base. Budgetary loss is, moreover, but one narrow, if important, element in the social costs of economic stagnation and unemployment, quite apart from the private costs to individuals in human and financial terms. Like health or good air to breathe, the social benefits of economic development may not be so perceptible when you have them; but their merits become patent when you have not. It seems hardly possible that the social costs, such as pollution or other damage to the environment, could outweigh the benefit of having much greater resources both for private consumption and for social expenditure, among other things on the environment itself. Where the damage is not acceptable, as it often will not be in a society that cares about the quality of life, the cost of preventing it can be met from the resources which economic development provides; and how far that cost is borne by the public or a private purse must depend on the relative balances of private cost and benefit and of social cost and benefit. The essential point for our purpose here is that the social benefit of development should not be overshadowed because some economists, influenced perhaps by the anti-industrial intellectual climate we have discussed, have been so much preoccupied by the social costs.

Nor should preoccupation with the costs of development in the sense of environmental damage and other such social costs divert attention from the costs of development in a more conventional sense: the money that has to be spent on training, research, plant, equipment and infrastructure without which modern development cannot take place. As technology has progressed, all these things have come to occupy a larger proportion of the growing value of total output; and despite the cheapness and efficiency of the new microelectronic technology, this general tendency is not likely to be reversed. The larger part of the costs of development can be borne by the firms that carry it out and recouped from the sales of the resulting products. But those costs which are incurred to provide conditions of development that are of benefit not just to a single firm but to the economy as a whole or to a sector, area or other wide group of economic agents, have become an increasing proportion of the total development costs. General education and fundamental research have already been mentioned. A substantial part of training is of this sort, because most of the people who are trained do not work for long with the firms that train them. The same can be said of much applied research, which promotes development far beyond the firm that undertakes it, as the new technology is diffused through the economy. Much infrastructure cannot easily be paid for by those who need it to carry through their developments, with roads an obvious example. There is evidently a case for public financing of such costs. In some instances, such as the most general education, the most fundamental research or the road network in towns, the case is almost incontrovertible; in others, such as training and applied research, it is a matter of economic judgement and political choice. But it should not be surprising if, in an economy that becomes increasingly complex, interdependent, capital-intensive and skill-intensive, the proportion of development costs with respect to which the case for public financial support is strong should tend to increase, because of change in the economic structure rather than in political philosophy. Of course attitudes towards public support for development have to change, if they have previously been based on the premise of laissez-faire; the support will not be effective if neither those who are giving it nor those who are receiving it believe it should be provided. This is, however, but one of the changes of attitude that have become necessary if the British are to get to grips with the conditions of development of the modern economy.

When attitudes have become fixed, as in Britain, in ways that place a severe constraint on economic development, one contribution that public policy can make to breaking out of the vicious circle of negative attitudes and poor growth may well be to provide greater incentives for firms to develop than would be necessary in countries where the interaction between attitudes and development is more benign. Attitudes are less likely to change if the financial rewards for changing them are seen as small or very uncertain, as they are likely to be in a slowly or uncertainly developing economy. The rewards during a period when attitudes need to be changed may therefore have to be larger than when appropriate attitudes have been established; and that can imply not only tax incentives for firms and individuals but also subsidies or other forms of support to promote development.

This argument for a special effort of public support for development to break out of Britain's secular industrial stagnation has been powerfully reinforced by the new stagflation of the past decade; and the case has been extended to the whole of Western Europe and North America. For the combination of pay push, low profits, deflation, weak prices, low investment and low growth has engendered pessimism within firms about the prospects for future development as well as depriving many of them of the financial means to embark on it. It may well be necessary to offer particularly favourable rewards for undertaking development as well as other public support for it, if the dynamism of the western economies is to be restored.

Inadequate skill and education
Since by far the most important resource of any economy is the human

skill and effort available to it, faults in this area must rank high among the potential constraints of effective economic development. The failings may lie in education or training, and in the quantity, quality or appropriateness of either. They may lie in attitudes and practices which governments can do little to change; but they may also lie in inadequate or ill-directed public provision, since education and certain types of training are prominent among the activities whose social benefits are such that there is a strong and almost universally recognised case for public support. There is a widespread belief that there are indeed serious faults, even if the evidence is difficult to interpret. Let us review some of it.

First, however, a word of warning. Much of the public discussion about training in skills and about education for jobs appears to assume that the typical worker is an operative in manufacturing industry or construction. But these are now minority sources of jobs, and there is every likelihood that the proportion of the labour force employed in making physical things will decline further, as automation advances. While the levels of skill required in manufacturing will rise, the 'typical' job is in the performance of services and in administrative and professional work, and this fact needs to be very much to the front of our minds as we think about preparation for jobs in the twenty-first century.

The Manpower Services Commission, in its consultative document, *A New Training Initiative* (May 1981), made a striking comparison with France and West Germany:

Table 6.1   Activities of young people after compulsory school period

	Full-time education		Apprenticeship	Row percentages Work or unemployment
	General	*Vocational*		
France	27	40	14	19
West Germany	25	18	50	7
Great Britain	32	10	14	44

Germany relies heavily on apprenticeship, and France on continued full-time vocational education: Britain does less of both, and the new schemes to be introduced in 1983 (1982 in Northern Ireland) will not be an adequate correction. Large numbers of our young people leave school with no qualification of direct value in the market place, and go either into unemployment or into jobs in which the training content is small.

A consequence of the inadequacy of vocational training is the existence of persistent skill shortages, even in times of depression and even in areas of the country that are particularly depressed. It must not, of course, be supposed that all skill shortages can be foreseen and prevented; some, which follow the unexpectedly rapid rise of a new technology, perform an economic function in stimulating the appearance of new supplies of trained manpower. At present both electronic engineers and computer programmers are in short supply and enjoy high earnings: the likely consequence is a massive increase in the numbers seeking training, so that in due course the supply will over-shoot the requirement. Shortages of this kind exist in all advanced countries, but they are self-correcting. What is a matter for greater concern is that the shortages may be corrected more slowly in Britain than in some of our main competitors, and that in some trades there has been a long-term *persistence* of a skill shortage. This may be due to an inadequate differential in pay between the skilled and the unskilled; or to restrictive practices which limit the numbers entering training; or to a general inadequacy of the training system, causing it to 'catch' too few entrants of the required ability. The lack of skill is both a cause and a consequence of the sluggishness of British industry in producing advanced products. It should be remembered that in agriculture, transport, distribution, finance, administration, and some forms of personal service our position in the world league is very much more favourable; but the slow progress of industry has been a critical drag on the economy.

A shortage of joiners or fitters or chefs, once identified, can be made the subject of a specific effort in training. But many people see also evidence of a more diffuse form of disadvantage, which arises from the nature of school education. One complaint is that professional educators have little idea of the nature and requirements of the economic system, and that they encourage in the young ideas which are harmful to economic success – such as that engineering is work for those who are too stupid to do other things. The Confederation of British Industry has done much to encourage in the schools a better appreciation of industry, but the gap in understanding is still considerable. It is indeed difficult to see how it can be bridged, while we continue to re-cruit teachers predominantly from those who have never seen life outside an educational institution (see p. 163).

There is, however, a more serious charge: namely that the content of education, particularly for those who leave school at 16, is inadequate as a preparation for the modern world. The number of hours of teaching in the school year has tended to become shorter, and the range of subjects and projects covered has become wider. In comparison with France and Japan, the requirement of hard work at school is con-siderably less. In passing from the, now despised, grind of the 3 Rs to a 'modern' curriculum, with its enjoyable diversity, we have still made it possible for children who are by no means mentally defective to complete their schooling barely literate or numerate. Whereas in some countries children in secondary school are required to carry until they leave a range of subjects, including language, mathematics and science, we permit to those who stay at school the choice of knowing virtually no science, or of giving up mathematics as hopeless, or of knowing no language but their own.

Fortunately, of course, children are educated by many influences other than school. Nevertheless, the ground-work – the ability to write a clear sentence, to understand instructions precisely, to perform the basic manipulations of mathematics, to appreciate essential facts about the physical world – is extremely important. Unless it is well done, young people will lack the ability to adapt to requirements for new skills that arise during their working life. It is not too extreme a statement to say that our present educational system is designed to provide large numbers of people who are unskilled or who perform unchanging routine skills; and the world no longer needs many such people in its advanced economies. Thus the educational system is turning out people who are likely to be unnecessarily deprived throughout their working lives.

The doubts about the appropriateness or adequacy of education extend to higher education. Here, however, the position is less clear. It is true that the proportion of each age-group entering higher education is much less than in (say) the United States. Probably, however, the opportunities given to first-rate origianl minds are fairly good in both countries. But the United States has a much larger number of more ordinary people who have received an extended general education; and both the United States and other leading industrial countries have more of their most able people suitably educated for business careers. This is of great value in improving the quality available for general management: too many British business men are lacking in the breadth of their education. But its relevance to the performance of technical functions is less evident. Rather than promote a flood of graduates, many of whom would be used on work which does not strictly require that level of preparation, it might be more cost-effective to expand facilities for industrial or commercial training below degree level – that is, in the British context, to expand 'further' education rather than 'higher' education.

Such a programme could be directed more precisely to specific need, whereas the balance of effort in higher education tends to be determined by ill-informed student choice. But there are problems in further education also. What is needed is a common effort by employers and educators, using 'real life' situations as much as possible as the basis for training, and altering the balance and content of training in response to expected future needs in employment. But Bernard Shaw's savage dictum, 'He who can, does. He who cannot, teaches', has an uncomfortable relevance in describing the division of attitudes that exists between teaching institutions and employers. As a PSI study[1] has shown, even the government's Skillcentres, existing for an immediate practical purpose, were oddly divorced from local industry in the areas which they serve.

Although many young people – even those coming from advanced parts of the educational system – have learnt very little about science, there is probably a growing diffused impression of its methods and results, as a consequence of the newsworthiness of scientific advances: for instance, the television programme 'Tomorrow's World' has a considerable following. But the understanding of technology – which is a practical art with a scientific foundation and an economic context – is more limited. It is not just applied science, nor is it coterminous with engineering; it requires the development of a range of qualities that can be brought to bear on the solution of specific problems. The 'two cultures' of which C. P. Snow wrote are more properly three – arts, science and technology; and it is a proper criticism of our educational system that it does far too little to break down the barriers to understanding between them.

There would unquestionably be social benefit in having a better educated and more appropriately skilled labour force: we would be much better able to seize new opportunities and to react flexibly and speedily to changing needs, and thus to generate higher incomes and more employment opportunities. Indeed, one aspect of the slowness of the output response, when the British economy is stimulated, is the difficulty which employers find in recruiting the skills needed for expansion. The real output per head in Japan multiplied by 3 in 16 years: any such expansion here would have been prevented by the inadequacy of skills. Of course, there is private benefit, or benefit to a particular enterprise or economic unit, also to be found in a higher level of education or skill. But efforts to 'privatise' the problem, to put the responsibility on to employers, run into two difficulties. First, it is very difficult to prevent some employers becoming parasites on the superior training facilities provided by others, and this implies that the better the training job is done, the more likely it is to be uneconomic, since many of those trained will be 'poached' by other firms long

---

[1] Richard Berthoud, *Training Adults for Skilled Jobs: Skillcentre Training and Local Labour Markets*, (Policy Studies Institute, Report 575, London, 1978).

before they have returned the value of their training. Systems of levy and grant have been used to try to overcome this problem, but they have proved unpopular – which probably means that (unlike Germany) we have a low level of 'good citizenship' among employers in the matter of training, so that the parasites tend to be in a majority. Second, employers can see that, if a form of training can be pushed into the State educational system, it will be largely free of immediate cost to them. The general charge on taxes and rates may be larger, but it is less easily perceived. If the big majority of employers were to adopt the German practice of training enough of their employees to the standards of skill needed in the modern economy, there would be less need for State support – although it should be noted that even in Germany, where employers are better citizens in this respect, State expenditure on training is very high. In Britain, so long as employers do less, the need for public support to break this constraint of human as well as economic development will be yet greater.

It can be argued that the costs of education and training should be paid by the individuals who receive it, out of their enhanced lifetime earnings; and indeed a number of studies have shown that the enhancement from *higher* education is considerable, and might well service the cost of a loan to pay for the education. But skill differentials in the workshop have become squeezed – indeed, they have sometimes become negative; so this would be a very uncertain means of financing that level of skill training. In any case, it is a condition of stronger economic development in Britain that we increase, as quickly as possible, the level and quality of education and skill obtained by young people, and a proposition which offers an immediate debt and a deferred benefit is very unlikely to be effective in achieving this. Here again, more of the responsibility could be placed on individuals if the practice came to be accepted as more normal and if skilled people were sufficiently confident that they would in future receive differentials adequate to finance the training costs. Meanwhile, particularly among skilled manual workers, neither the practice nor, in some cases, the differentials are conducive to a change in the present practice. On the contrary, more public support and greater incentives would seem to be required if skills are to become sufficiently abundant.

Our own proposals for dealing with the problem will be found in chapter 9. For the present purpose, it is sufficient to say that – although the 'adequacy' of education and training is something very difficult to define – there seems good reason to think that certain faults of the British system are serious constraints on the economy. Britain's training effort needs more public support than it has had in the past if the constraint of skill shortages is to be overcome. But even though public money is necessary, the case of education shows that it is not enough. Attitudes, policies and institutions have to change if the expenditure is to be effective in breaking the constraint.

Technological development

The development of technology is closely related to the development of skills. Deficient education and training place a severe constraint on the invention and application of new technologies. There is, indeed, a wide border area between training and technological development, in the process of diffusion of new technologies among firms that are not in the forefront of technological progress; and public policy can justifiably assist the information and awareness aspects of the diffusion process just as it can support training, in view of the social benefit of technological advance throughout the economy. But there is also an increasingly formidable constraint on economic development in the form of the ever-rising costs of research and of the development of its results into saleable products. Let us consider how the social benefits of this sharper end of technological development relate to the private costs and benefits, and how British attitudes and practices have influenced the effectiveness of the public policy that has been intended to promote it.

The word 'technology' derives from the Greek word for an art or craft, that is a practical means of doing things by the exercise of human skill. In this general sense there can be a technology of banking, or administration, or education, just as much as a technology of manufacture. By a transference of ideas, the word has come to be associated with 'industrial arts' and with the machines by which things are made. But this is an unfortunate limitation, tending once again to give exclusive prominence to the manufacturing part of the economy, and even for that part leaving us with no convenient collective description for improvements of method which are not embodied in hardware. In any case, a 'technological advance' can be – and often is – derived in part from a new machine, and in part from a new system or method of organising work. This is a very familiar thought in relation to the uses of computers, where the 'software' – that is, the development of systems of use – may cost a lot more than the 'hardware', the computer itself.

It is better, therefore, to give to 'technology' a broad definition, applicable to methods in all parts of the economy whether or not they are primarily embodied in machines. Technology alters by 'invention', that is the contrivance of a new method or means of doing something, or of a new product; but invention, in this general sense, is not a sufficient condition for change. An actual process of change we describe as 'innovation', that is the act of carrying into practical effect the potential of new methods and new products.

The general state of technology in a country is not susceptible to very rapid change, since part of it is embodied in long-lasting investment and much is inter-related with the developed abilities of the labour force. If the state of technology has become in some sense inappropriate, this operates as a constraint preventing the satisfactory development and working of the economy; and the seriousness of that constraint is greater if there are frictions and barriers which prevent or slow down the correction of inappropriateness of technology.

But the meaning of 'inappropriate' in this statement is elusive. A failure to use in country A the newest technology developed in country B is not of itself proof that A has missed an opportunity. The 'factor endowments' of the two countries will differ; the new technology may be intended to overcome some factor shortage in B which is not present in A. The appropriateness of a technology has to be judged in relation to the expectations which a country seeks to fulfil through its economic activity. Thus it might be theoretically possible for Britain to revert to being a nation of craftsmen, working long hours with simple methods; but though such an economy might incidentally produce work of great quality and beauty, its general standard of living would be very much lower than is now considered tolerable. Since we have chosen to compete with, and to seek to equal in wealth, other 'advanced' nations, it is necessary that our technology should broadly match theirs in the specification and quality of what is produced and in the efficiency of production.

There is a general impression that British technology has, on average, become backward, and that this is a process which can be traced over a long time – perhaps for 120 years. It is easy to set down a list of industries in which we have been overtaken, and defeated in trade, by other countries; and to show that in some branches of engineering we have become producers and exporters of old-fashioned and unsophisticated equipment, but have had to import the high technology versions of the same equipment for our own use. This evidence suffers, however, from the effects of the general tendency to equate the economy to manufacturing industry. In the oil, natural gas and coal industries there is no evident technical lag; and – using 'technology' in the broad sense we have chosen – the methods of (say) the finance sector, of agriculture, of government administration, and of sectors of retailing and tourism are, though certainly imperfect, well up to the standards achieved by other nations. Furthermore, every nation must expect to be only second- or third-best in some areas of its technology; cycles of replacement are not synchronised, and areas of concentration of interest differ. The fact that France and Japan have faster railway trains is not sufficient evidence for making a general charge of technical backwardness against British Rail.

It is often assumed that technology alters mainly as a result of research and development expenditure. This, however, may be misleading. What is identified as 'research and development' is deliberate and segregated expenditure *intended* to discover new products or processes and to bring them to the point of commercial application. A planned and identifiable research and development activity is often to be found in large organisations; but it must not be concluded that, because a small firm has no 'research department', therefore it never improves its products or processes. Indeed, even in a large organisation much technological progress arises by piecemeal improvements made on the shop floor, or by new ideas or systems being tried out by people who are not identified as having a research function.

Nevertheless, research and development expenditure is obviously a key variable related to technological change, and there is evidence that, over the 1970s, this expenditure as a percentage of gross national product was static or declining in the United Kingdom and in the United States, but rising in West Germany and Japan; and other bits of evidence, for instance from patent applications, can be used to suggest an unsatisfactory state of innovation.[2] But this is very treacherous territory. The relation between research and development expenditure, in total, and economic success is not at all a direct one. Apart from the fact, already mentioned, that technological change is not wholly dependent on identifiable research and development, one reason for this is the tendency for the bulk of expenditure to fall in narrow fields – such as defence, aerospace, nuclear energy – which have different importance to different countries. Even industry-financed research and development tends to be heavily concentrated on chemicals and electrical engineering. Furthermore, much new technology can be bought on licence, or obtained embodied in equipment imports, provided that there is enough technical expertise to make proper use of the incoming technology. Japanese research and development expenditures have indeed been rising, but they were quite low through the great period of Japanese success – and, of course, they remain much lower in absolute terms than expenditure in the United States, and it could be argued that it is the *absolute* size of this spending which ought to be relevant to the rate of innovation and of technical advance. Yet from 1967 to 1978 real gross product per employee rose

---

[2] See Kerry Schott, *Industrial Innovation in the United Kingdom, Canada and the United States*, (British-North American Committee, London, 1981).

by 13 per cent in the United States, by 28 per cent in the United Kingdom, but by 95 per cent in Japan.[3]

A further line of argument is that Britain gives too much attention to basic discovery, which others then exploit. It is true that we have a very distinguished record in basic science, evidenced (for instance) in the roll of Nobel prizewinners. But the use of resources for basic science is in all countries small compared with the use for applied science and technological development; so the argument from diversion of financial resources is a weak one. The belief that 'foreigners take our ideas and make a success of them' is not confined to Britain, and is not satisfactorily established by quoting individual cases. Nevertheless, the idea of a British weakness in exploitation does have something in it; it would be an expected result of the deficiency in the flow of high ability into certain industries.

It looks as if we need a more cautious statement of the nature of the technological constraint. Because, apart from energy, the British economy is not (in relation to its population) well endowed with natural resources, the fulfilment of expectations of a high standard of living is crucially dependent on the use of brains – that is, on the development of better products and services and better ways of producing them. The 'technological constraint' is seen in an inability to show success in keeping up or moving ahead of other advanced nations *over a sufficient range* of economic activities. We have the wrong ratio of lame ducks to swans.

Such a constraint could be self-perpetuating, because economic ill-success erodes the profits that are needed to finance new products and new methods. In some trades, such as aircraft manufacture and pharmaceuticals, the costs of development are a very high proportion of the costs of the finished product, and there may be problems in mounting a development programme with a long-deferred pay-off when profits are low. However, the aircraft industry depends, in all the main producing countries, on the defence interest; it is difficult to argue that aerospace research has been starved of resources in Britain, because the significance of the defence element cannot be assessed by outsiders. (Some people have argued that aerospace industries have taken far too large a proportion of scientific manpower.) More generally, the cost of investment associated with technical change is more likely to be a problem than the cost of finding out what change to make. Returning to the international comparisons of research and development expenditure, we see that, although the British *trend* is unfavourable, the *amount* is not exceptionally low. Rightly distributed, and with due ingenuity in searching out and adapting developments

[3] See table on p. 28.

made in other nations, the expenditure looks as if it ought to have been able to support a sufficient rate of technological advance; remembering that in all countries there are social limitations to the speed with which change can be made.

It is necessary at this point to beware of the illusion of insularity. It is obviously not appropriate for Lancashire to mount research and development programmes to meet every requirement of technological advance in Lancashire industries. The smaller the area we take, the more it must depend on inflows of technology. Yet the problem is sometimes discussed as if Britain must be self-sufficient in developing new technology. This is impossible; and the attempt to be self-sufficient, to re-invent wheels which have been invented elsewhere, is a potential waste of resources. A sovereign State, divided by geography, laws and language from other States, will need to mount a sufficient scientific and technological effort of its own to be able to appreciate the significance of international flows of knowledge, to adapt technology to its special needs, and to overcome limitations produced by secrecy. That implies having technologists working at the frontiers of knowledge; but Britain, as a small country, must expect a large part of its advances to come from pulling in ideas originated or developed abroad.

The effect of low profits on investment is discussed elsewhere (p. 63 ff). Apart from this aspect of the problem, the difficulty in breaking through the technological constraint seems to lie in a lack of drive and ingenuity in adapting and adopting new ideas. This brings us sharply back to issues of the recruitment of high ability to management, and to the training of management (including a sufficient education in the possibilities of new technology).

That these are indeed the central issues is confirmed, both by examining the history of some of the 'lame duck' industries and by observing the weakness of some of the alternative excuses for failure. Thus, there is little evidence that technological advance is often *prevented* by resistance from the workforce. It may often be delayed, and sometimes too high a price in compensation for change is demanded; but, more typically, workers have been proud to be associated with using advanced technology or making advanced products. and have seen this as an assurance of stability in employment. Nor is it usually plausible that advance has been prevented by inability to get some specialist type of manpower; those who put forward this reason are usually found to have done little, either by offering higher salaries or by developing special training, to overcome the shortage of which they complain.

There are very evident social benefits in improving the ratio of swans to lame ducks. If (apart from the finance of investment) the main issue is one of awakening sluggish managers to their opportunities, and raising the general quality of entrepreneurship, what can government do to help? Evidently part of the problem lies in the educational system (p. 102 ff), and a special drive to improve the quality and toughness of training for management would help. But this is a very slow-acting remedy. What can be done in the short and medium term?

One answer is to sharpen competition, and let the inefficient know that they will be driven to the wall rather quickly. Associated with this could be the break-up of very large enterprises, so as to introduce a competition of ideas instead of a monolithic structure which invites lethargy. Observation of highly competitive industries, however, suggests that management is forced to take very short views, which may make it impossible to plan a long-term improvement – particularly if, as we argue later, British financial institutions tend to take too short-term a view in the provision of funds for industrial de-velopment. The right object of policy, therefore, is to have a reasonable balance of safety and competition. Monopoly certainly needs to be challenged – the example of British Telecom shows how even a marginal threat produces a much greater openness to new ideas. But equally some industries may need help and protection, or amalga-mation of firms into larger units, if they are ever to be able to develop a viable continuing policy of technological improvement.

Research and development costs are given favourable tax treatment in many countries, but the uneven incidence of company taxation in Britain suggests that further tax benefits might not contribute a great deal to inducing technological change. Alternatively, there can be direct subsidies to research and development costs (in Northern Ireland, for instance, grants of up to 50 per cent are available); or government can help co-operative research in industry, through commissioning work by research associations; or it can make a contri-bution through its own laboratories or (more distantly) by the support of research in higher education institutions.

All these measures have been used, and are a proper recognition of the social benefit that might be gained. But their effectiveness lies more in encouraging those who are already awake to possibilities than in awakening the sleepers. A further approach, therefore, is to con-centrate on encouraging awareness of new technology – for there are evident benefits from speeding up the rate at which it is diffused, and smaller firms (not supporting their own research) may suffer from simple ignorance of what is available. An example of this approach is the Microprocessor Applications Project, which has three arms: intro-ductory 'awareness' courses, subsidies for consultancy to identify particular uses, and subsidies for putting in applications. But an even more significant example is to be found in agriculture. Here it has been the practice over a long time to provide advisory services to help farmers to use new 'technology' (including breeds of livestock or types of crop) sensibly, and to assist them to adapt to changing market conditions. Although this is an industry of small units, many of them run by people with no extensive educational background, the efficiency of agriculture has been remarkably well advanced. Part of the credit no doubt goes to the protected markets that can be enjoyed in some products; but the importance of the advisory services is considerable, and one wonders why similar methods are not applied in other sectors.

In all the interventions so far listed there is a distant memory of laissez-faire: they induce, encourage or advise, but ultimately the action rests with the individual enterprise. But what about government direct action to develop high-technology enterprises? The route to this by way of nationalisation has been comprehensively devalued by the British experience, though this may be blamed more on the form of organisation used, and its tendency to foster cosy arrangements between management and workers, than on any necessary fault in public ownership as such. Nor has there been a very happy experience in the support of enterprises operating in competitive conditions; too many of them have been lame ducks. But the example of Amersham International PLC can be quoted to show the possibilities of the development, and subsequent successful sale to the private sector, of a high-technology firm.

Another possibility is the use of government contracts, as extensively practised (to the benefit of technology) in the field of defence. Or there could be the sort of close partnership between government and industry that has been so successful in Japan, the essence of which is an agreement to foster a particular line of development, government taking a share in underwriting risks and ensuring that capital is available. All such plans for direct action by government presuppose, however, that the State and its satellites are well placed to make the right decisions. Few people believe this to be true in Britain; from the groundnuts scheme to Concorde, from nuclear energy to telecommunications, there are too many examples of very expensive mistakes. This is not at all surprising, since a civil service of generalists, shifting from post to post (but seldom having extensive commercial experience), is not well adapted to advise on technological decisions which have a market context. A condition for successful direct intervention by government, therefore, may be the development of much greater mobility between industry and government bodies, and of new ways of recruiting and training those who will have the ultimate responsibility for advice to Ministers on industrial matters.

Some people consider that the necessity for the direct intervention of government (which will always carry some political risks) could be much less if the banking system was more supportive of efforts to develop and use new technology. It is of course far from true that British banks are only interested in short-term finance of going enterprises. Bodies such as Finance for Industry have been developed with a capacity for technological assessment, and a readiness to finance new ventures and to act positively to help with successful development, providing for this purpose a wide range of advice. Indeed, the general complaint of those concerned with 'development banking' of this kind is that there is a shortage of people with good ideas to whom their help can be given. If, however, the main joint-stock banks had a closer involvement with the policy of their customers, they might be able to stimulate a more adventurous attitude to new technology. The banks in Germany and Japan, starting from a strong tradition of long-term support (and therefore of close involvement), are probably on balance more effective in stimulating the production of 'winners' in high technology.

In discussing major financial support by government or by the banks, however, the problems of technology merge with those of investment in general, to which we now turn.

Investment

While better working practices can secure more output from existing equipment, economic development generally requires investment in plant and equipment as well as in R and D. It is not surprising, therefore, that Britain's poor industrial performance was for long periods associated with a lower rate of investment than in more successful industrial countries, or that investment rates in the West as a whole have declined since the period of stagnation that started in 1974. The statistics of investment are difficult to interpret, because they include a large element of social investment (particularly in housing). Total British investment in fixed capital assets has remained rather low by international standards; but investment in plant, machinery and transport equipment (which is the relevant figure to relate to economic development) has recently been rather *higher* as a proportion of gross domestic product than in other major developed countries (with the important exception of Japan). This is encouraging, and demonstrates the vitality of which our industries are capable. However, three things must be remembered. First, gross product per head in Britain is now much less than in several of our major rivals: so that – if we could overcome problems of valuation – we would be likely to find that the *amount* of investment in plant and machinery per head of the population was very *low* by international standards. Second, gross investment includes replacement, and it may be that – as a consequence of past neglect – an unusually high proportion of British equipment needs to be replaced. Third, the rate of net manufacturing investment has probably declined quite sharply since 1979 (see p. 25). So there is no ground to be satisfied with our rate of investment. Despite the statistical evidence that high investment is linked with strong development, the common sense technological grounds to suppose that the investment is a condition of the development, and the stronger trend of industrial investment in some recent years, prevalent British attitudes remain ambivalent or even resistant to investment. There is evidence, too, of a misdirection of investment, and of very poor returns on some of it.

The concentration of public attention on the jobs that might be lost through the application of microelectronics, rather than on the improvement of living standards and of the quality of work that should result, is an example of the unhelpfulness of attitudes to investment. Most of the prognostications that x million jobs will be lost ignore the potential for higher incomes and hence demand to absorb the higher output; the new demand for equipment that the new technology generates; and the loss of (probably x + y million) jobs that would follow from a *failure* to apply the technology and thus be competitive in the international market for manufactures and many services. The prognostications are implicitly Luddite, without the much better grounds that the original Luddites had for their actions: almost complete lack of labour market policy to help them through the process of change; lack of previous examples of industrial development to show that living standards rise without any necessary decline in the amount of employment; and the absence of a numerous profession of economists to explain such things.

The latter point is not quite fair to the general public, however, because the economists themselves have been less helpful than they should have been in explaining the role of investment. This has been partly due to the tendency that we noted earlier to analyse the economy in static terms. Thus the Keynesian adaptation of the classical theory was focused on the amount of global demand that would evoke full employment given the existing technologies and factors of production, not on the development of the economy to produce higher output and incomes. Investment, despite its essential role in the development process, was treated by Keynes as a secondary instrument, to be contracted or expanded as required to give full employment in the short term. Too many of those who adhere to the monetarist theories seem to believe that, if the quantity of money is right, investment will look after itself, thus in fact leaving it to be squeezed by pay push and hence by consumption. Economists who *have* recognised the need to focus on investment have too often regarded it as not only a necessary but also the sufficient condition of growth, laying themselves open to the criticism, particularly telling in Britain where industrial equipment has been badly used and the ratio of output to capital therefore low, that investments are no use without efficiency on the part of those who operate them. But too many of these critics have gone on to assume that because investment is not sufficient it is not necessary either, which happens to be as damaging to attitudes and policies, and consequently to British economic performance, as it is illogical.

We now have hindsight over the last few years to drive home the lesson that jobs lack durability if they have been evoked through the pumping in of demand by conjunctural policy and not through an efficient response to the evolving demands of an internationally competitive market. The prospect of sufficient demand is of the essence in the creation of durable jobs; but the scale in time and space is quite different from that which is implicitly assumed by the conventional demand management. For the durable jobs will often be associated with investments in plant and equipment which require anything from one to five years or more before production can start and which must then be operated for five to ten years or more before they can be proved financially justified, and thus contribute to the further development of the firm and the continued provision of jobs. If these investments are to stand a good chance of success, moreover, they will probably be part of a firm's industrial strategy with a time scale measured in decades rather than years, in which technologies and then products can be developed. In space, only a minority of the sales that will result from such strategies and investments may be made in the home market of a country the size of Britain; production that is oriented mainly towards the British market will in many sectors not be on a scale to be competitive with that of companies, wherever they may be located, whose horizons are those of the world market. The majority of jobs in the economy may indeed not have to be seen in such a large perspective of time and space. But those for which this perspective is essential have a powerful influence on economic development and international viability; and, for them, the state of domestic demand over the short term may be significant but is certainly less important than the conditions of development with which we are here concerned – among which the longer-term prospects for a steady development of real demand in the home market and for reliable access to the world market are both of critical importance.

It follows that short-term equilibrium should be a secondary aim of policy, *after* the basic aim of developing the productive strength on which durable jobs, and hence lasting full employment, must depend. The focus of policy needs to shift from short-term or proximate phenomena such as a demand gap or the money supply to what might be called a development gap: that is, the difference between on the one hand the number of jobs being created at present through developments that comprise a technologically efficient response to evolving market demand (which for numerous goods and services means world market demand), and on the other hand the number of jobs needed to provide full employment. It may be objected that although economists and officials are fairly good at measuring global demand or money supply, they are unable to estimate how many jobs are being created through developments of this sort; they can measure the quantity of employment but not its quality. Given that the quality of employment has not been regarded as the direct concern of economists or of officials responsible for macroeconomic management, it should hardly be surprising if they are unable to estimate it. But it does seem to be a matter of central concern in Japanese economic management; British officials with responsibilities for industrial policy have been acquiring skills in it, with some help from industrialists whose success has depended on precisely such abilities; and there is surely no reason why the British should be unable to evaluate the quality of employment created as well as its quantity, if this is indeed necessary for successful economic management. The question may seem academic at present, when the development gap is obviously enormous. But it would have been highly relevant in the early 1970s, and will likewise again be relevant when full employment is regained.

Meanwhile, it is not so much an attempt to measure precisely the size of the development gap that is required as a view of the conditions that favour development and the measures that will help to bring them about, together with support for the development efforts of firms and hence, to some degree at least, an assessment of the quality of firms' development plans and of the employment they will generate. The state of the art of development management for advanced industrial countries may perhaps be compared with that of demand management at the time of the New Deal, when Roosevelt's measures preceded Keynes's theory and the development of national accounts on which demand management was subsequently based. When theory and measurement lag behind events, action will often, rightly, precede them.

The case for public policy to promote investment depends, again, on the relationship between private and social costs and benefits. We have seen how firms' returns from investment, in the form of profits, have for nearly a decade been squeezed between pay push and weak prices;

and even if there is some cyclical improvement, firms are not likely to be confident that profit margins adequate to finance a strong development will be restored, until there has been at least some experience of a method of economic management that gives a reasonable assurance of this. In Britain, such confidence is harder to engender against the background of a century of attitudes unfavourable to development. While the expectation of profit has become weak and uncertain, moreover, the cost of investment has, with growing capital-intensity and with the fast growth of construction costs,[4] continued to increase; and public support is justified for a significant part of it, because there is a social benefit beyond the expected private benefit. As long as private gain is depressed by stagflation, the social benefit of more investment leading to industrial development will remain very large. But even when stagflation is overcome and profits return to a level that provides for more normal rates of investment, there will remain a variety of market imperfections and externalities, inherent in the modern economy, that justify the use of public policy to secure a social benefit.

The social benefit of much R and D is such as to justify public support that will evoke a more ample effort than will spring from calculations based on private gain alone. We have also noted the need for public provision or support with respect to much of the infrastructure required for modern industry. The encouragement of new or growing small firms is an object of public funding in most countries, to offset the many difficulties and costs that face such firms. Fields such as energy conservation have a macroeconomic significance that marks them out for public support. There are also projects, such as the development of major aircraft or families of aero-engines, which are so big that private capital markets are not prepared to supply the necessary funds, given the long lead times and the political uncertainties associated with them, and so important for the economy that it is legitimate to underpin them with public money, provided that they are soundly enough based. In addition to new investments such as the foregoing, which characteristically in the modern economy require large resources of which a significant part needs to come from public funds, there is the high and growing cost of winding up old production capacity which changes in technology or markets are making obsolete. Such capacity can be a drag on economic development, because it locks resources into dead-end activities when they should move into activities with a prosperous future which could then expand more quickly; and because production

---

[4] For ten types of plant in Canada, the UK and the US, capital costs per unit of output were rising, in the early 1970s, by two to seven times the general rate of inflation. See *New Investment in Basic Industries*, (British-North American Committee, London, 1979).

from the obsolete capacity can weaken the market so that efficient capacity becomes unprofitable. When resources are fully employed, the former is more important; when there is high unemployment and below-capacity working, the latter is. In either case, the old capacity imposes a social cost for as long as the firms can struggle to survive or so long as the obsolete plants place an excessive burden on otherwise healthy firms, which may keep them in being in the hope that demand will turn up again. Here again, there is a case for public support, this time to wind up redundant capacity rather than to promote new investments – although the promotion of new investments in a particular area may be a corollary if such closures destroy old jobs there much faster than new ones are being created.

Even in normal times and countries, that is when stagflation is absent and attitudes to development are positive, cases such as these justify an active public policy in relation to investment. Without such a policy, industrial development is likely to be impaired, however efficient the bulk of industry may be. Indeed, one of the reasons why Japanese industry has become so efficient and dynamic is that such a policy is regarded in Japan as a matter of course. Partly as a consequence, Japan is the only advanced industrial country that is not now in urgent need of a special effort to revive investment. Elsewhere, the social costs of low investment and slow development are so great that the case for measures to promote development, and hence among other things to raise investment, must be very strong, provided only that the measures are likely to induce viable activities. In Britain, the need to break the constraint of anti-industrial attitudes and expectations of slow or zero growth adds yet more strength to the case. Yet the management of the economy, despite a number of measures such as generous tax allowances intended to promote investment, has only too often in fact been inimical to it.

Probably the most important determinant of decisions to invest in industrial development is the expectation of a sufficient market for the products in future, that is to say of a growth in demand. We have seen that for the more important investments the British or world market must be expected to be sufficient for a good many years ahead. The macroeconomic policies of successive governments have given industry no grounds for confidence that this will be so as far as the British part of industry's market is concerned. Even if stop-go would have been inevitable under any government, given the pay push and anti-development attitudes that have been endemic in the British economy and the primitive state of the art of dealing with such constraints in this country, the electoral cycle has undoubtedly aggravated it. Governments may have become less prone to unleash pre-electoral inflationary booms, but they have at the same time become more addicted to post-electoral ideological programmes that have exaggerated the swings of inflation and recession, quite apart from the disruption of any steady development of industrial, incomes and manpower policies. The design of a macroeconomic policy that would give industry grounds to expect a steady growth of non-inflationary demand would set the best context for investment and development. In the absence of this, the parties should at least eschew the excesses of adversary politics.

Demand in export markets has grown faster and more steadily. But the relationship between British industry and these markets has been upset almost as much by the movements of the exchange rate as the home market has been by the movements of domestic demand. Reflecting the long history of Britain's neglect of industrial development, anti-industrial exchange rate policies have almost venerable roots. In the 1920s the restoration of the prewar parity was a major reason for the stagnation of British industry and the cleavage of British society. In the 1950s and 1960s, the attempts to defend sterling at fixed parities involved for much of the time exchange rates that made industry internationally uncompetitive and deflations that undermined the home market. Through most of the 1970s it appeared that the lesson had been learnt and that policy was aimed at an exchange rate which allowed industrial competitiveness to be maintained; the policy was broadly successful and, for the first time in a century, the ratio of the volume of British to world exports stabilised and even rose a little. The advent of North Sea oil was bound to make sterling stronger than it would otherwise be; but instead of moderating this tendency, government policy at the beginning of the 1980s has sharpened it. The intention was to bring down inflation as the pre-condition for growth. The method made interest rates particularly high and thus strengthened the exchange rate. Nor was this unwelcome to the government, because a rising exchange rate reduced the pressure of inflation, and the main alternative instrument for countering pay push, that is pay policy, had been explicitly renounced. Ministers argued, moreover, that the high exchange rate also helped to weed out the industrial weaklings. At the same time, however, it cut the profits of efficient companies by reducing or eliminating the margin earned on exports, reduced their share of the home market in favour of imports, and set the ratio of the volume of British to world exports once more on a downward path. At the worst, early in 1981, the loss of competitiveness was estimated at more than 50 per cent; a year later, it was still about one-third. So far from this government having an anti-industrial attitude in principle, the strength of industry is one of its highest priorities. But in practice, exchange rate policy, or more precisely the effect of other policies on exchange rates, has once again undermined profit-ability and hence industry's capacity to invest.

Competitive strength in the world market is essential if firms are to sell enough to cover the high fixed costs of modern industrial develop-ment. We will therefore return in the next chapter to Britain's relation-ship with the international economy, in which the exchange rate is a decisive element. Closely linked with the exchange rate is the interest rate, which represents the price of financing investment and hence an important part of development costs.

Like the exchange rate, British interest rates have often been higher than would be the aim of policy if the strength of industry were a more central objective. As the high interest rates have tended to coincide with the high exchange rate, the one being a cause of the other, industry has suffered a double blow. It is hard to imagine a Japanese policy in which the interests of industry so often take second place; and the benefit which the Japanese economy and society now derive from the strength of industry owes much to the constant care that the managers of the Japanese economy have given to industrial interests, in devising the mix of fiscal, monetary and exchange rate policies as well as in other ways.

Not only has macroeconomic policy in Japan been as constantly benign to industry as in Britain it has been capricious; it is also incon-ceivable in Japan that the fiscal system should, as in Britain, have benefited house ownership and life assurance so much more con-sistently than direct industrial investment. While the tax treatment of investment, including research and development, has been much improved in recent years, there still appears to be room for improve-ments in the treatment of rapidly developing firms. Another way to make public policy more helpful to industry would be by subsidising the interest rates for at least a significant part of industrial investment. The idea of a special interest rate is not familiar to the British. But it should be remembered that special favours have long been available in important sectors of the financial markets, such as housing. The French have, moreover, a large and successful experience of redis-counting loans to industry at low interest rates through the Crédit National; and the Germans have, on a smaller scale, done the same for small and medium firms through the Kreditanstalt für Wiederaufbau. Both governments have, in the last year or two, expanded their use of subsidised interest rates. The present British Government introduced a small firms loan guarantee scheme in 1981, which has been proving remarkably successful. Beyond this special measure for the small firms, however, serious consideration should be given to the idea of subsi-dising interest on loans to finance industrial investment. A general fall in interest rates would no doubt be better; but the influence of American rates on those in Britain and other European countries is strong, and the combination of large budget deficits with tight money seems likely to keep the American rates high for a considerable time ahead. This is just one example of the factors outside the control of governments in countries such as Britain, which make it hard to be confident that interest rates will be reasonably low even if macroeconomic policy is directed to that end. Other market forces as well as political constraints make a reduction of general interest rates to levels that would really stimulate industrial investment hard to achieve. A subsidy limited to industry would make it possible to guarantee a low rate for loans for industrial investment, and could thus make a substantial contribution to the revival of economic development. Such a subsidy would be appropriate only for so long as investment and development remained slack and employment low; as the economy became more dynamic and the momentum of investment likely to lead on to full employment, the case for a subsidy designed to raise the general level of investment would disappear, confining the justification for public support to the particular kinds of objective we noted earlier, where there is a need to offset certain imperfections and externalities that inhere in the structure of contemporary markets.

It may be objected that an interest rate subsidy which would be enough to influence investment decisions would be too much to spend at a time of public expenditure cuts. It could certainly be costly; but not more so than measures such as further abatement of the national insurance surcharge or a small reduction of income tax rates, which are regarded as serious options for British budgets at a time when revenue from North Sea oil has begun to flow at annual rates which are a multiple of the sums that could be expended on subsidising industrial interest. The question is not whether the money could be found but whether it would be the best use for it; and if a scheme could be devised that would really stimulate viable investments, there can be little doubt that it would.

The argument should not, then, be about the principle of public spending to give a major impulse to industrial investment, but whether an interest rate subsidy would be the best method, and if so what form it should take. Although British firms do not pay high corporation tax by international standards, fiscal incentives have been suggested with respect to the timing of tax payments and the treatment of index-linked industrial bonds, and it might be better to confine general measures to such fiscal incentives. It could be argued that the finances of most industrial companies have deteriorated so far that a subsidy for all industrial investment would be justified for a period, the boost to investment by efficient firms outweighing any encouragement given to investments that will never yield a return. But the argument that public subsidies intended to make investments profitable may instead be pre-empted by pay push is a serious one; and it would anyway be better if the subsidies could be concentrated on investments that are likely to be successful. The subsidies could therefore be offered, not to all firms, but to those with adequate development programmes, and in particular to those with development contracts with their employees to ensure that the success of the programmes is not undermined by pay push or failure to adopt the necessary work practices.

This brings us back to the question, raised in the last chapter when we considered public policy in relation to development contracts, of the ability to judge whether development programmes are adequate and whether pay settlements and work practices are conducive to their success. Doubts are often expressed in Britain whether anybody who is implementing public policy could make such judgements.

These doubts may be linked with the relative lack, in Britain's financial system, of institutions which are particularly strong in Germany and Japan and which may be called industrial banks. The function of these institutions is precisely to judge the design and implementation of firms' development plans; and they are staffed with enough engineers and others who have worked in the sectors they finance, to be qualified to form such judgements. This enables them to finance those investments for which a healthy balance sheet in previous years is not an adequate guide: expensive technological developments that are risky, long-term and yet essential for competitive survival; fast-growing firms; and firms in trouble which can nevertheless be turned round. These are precisely the kinds of firms that need to be intelligently financed if Britain is to enjoy a healthy industrial development. Yet our otherwise strong financial institutions are still weaker than those of our main competitors in their capacity to judge such situations; and the absence of a tradition of industrial banking may have led to a belief that the judgements cannot be made, except perhaps by the industrialists themselves.

The capacity to judge industrial firms' development indeed lies mainly, as it should, within the firms. But the institutions that finance industrial development need to have a share of this capacity, if they are to facilitate promising investments, deter unpromising ones, and help to ensure that firms' managements are of the quality to cope with their firms' development. There is indeed a growing awareness of this need and some progress towards fulfilling it, both in organisations such as Finance for Industry which have been established for the purpose and in other financial institutions, but much more is needed. Proposals have been made for accelerating the progress by a transfusion of industrial experience to the service of financial institutions.[5] Such arrangements could likewise help to improve the capacity to make wise decisions in implementing public policy, partly by employing the financial institutions that would possess the industrial experience to participate in making the necessary judgements and partly by employing such capacity in the public service. Both these methods are already used to some extent; but the limited capacity remains a constraint both on the ability of the private financial sector to contribute to successful development and, more markedly, on the effectiveness of public policy.

Since history has endowed us with a financial community that, despite a high general level of efficiency, has institutions and attitudes that are less than favourable to investment in manufacturing industry, and since this constraint on our economic development implies a substantial social cost, there is a *prima facie* case for public policy to encourage the building of a capacity for industrial banking. Here again, as in so many other fields, the development of policy has been dogged by the ideological quarrel over private and public ownership. Labour governments have established public bodies with industrial banking functions, such as the Industrial Reorganisation Corporation and the National Enterprise Board, even if the latter was for a time too much encumbered with lame ducks; but Labour governments have not carried much weight with the private financial institutions, who tend to treat them with suspicion. Conservative governments have abolished the IRC and curtailed the functions of the NEB, without using their friendly relationship with the private institutions to encourage industrial banking in the private sector.

The financing of investment in State enterprises should also be seen as an industrial banking problem. Instead, the alternating governments have chosen different ways to undermine the nationalised industries' ability to invest: Labour governments by keeping their prices down at levels that left no room for profit; Conservatives by cash limits applied without due regard for commercially viable investment proposals, combined with a reluctance to let the corporations raise money in the capital markets. Under all governments, official methods of vetting investment plans have involved delays that would in the private sector be regarded as ruinous, and would never be imposed by industrial banks. The weakness of the industrial banking function in relation to State enterprises is yet another constraint on Britain's in-

[5] Sir Arthur Knight, *Wilson Revisited: Industrialists and Financiers*, (Policy Studies Institute Discussion Paper 5, London, 1982).

dustrial development, impeding the progress of a substantial sector of the economy and reducing its ability to contribute to investment-led growth.

A national development programme

Our examination of education and training, technological development and investment has shown that deficiencies in quantity and quality are a severe constraint on economic development, long-standing in Britain and, at least with respect to technology and investment, lasting nearly a decade by now in most other western countries. Without support from public policy, economic development will be confined to those investments that firms expect to yield a profit after all the costs have been met. In the most dynamic of economies, there is a variety of elements in economic development which bring a substantial social benefit but would not satisfy the condition that private benefits exceed private costs, so that public support is required if the social benefit is to be obtained. Japanese industrial policy is the outstanding example of this principle being applied. In a less dynamic economy, such as the British, slow growth and an unfavourable environment have reduced the prospect of private benefit, and attitudes that have accompanied a century of poor performance further dampen the expectation that industrial development will be profitable. On top of this, expectations of profit have been sharply reduced by the recent period of stagflation, while the costs and risks of investment have continued to rise. So long as the bias against development remains, because of the stagflation and, in Britain, the unfavourable attitudes, there will be a powerful additional justification for public support, in the form both of money and of policies to change institutions and attitudes. Without changes in institutions and attitudes, too much of the money would be wasted; but expenditure, if wisely directed, could do much to promote such changes. Our specific proposals for policy to these ends will be found in the concluding chapter. Here we will draw together the threads from this chapter and relate them to the conclusions of the preceding chapters to derive some principles on which policy could be based.

Successful industrial development requires a development programme designed by the managers of a firm, employees' co-operation in implementing it and money to pay for it from financial institutions whose managers judge that the investment will bring a return. Particularly in Britain, the attitudes of each group are inhibited by what they expect from the others; and as far as long-term development is concerned, the stagflation has turned these British inhibitions into something approaching a stalemate. In order to break this stalemate, the managers need not only to design long-term development programmes for making their firms highly competitive in the world market, but also to persuade the employees to accept pay and work practices that will enable the programmes to succeed; the employees need to share the responsibility of successful development, and to obtain their share of its benefits without eroding the profit on which it depends; the financiers need to be ready to finance long-term development plans on a large scale, for which the institutions require the capacities of industrial banks. We have seen that there is a strong case for wide-ranging public support for industrial investment in order to push the economy out of its present depressed state, provided that the expenditure is not wasted on unsuccessful investments. The key is to provide the expenditure in ways that encourage the attitudes and practices that favour successful development.

We have suggested that an interest-rate subsidy would help to revive industrial investment; and there would be much to be said for offering the subsidy only on loans to finance such of firms' development programmes as are judged to have good prospects of success, provided that there is enough capacity of the industrial banking type and of the quality to make the judgements well. There is certainly a need for some such capacity in government departments, and some has been acquired in administering grants under the Industries Acts. There is also a capacity of this kind in public-sector financial institutions such as the Scottish, Welsh and Northern Ireland development agencies and the British Technology Group. But it would at the same time be possible for public policy to help build industrial banking capacity in private sector financial institutions by paying the subsidy on loans they make to industry on condition that a satisfactory appraisal of a development programme, within the context of a firm's industrial strategy, has been prepared.

The development programmes would not be convincing unless they were accompanied by evidence that the employees were likely to accept pay and methods of work that would allow profits and productivity to be sufficiently high. This evidence could consist of a past record which amounts, implicitly, to a development contract between the firm and the employees, on the lines we have observed to exist in Japan. In the smaller British firms, a credible development programme combined with a record of good labour relations or with a commitment by management to take steps necessary to secure employees' co-operation in future should be enough. But in the larger firms, which are better suited to more formal arrangements and from which inflationary pay push can be rapidly transmitted into the economy as a whole, an explicit development contract could be required, which commits the firm to use its best endeavours to carry out the development programme and the employees to accept non-inflationary pay settlements and necessary changes in work practices; and such contracts would become part of the case for justifying the interest subsidy on the loan to finance the programme. Thus the firm and the employees would have a powerful incentive to make a development contract. It is usually a number of years before a loan can be repaid, and annual payments of the subsidy could be conditional on the contract being respected, so that the incentive to respect the contract would be maintained. Eventually, the existence of such contracts, explicit or implicit, and respect for them should become a matter of course, not requiring any special incentive because they are so strongly in the interests of firms and employees. But in Britain, such habits have yet to take root, and a conditional subsidy could help to establish them.

It may be objected that development contracts would have something in common with productivity bargaining agreements, which got a name, when they were used as a criterion for pay increases under incomes policy, for being a figleaf to cover up naked pay push. Although the evidence was not all in that direction,[6] the point is well taken that such arrangements, if they are to be a criterion for benefits from public policy, need to be very carefully evaluated. This brings us to the tribunals which we considered in chapter 5 in relation to incomes policy and development programmes. Such tribunals would require the capacity to evaluate the viability of development contracts as far as pay and working methods are concerned and to monitor adherence to the contract in order to ensure that the development programme was not being endangered. This would have to be thoroughly enough done to carry the confidence of the government, which would depend on the tribunals' advice as to whether one of the main criteria for the interest rate subsidy was being respected, as well as of firms and employees in general, whose co-operation is required if any such scheme is to work. We have already suggested that the full scheme, that is the linking of interest rate subsidies with development programmes and development contracts, might apply only to the larger firms, perhaps the top four hundred. If these firms develop well then the economy will develop well, at least for a decade or two ahead; and if their employees' pay is kept within bounds that allow the firms to keep the prices of their products stable, while pay in the public sector does not get out of line, pay trends will be such that prices will be stable in the economy as a whole. The number of firms would not be too great for a system of tri-

---

[6] See W. W. Daniel, *Incomes Policy and Collective Bargaining at the Workplace: a study of the productivity criterion cases,* (political and Economic Planning – now Policy Studies Institute – Broadsheet 541, London, 1973).

bunals with fairly modestly-sized, though high-quality, staff to examine each development contract sufficiently thoroughly. It could be hoped that breaches of contract serious enough to endanger development programmes would not be very numerous; but the numbers should anyway be manageable and the cost of the work involved insignificant compared with the benefits that would flow from stable prices and healthy development.

For smaller firms the less elaborate system suggested above should be adequate. Interest rate subsidies could be made widely available by official rediscounting of commercial banks' loans, after the pattern of the Crédit National, and low-interest loans can be made through public bodies such as a number that already operate successfully, including the Scottish, Welsh and Northern Ireland development agencies, COSIRA (the Council for Small Industries in Rural Areas) and the Highlands and Islands Development Board. The former method has the merit of encouraging industrial banking in the commercial banks, as the rediscounter can press for good investment appraisals to be made; some of the latter bodies provide a wide range of advice to small firms, almost amounting to extension services of the type whose value was stressed earlier in this chapter.

The interest rate subsidy with the associated conditions and institutions could be central to a national development programme: a coherent set of policies for development which would also include measures to increase the quantity and quality of training, to inject a greater element of practical usefulness into the education system, promote technological development, improve infrastructure and increase public sector investment more generally, and provide special support for objects such as energy conservation. The aim would be to close the development gap between the existing level of employment and full employment on the basis of jobs that are reasonably secure because they result from healthy economic development. The closer that end was approached, the more vigorously the development programme would turn to the eradication of obsolescent capacity and the transfer of resources into activities with a future. So long, however, as the development gap remained, a major contribution of macroeconomic policy would be to keep general interest rates and the exchange rate as low as practicable; and schemes for training and temporary employment could be used to reduce unemployment as far as possible.

Financially, such a programme would contribute to a revival of development by providing incentives to training, R and D and investment. More crucial, it should promote a shift towards more productive attitudes not only in industry but also in finance, education and government. Yet while a realistic national programme should be an important focus for public policy and for attitudes towards development, it should not loom too large in thinking about development. It should not be forgotten that most of the seeds of development are sown in individual firms, and that the firms' efficiency in bringing them to bear fruit is decisive. Nor should the idea of a national programme distract attention from the detail of particular aspects of public policy, because the usefulness of such a programme depends on the soundness of the detail. Nor should it be thought that public policy for development stops at the national frontiers. We have already stressed the importance of the world market to industry in a country the size of Britain. In the next chapter we will consider some of the implications for policy of this fact.

7 Britain and the International Economy

The high costs of modern economic development have been a constant theme of the preceding chapters. Their continuing growth has made fixed costs a high and growing proportion of total costs; and we have seen how this has caused average costs in firms with such a cost structure to diminish as output increases. This can give a decisive advantage to firms that produce a high volume, which can sell at a competitive price while still earning the margin they need to finance further developments.

It is by now normal for manufacturing firms in Western Europe to sell half of their output in other countries; and this reflects the importance of the wide international market in enabling firms to cover the cost of developing technologically more advanced production. It is because they grasped this basic need of modern industry that the most successful among the advanced industrial countries have consistently pursued policies that strengthened their ability to export.

After their postwar currency reform in 1948, the Germans kept their exchange rate low and seized all opportunities to improve their access to export markets. The high value of the mark which has become so familiar to us was a consequence of the success of German exports, which had in turn been much helped by the low exchange rate of the 1950s and 1960s. The Germans also strongly supported the moves to free trade in the European Community and towards freer trade in the wider international economy. German governments have been alert to detect and correct any policies that might be damaging to industry's international competitive strength, and have thus played their part in fostering a benign circle of rewards and attitudes that favour exports.

The Japanese likewise kept their exchange rate low as long as this was needed to establish a rapidly growing share of export markets, and only then had to allow the strength of their exports to draw the exchange rate up. Entry into the General Agreement on Tariffs and Trade (GATT) and other international organisations was a major objective of Japanese diplomacy in the late 1950s and early 1960s, which gained for their industries the necessary access to foreign markets. The only flaw in an otherwise masterly application of the principle that modern industry must have the widest possible market has been a failure to satisfy Japan's trading partners that the access to their markets is properly reciprocated, when non-tariff barriers and private arrangements that restrict Japanese imports are taken into account as well as formal liberalisation of tariffs and quotas. When penetration of imports from Japan really begins to hurt, the case against protection is undermined if too many difficulties are encountered by trade in the other direction. Without energetic reciprocation, there is a danger that the Japanese will lose the access to export markets that is one condition of their industrial strength.

The French, like the Japanese, protected their home market during the 1950s when they established the foundations of their modern industries. But these industries would have been unable to develop had the French not widened their market by participating in the European Community, with its internal free trade and its generally liberal external policies for industrial trade. In the 1970s, the French government has been extremely active in promoting the exports of France's advanced industries, such as aircraft, nuclear power and telecommunications.

The American experience has been different. The size of the home market enabled the Americans to develop what was by the 1950s by far the most advanced economy in the world, without much concern for exports. A liberal trading policy, based on the GATT, was the context for an expansion of American exports of manufactures during the 1950s and 1960s. But the strength of the dollar led to a decline in competitiveness, and the defence of the over-valued dollar in the latter part of the 1960s damaged American industry as the defence of the pound had earlier damaged the British. Since then, policy and the exchange rate have fluctuated, and this inconstancy in the defence of industrial interests has accompanied an erosion of competitiveness in relation to the industries of Japan, Western Europe and the newly industrialising countries.

The saddest story of neglect of industrial interests in external economic policy is, however, that of Britain. We have already shown how the double bind of an over-valued pound and its defence through deflation weakened British industry in the 1920s, the 1950s and the 1960s and how, unmindful of this experience, policy has exacerbated a combination of high interest and exchange rates in the last three years. The old free trade tradition led Britain to be a strong supporter of the GATT; but the newer practice of Imperial Preference impeded British attempts to join in creating a single market with our continental neighbours. The failure to join in establishing the European Community became a serious disadvantage to British industries in the 1960s, when the expansion of trade among the Community members averaged 20 per cent a year, reflecting the pace at which markets were widening for their industrial firms. The response of British exports to the other members since Britain joined in 1973, growing from 29 per cent of total exports in the year previous to joining to 43 per cent in 1980, has shown how much British industry needed this wider 'home' market. But, apart from the years lost in the 1960s when Continental firms had this important advantage while ours had not, British accession when it did come coincided with the onset of the great stagflation, which became a new source of weakness for our industries and prevented them from benefiting as much from the wider market as they could otherwise have done. Thus the hesitations of Britain's European policy in the 1950s turned into yet another cause of British industrial weakness, which would hardly have been allowed to occur had the need for industrial strength been better understood and more highly rated as an objective of our foreign policy.

Unfortunately, the need to maintain access to the wide tariff-free market is still not understood by all those who may form British governments in the coming years. The Labour Party is committed to pull Britain out, without any assurance or even likelihood that the open trading relationship would survive. Although a market that will carry the volume of sales required to enable modern industrial production to develop has become more and more evidently essential with the technological progress of the past quarter of a century, the mistake that Britain committed in the 1950s when it failed to take part in establishing the Community would be repeated if the Labour Party's policy were implemented. It can be argued that membership of the Community is not the only form of access to a wide market: we could sell into the Community from outside it and there is all the rest of the world as a destination for our exports. But the Community is a large market that is securely open to us, which cannot be said of any other large market. Access to most other markets is liable to be impeded from time to time, sometimes arbitrarily and suddenly; such hazards offer an insecure basis for costly investment decisions, and hence for the modern industrial economy. The nature of the modern economy is moreover such that non-tariff barriers to trade are becoming increasingly important, so that a constant effort to reduce them is needed if any open market is to be maintained; and for all the imperfections in its institutions and in the behaviour of the member countries, the Community is better able to deal with this effectively than any other group to which Britain might belong. It can on the other side be argued, in a more defeatist vein, that the obligation to keep the British market open to imports from our Community partners does more harm to our industries than access in the reverse direction can do good. We will return to the question of Britain's competitiveness within the Community market. Here we need only note that if Britain does not by and large reciprocate the access it obtains to the markets of others, that access will sooner or later be withdrawn. Thus a British reversal of free trade, unless it is undertaken temporarily and by agreement in order to solve a particular problem, implies a market permanently narrower than it would otherwise be, and narrower than is available to our competitors in the larger markets of the Community, the United States and Japan. Policies to this end can be based only on a failure to understand the necessity of a sufficient volume of production to cover the high costs of contemporary development. Suspicion that an element in the advocacy of withdrawal is unawareness of the implications of the past two decades of technological advance is heightened by the use, in one of the books that advocate this course, of sources 20 years or more old as evidence that in Britain itself we may have the necessary 'minimum market-size' and that 'a large enough domestic market already exists for economies of scale in the production of all except a few advanced technology products and aerospace'.[1] When these earlier texts were being written, there was already enough understanding of the need for the wider market to induce the British government to try to gain free access to it, though it was not seen as urgent enough to motivate a policy that was sufficiently effective to bring this about. Now, after output per head has doubled in West European economies and quadrupled in Japan, bringing still sharper rises in the costs of development and hence in the need for a correspondingly larger volume of production, not just for 'a few advanced technology products' but over a whole range of modern industrial sectors, it seems that British industry still faces some ignorance of its basic needs. After a monetary and exchange rate policy on the part of the present government which has for a substantial period pushed the terms of trade to a point where a large proportion of exports to all markets have been unprofitable while British imports of manufactures have become all too profitable for our competitors, we have on offer an alternative government which, in the face of the realities of modern industrial costs and structure, would reverse the progress that has been made towards secure and favourable access to the bulk of the West European market.

Partly as a legacy of its free trade tradition, partly because of the

---

[1] Stuart Holland, *UnCommon Market: Capital, Class and Power in the European Community*, (Macmillan, London, 1980), p. 54, citing C. D. Edwards, 'Size of Markets, Scales of Firms and the Character of Competition' in E. A. G. Robinson (ed.), *Economic Consequences of the Size of Nations*, (Macmillan, London, 1963) and Tibor Scitovsky, *Economic Theory and Western European Integration*, (Stanford University Press, 1958).

relatively slow growth of the domestic market, Britain exports over one-third of its gross domestic product, a higher proportion than any other middle-sized advanced industrial country. This should be a source of strength for modern industry since growing participation in the international economy is a condition of technological advance. It will be a source of weakness if policy impairs the terms on which British industry participates. We do not propose to dwell on the implications of a return to the highest exchange rates of the past three years or of the extraction of Britain from the European Community, because either would undermine the industrial and economic development we wish to see. Instead, we will consider the implications of participation in the Community and the wider international economy, on the assumption that policy will endeavour to enable British industry to participate in them effectively. Policies such as continued membership of the Community are in Britain's own hands. Many other policies that affect the terms of access to other countries' markets, including exchange rate as well as trade policies, are however not within a British government's exclusive control; and this brings us to the subject of international policies for an international economy.

International policies for an international economy

Neither a siege economy nor laissez-faire is a viable option for an advanced industrial country. Such a country has to be part of an international economy, in which a range of macroeconomic and microeconomic policies have to be pursued. Most of these policies are made by national governments. But the more interdependent the several national economies become, the more the policies of one country impinge on the economies of others. At the least, an escalation of beggar-thy-neighbour policies has to be avoided, or the international economy will disintegrate and revert to a set of national siege economies. More desirably, a mutual accommodation of national policies could be devised to maximise welfare in the international economy as a whole or, more realistically, to leave the average country better off and no country worse off than it would be by going it alone. Such, in the field of tariffs and other barriers to trade, has been the principle of the GATT. Beyond that, when internationalisation of the economy reaches a certain degree of intensity, it becomes less likely that the mutual accommodation of national policies will lead to a satisfactory outcome, and more likely that a common policy, designed to look after the international economy as a whole, will better meet the interests of each country involved. That is the principle of, for example, the internal free trade and the common external trade policy of the European Community. As the country which, among the

middle-sized advanced industrial economies, is the most interdependent with the international economy, Britain has a strong interest
in improving the intergovernmental co-operation and the making of
common policies in both the European Community and the wider
international economy, together with the weight to promote this
interest effectively. Rather than complain about what others have
done, which seems to have become the British practice in relation to
both European and international policies, let us consider what policies
would be in the interest of Britain as well as other countries, in the light
of the problems and possible remedies that we have considered earlier.

Nothing is more obviously a matter of common interest than the
exchange rate, because it influences the terms on which almost all
transactions between a country and its economic partners take place.
Exchange rate policy clearly cannot ignore the market forces that lie
behind the purchase and sale of currencies; but policy can influence the
reactions of exchange rates to the impact of such forces. The common
interest in the ways in which such policy is applied has been recognised
in the exchange rate regime of the European Monetary System (EMS),
in which all the member countries of the European Community other
than Britain and Greece participate. Participants' exchange rates can
be devalued or revalued beyond the System's normal limits of
fluctuation, but this must be by agreement among them. Britain has
not adhered to this regime, because of the view that sterling is subject
to unusual pressures as the petro-currency of a weak economy with
strong inflation, and also because, for a time at least, the present
government has given such central priority to its targets for control of
the money supply, which could be upset if a second, exchange rate
target were also adopted. If the other members did not allow us to
adjust our rate, the argument runs, our economic management would
be disrupted; if they did allow it, we would disrupt the EMS. But we
have argued that an exchange rate which enables British exports to be
generally competitive is a fundamental condition of our industrial development; and if we can fix sterling at such a parity in the EMS, the
backing which other members would then give the parity would make
it possible to take strains on it of a magnitude that we could not otherwise support. The question is, then, not whether a stable and
competitive rate for sterling is desirable, but whether we can secure
agreement on such a rate in the EMS; and this may imply not only
entering the EMS regime at a competitive rate, but subsequently
adjusting the rate downwards or upwards if we become less or more
competitive in relation to our partners, which is largely determined by
the relative rates of inflation. It may also imply a sustained policy for
the export of capital, whether private or through official purchases of

international assets, in order to offset part of the large but temporary income from North Sea oil. If our partners would not accept that we enter at a competitive rate and if necessary adjust it in order to remain competitive, then we would do better not to apply the regime until our economy becomes sufficiently strong and stable or the regime adapts itself to cater for the weak; the danger that most of the United Kingdom could become a depressed region for a long period is not so remote that policies which sharpen that risk can be justified. But there does not seem to have been any sustained and energetic endeavour to find out whether the other members would in fact agree, let alone to persuade them to do so. Since over two-fifths of our exports go to our Community partners, with another one-fifth to other West European countries associated with the Community and more or less closely linked to its currencies, such a policy of stabilising the exchange rates we share with them at levels that enable British industry to compete profitably would satisfy a large part of the exchange rate condition of our economic development.

The rate of exchange with the dollar is less important for our industrial trade than the rates of exchange with our European partners. But it is significant for Britain's overseas trade, particularly for our imports of raw materials; and it is more than significant for our interest rates, because the defence of the rate of exchange with the dollar at a time of high American interest rates implies correspondingly high interest rates in Britain. American interest rates are a major influence on the conjuncture and on economic development in Western Europe, and the European countries have a common interest in securing influence over American interest rate policy and over the effect of that policy on interest rates in Europe – none more so than Britain with its weak propensity for industrial development. The ability to pursue a more effective policy with respect to the dollar exchange rate would help to offset some of the influence of American interest rates, as well as enhancing the capacity to use exchange rate policy as an instrument of external trade policy. It has been argued that Europeans can do little about the dollar exchange rate without American co-operation; but the Americans would be more likely to co-operate if the Europeans had stronger collective instruments of exchange rate policy, with which the dollar rate might be influenced even in the absence of American co-operation. Such an instrument could be a substantial Community Reserve Fund, as a basis for buying and selling dollars for Community currencies and, eventually, for the European Currency Unit. It was agreed when the EMS was founded that a Reserve Fund would be created, to which one-fifth of the member countries' reserves would be transferred; but the member governments have delayed its establishment. It would be to Britain's advantage, as much as that of any other member country, if the Fund were established and enabled to intervene to influence the dollar exchange rate.

The Americans initiated the Kennedy round of GATT negotiations, which resulted in tariff cuts of about one-third by the advanced industrial countries, after the EEC had been established with its common external tariff. Before that, the Americans had lacked a trading partner with weight equivalent to that of the United States; but the Community, with its common instrument of external trade policy, became an economic power important enough to justify such a substantial American initiative. A major aim of establishing common Community instruments of external monetary policy would be to induce a similar policy of co-operation on the part of the Americans, whereby the mutual exchange rates would continuously be treated as a matter of common interest as they are in the EMS, instead of being subjected to alternating bouts of mild co-operation and so-called benign neglect, whose effects can be far from benign. The mechanism would doubtless be simpler and less binding than that which Community members apply among themselves in the EMS, for example swap arrangements backed by massive resources. Such co-operation would not only help to make the trade and financial relationship between the Community and the United States more mutually beneficial. It would also enable the two principal pillars of the western economy to deal better with one of their most difficult long-term problems: relations with Japan and with the newly industrialising countries.

Despite the alarm caused by imports from Japan, the Community lacks an instrument with which to effect a common policy towards the yen, even though the exchange rate is one of the most potent instruments of trade policy. The purchase of yen would stiffen the prices of Japanese exports or reduce their profitability or both, and thus reduce pressure for particular measures of trade protection which are a danger for the open international trading order. In a longer term perspective, it seems likely that both Japan and the NICs will continue to develop faster than Western Europe or North America, the Japanese because of their superior economic aptitudes and the NICs because countries catching up can usually grow faster than those that are ahead; and there will be a lot of NICs catching up on the western economies for a long time to come. There is a serious danger that the unremitting encroachment of highly competitive imports into the western markets from these sources could undermine the dynamism of western economies, just as the dynamism of a number of regions that were industrial leaders in the nineteenth century has been undermined. We considered in chapter 4 how such competition can disrupt the price structure in sectors where modern industrial development has necessitated high fixed costs and hence produced vulnerability when capacity-use falls below normal levels. Without the profits to pay for future development, such sectors will be unable to progress. But they are likely, unless decisive action is taken, to be a long time dying. Meanwhile they will constitute a drag on the rest of the economy; and there could well be enough of them to cause the economy as a whole to stagnate. We have suggested measures such as development contracts and rationalisation cartels to help avert this. But rationalisation cartels imply at least temporary protection; and it should be possible to minimise protection, with its dangers for the open trading system, if exchange rate policy can be used to keep trade as a whole in equilibrium. Thus if, as seems likely, Japan and the NICs will be developing faster and thus steadily improving their competitive edge over the western economies, trade as a whole might nevertheless be kept in balance by a steady depreciation of the western currencies in relation to the yen and the currencies of the NICs: a sort of crawling peg to enable the dollar, the European Currency Unit and the currencies associated with them to be incrementally and hence undisruptively devalued in relation to the currencies of the fast developers. Such a policy would be considerably more powerful if undertaken jointly with the United States; but in the absence of American co-operation, it could still have some effect if undertaken by the Community as a whole.

While the primacy of the dollar in international capital markets makes the influence of American interest rates on European economies particularly strong, there is also a mutual influence among the interest rates of the Community countries. Exchange controls can moderate the influence to some extent. The French have proposed that the Community apply exchange control on transactions with non-members of the Community, precisely in order to insulate Europe's financial markets from the American influence; and most member countries do in fact apply their own exchange controls on some transactions with other members as well as with third countries. But although the influence of other countries' financial markets can be moderated, it cannot be excluded unless a country separates itself from the international economic system to a degree that would hardly be compatible with the requirements of an advanced industrial economy. We therefore have to consider how the international financial markets, and those of other Community countries in particular, may affect British interest rates, and how far it is desirable and feasible to influence the other countries' interest rate policies.

International financial markets can either inhibit Britain's develop-

ment prospects by drawing our interest rates upwards to higher levels
or thwart our anti-inflation policy by pulling our interest rates down.
This can of course happen whether we join the EMS exchange rate
regime or not, and indeed whether we are members of the Community
or not, so long as we do not insulate ourselves completely from international financial markets; and we are particularly wide open to such
influences when we have, as at present, no exchange control at all. But
if Britain participates in the exchange rate regime, even at a parity that
enables our industries to be competitive in European trade, one means
of moderating the influence of continental interest rates is thereby
limited, unless we can also change the parity whenever these interest
rates become inconvenient. Thus there may be a cost, in terms of influence on our interest rates, to set against the advantage of our
partners' help in stabilising our exchange rate at a competitive level. In
the last three years there would in fact have been a gain on both counts,
because both interest and exchange rates would have been kept at a
more moderate level, less detrimental to our industrial development.
In so far as continental interest rates draw ours upwards in a way likely
to inhibit development, this could be offset by adjustment of any
interest rate subsidy for industrial investment, of the sort that was discussed in the preceding chapter.

We will return to the question of the impact of Community membership, and of participation in the international economy more generally,
on a weak economy such as that of Britain. Meanwhile, before leaving
the subject of interest rates, we should consider what effect Britain
could have on the Community, as well as the effect that the rest of the
Community may have on us. The Community as a whole has suffered,
since the stagflation began, from low profits, low investment, high
unemployment and weak development, and like Britain the rest of the
Community needs effective development policies. Britain's need is
greater and longer-standing, so that we have an even stronger motive
to pursue development policies than our partners do. But they too have
a strong motive, as the common urge to escape the influence of high
American interest rates has shown. A British government that intends
to pursue a serious and sustained development policy would, therefore,
put a great deal of effort into persuading our Community partners to
adopt similar policies, within the framework of a common development
policy for the Community as a whole. Low interest rates on loans for
industrial investment could be one element in such a policy. France
and Germany have both recently made increasing use of government
subsidised investment loans. The Community itself has rapidly
expanded its investment financing with the new 'Ortoli' loan facility as
well as the European Investment Bank; and a common Community

subsidy for industrial interest rates would offer a way to stimulate development that would fit well with these policies and would remove any question that individual member countries' subsidies might give them an unfair competitive advantage. Because of the mutual influence of member countries' financial markets and policies, a common policy would be more powerful and effective than conflicting national policies; and because of the high proportion of exports that go to other Community countries, each member country benefits considerably from policies that induce prosperity in the rest of the Community.

Both external trade policy and industrial policy also have to take full account of interdependence in the international economy. About half of manufacturing output of the average Community country, and of Britain in particular, is sold abroad and hence subject to the import policies of other countries and affected by their industrial policies; conversely, the price and quantity of imports is affected by other countries' export and industrial policies. These policies are clearly a matter of mutual interest; and as we shall see, in an international market for manufactures some industrial policies can hardly be effective unless they are made in common by a group of countries comprising at least a substantial part of the international market. Since the Community member countries conduct half their external trade with each other, trade and industrial policies within this group are of particular importance to all these countries, including Britain.

Of the Community's trade and industrial policies, by far the most important has been the removal of tariffs and quotas on trade between member countries, which enables firms to invest and develop, confident that they will not be deprived by the partner countries' trade policies of the market they need to recover the cost. The free trade associations with other West European countries have extended this free trading area so that it now takes about three-fifths of total British exports. Without free and secure access to such a market, the prospects for modern industrial development in Britain would be severely restricted. Yet many non-tariff barriers to trade among member countries remain, in the form of public purchasing practices, national specifications and other national regulations that, by accident or design, still impede this trade. It is important for industries in Western Europe that such barriers are removed, so that the best firms can base their development on a home market as big as that of the United States or Japan. For Britain, the removal of such barriers to trade in service industries, where we often have an advantage over other member countries, is particularly significant.

Complementary with the internal free trade is the Community's common external tariff and trade policy. As the world's biggest importer, the Community has a bargaining strength that is not available to individual member countries. This has generally been used in the reduction of tariff barriers in successive GATT rounds, with the central bargain being struck between the two largest trading partners, the Community and the United States. Since the need to widen the market continues to increase with the growth of specialisation, scale and the costs of development, free access to the American market remains a highly desirable objective for industries in Western Europe, which of course would imply reciprocal access for the Americans to the Community. The present unemployment on both sides of the Atlantic makes adjustment to new trade penetration difficult, so that the tariff cuts following the Tokyo round are probably all that can be managed until the stagflation has been overcome; and even then, the differing ideas and traditions regarding industrial policy between the two sides of the Atlantic are an obstacle to free trade, which requires some harmonisation of industrial policies. But the levels and structures of these two major economies, as well as their economic and political systems and cultural backgrounds, are similar enough to make a free trading system economically appropriate and politically manageable, and hence a suitable objective for Community policy, when the economic conjuncture becomes more favourable.

Japan is a less comfortable partner, with its rate of development twice as fast as that of the Community and its exceptionally rapid penetration of import markets in a number of sectors. The Japanese market is big and competitive, so that access to it is both quantitatively and qualitatively important; and the Community has been using its considerable bargaining power in order to secure better access. We suggested earlier that a common Community policy towards the yen could also improve the terms on which European industries compete with the Japanese. But so long as the pace and style of Japanese development remain so different from that in Europe, there will be sectors of European industry that require temporary protection and industrial policy to promote their adaptation or contraction, if they are not to remain for too long a deadweight in the economy and a source of deprivation in the society. The need for such policies is accentuated by high unemployment and low growth; but it is not likely to disappear even when full employment and faster growth have been restored. Indeed, the Japanese example itself indicates that a judicious use of temporary protection combined with industrial policy may be one condition of maintaining economic strength.

Some of the newly industrialising countries present Europe with a similar problem, not because they have achieved the Japanese standards of excellence but because industrial growth, and hence the penetration of export markets, is particularly fast at their stage of development. Here again, the Community may be able to minimise the use of protection when its employment and development have become healthier again and, perhaps, if it can apply an exchange rate policy that helps to retain a balance of competitiveness with the NICs; and, looking to the future, the Community should seek better access to the growing markets of countries such as Brazil, India, Mexico and South Korea, so as to ensure a world-wide market for the industries of the next century. But the NICs have their reasons to maintain protection for their newly-established industries, long since made respectable among economists by the infant industries exception to the principle of free trade; and advanced industrial economies such as the Community also have their reasons for selective protection when competition from the NICs is such as to undermine the conditions for their further development. Prolonged pressure of low-cost competition in sectors with high fixed and development costs can result not in the rapid demise of the sector and its replacement by new and more competitive activities, but in the sector's prolonged stagnation and, if such sectors come to comprise a substantial proportion of the whole economy, in a reduction of the economy's profitability and hence of its ability to generate new development. Prolonged protection, on the other hand, can also sanction prolonged stagnation. The way through this dilemma is to combine any protection with an industrial policy designed to promote development.

Although adjustment to competition from Japan or the NICs is one motive for the Community to have an industrial policy, it is not the only, or even the most important one. Subsidies to promote investment or research and development or just to rescue lame ducks in one member State may damage competing firms in other member States unless they receive similar subsidies. Such subsidies are therefore a matter of mutual concern and the Rome Treaty provides against 'State aids' which 'adversely affect trading conditions to an extent contrary to the common interest' (Article 92). The Commission of the EC has been inclined to take a fairly rigorous view of what would be in the common interest, while the member governments have usually defended their existing subsidies. If the member governments have very different ideas as to what subsidies are appropriate and succeed in defending them, they may eventually place the common market at risk, because the member governments that subsidise the least would be tempted to erect barriers against the subsidised imports; the German government has in fact warned that it might do this if other member governments do not progressively remove their steel subsidies. If on the other hand governments that use subsidies as an instrument of active industrial policy were forced to abandon them, they too could find it against their interests to comply with Community rulings. Hence the Community needs a policy towards subsidies that reflects the requirements of industry that we have earlier discussed and the differing circumstances of different member countries, while preventing excesses which would damage the countries that do not indulge in them.

Where subsidies result from weakness in a sector that suffers from over-capacity, Community policy may need to go beyond limitation of the subsidies and attack a cause of the weakness by securing a reduction of capacity. For where there is free trade among a group of States, each country will be reluctant to reduce capacity in its own industry if the outcome will be continued over-capacity in the sector because other members of the group have failed to cut their own capacity, thereby being rewarded for their unhelpfulness by increasing their market shares. This has, indeed, been the complaint of the British steel industry, which has cut capacity while some other Community countries have not, so that despite its sacrifices, weak prices still threaten viability. Thus a rationalisation cartel, which as in Japan requires adequate cuts in capacity and programmes for a return to profitable development as a condition of price support backed by production and import controls, has to be organised by the Community as a whole if it is to be effective. Yet the Community lacks the powers to secure the capacity cuts, and the arrangements for the steel industry have shored up prices with the help of production and import controls without establishing a basic condition of healthy development in the future. In the case of shipbuilding, where the need for capacity reduction has been still greater, the instruments of Community policy were yet weaker than for steel, where the Treaty establishing the European Coal and Steel Community provided for price support and production controls at times of 'manifest crisis'. The Commission has used its powers relating to State aids in the steel industry and has persuaded member governments to accept a number of Directives on aids to shipbuilding; but the Community's powers regarding State aids have not yet been used in a way that will effect enough capacity reduction in such heavily subsidised sectors.

Just as the creation of a common market implies that rationalisation cartels, if they are to be used, have to be organised by the Community as a whole, so anti-trust and competition policy are best conducted by the Community in so far as the competition in question involves firms of two or more member states. The Community's competition policy is indeed quite effective, consonant with the liberal philosophy that underlay much of the Rome Treaty. This has, on the other hand, prevented the competition rules from being interpreted by the Commission in a way that would help to deal with problems of over-capacity, as might have been done when the manufacturers of man-made fibres approached the Commission with their plan for agreed capacity cuts. A combination of the rules on State aids and on competition should have enabled the member States to deal with the sort of over-capacity that has dogged several major industrial sectors since the mid-1970s, had the member governments understood that it was in their common interest to deal with the problem as the Japanese have done.

Although the need for such Community industrial policies arises irrespective of the pressure to adjust to wider international competition, Japan and the NICs have made it much more urgent. The spread of protection from one product to another, while it may be justified in each case, will if there is no force working in the opposite direction reverse the trend towards a wider international market that meets the developing requirements of modern industry, and it may well allow European industries to become progressively less competitive. If the pressure of competition requires a sharper adjust-ment than can be effected with economic efficiency and social accept-ability by free trade alone, therefore, industrial policy should seek a reduction of as much capacity as is held necessary and the redevelop-ment of the firms that remain. Capacity reduction can be accelerated by buying it out, perhaps with the help of a levy on the firms with the remaining capacity, which will benefit both from protection and from the reduction of capacity; and special measures of manpower policy can be taken to help displaced workers to get new jobs. The firms that remain can redevelop either by improving their production processes, usually through more capital-intensive methods; or by improving their products, usually by moving up-market within their sector; or, if they are adaptable enough, by shifting into another sector with more promising prospects: the aim of the whole programme being to restore the firms' capacity to develop without special protection against inter-national competition. Moves in each of these directions have been pro-moted by policy, most of all perhaps in Japan, but also in European countries such as France, Germany, Sweden and Britain. The countries that have done it the most effectively are those where there is a strong industrial banking capacity to judge the prospects for each type of solution on the part of each firm that requires funds to carry it out, with a government that is able to relate the industrial banking judgements to a realistic view of the political, social and macro-economic constraints. The same applies, *a fortiori*, to the process of organising rationalisation cartels in sectors dominated by a small number of large-scale producers, where judgements have to be made about reasonable oligopolistic behaviour and the big firms' very complex development plans.

Since external trade policy is a responsibility of the Community, the Community has to take a collective view as to the scope of the industrial policy measures that should accompany protection. With several different views among the ten governments and a heavily intergovernmental way of taking decisions, this is a slow and laborious process, liable to produce inconclusive results. But this is hard to escape, so long as the responsibility for industrial policy and the instruments for carrying it out remain predominantly with the member governments. Since pressure from the NICs is almost certain to be long-lasting, and since the need for measures of industrial policy is likely to continue to intensify with growth in the costs of development and in the incidence of social costs and benefits, the Community's inefficiency in combining trade and industrial policy can be expected to become an increasing liability. Hard though it may be for some member governments to accept, there can be little doubt that the member countries' interests would be better served by giving the Community stronger instruments of industrial policy to combine with its instruments of trade policy, and by strengthening the capacity of its institutions to use them – which implies a move away from the practice of unanimous voting, whereby decisions can be prevented by a single government. The British in particular have resisted majority voting, and felt themselves the victims of the majority votes on agricultural prices in May 1982. But if the Community is to deliver the effective industrial and trade policies that the member countries' industries need, the practice of majority voting must be developed; and the British interest is to ensure that this is done in an orderly way through acceptance that majority voting will be the normal procedure where this is stipulated in the Treaties and in other fields where decisive action is required, rather than by *ad hoc* acts of political expediency which will inevitably appear to be directed against a particular member country.

Adjustment to import penetration is bound to be hard in times of high unemployment and stagnation. The more new employment is being created in the economy, based on firms' healthy and competitive development, the easier adjustment will be, and the better placed our economies to participate in the world-wide division of labour, to our own benefit as well as that of our trading partners and of the world economic and political system. Industrial policy focused on adjustment to international trade pressures is not, therefore, likely to be very effective, unless it is accompanied by a wider programme for economic development such as we considered earlier, with policies to promote training, research and development and investment, as well as to ensure that pay push does not erode the profits needed for development and that, perhaps through the practice of development contracts, the bulk of firms do in fact develop. While such programmes are no doubt mainly a matter for the member States, the Community as a whole has a strong interest in their success, if its economy is not to be burdened with weak regions and its trade policy hampered by excessive demands for protection.

This brings us to a wider case for Community support for member countries' industrial policies and to the more general issue of the relationship between the Community and member countries with weak economies. The weaker economies carry the heavier burden of adjustment to the Community's internal free trade as well as to imports from outside the Community. This argues for support from Community funds to help finance the public expenditure incurred in facilitating the adjustments. Not only does this seem just; it is also politically expedient if the governments of economically weaker countries are not to stand in the way of liberal external trade policies, or the removal of internal non-tariff barriers, that are in the interest of the Community as a whole but likely to impose higher adjustment costs on the weaker economies. Thus the Social Fund and the Investment Bank were provided for in the Rome Treaty because the Italians, with the least developed economy of the six founder members, felt the need for such support; and the regional development fund was established on Britain's entry into the Community.

Some people believe that the British economy cannot become more dynamic while it is open to free trade with the other Community countries, but will be condemned to continue the relative decline that started when our European neighbours began to erode our lead in the great nineteenth century industries of textiles, coal, iron and steel, and shipbuilding. They therefore advocate protection against imports from across the Channel, hoping that our industries will regain their original dynamism behind the protective wall. It is just possible that this would happen if Britain's access to export markets in the Community and elsewhere remained unimpaired. But if, as is much more likely, a return to protection against imports from the Community was accompanied by a deterioration of our access to the Community market, a prime condition for development in modern industry, that is a secure and widening market for its products, would no longer apply. Nor does experience seem to show that protection leads to dynamism in British industry. If exports of British manufactures to other Community countries had been a failure since our entry, there would be a more plausible case for risking the narrowing of our markets abroad and the sluggishness that protection at home might well induce. But Britain's exports of manufactures to other Community countries have in fact grown rapidly. Rather than risk damping this source of growth for our most competitive firms, it seems more sensible to maintain Britain's position in the Community, while promoting Community support for a positive industrial policy that will be of particular help to the weaker economies.

It is fair to argue that, instead of helping the weak British economy, the Community's budget is so constructed as to exact a heavy toll on it, because of the cost and the financial arrangements of the common agricultural policy. While it is important to keep the cost of this policy under control, which could be done by transferring more of the social burden of supporting small farmers to the budgets of the member States, it is much more important to strengthen British industry, and neither the agricultural policy nor its financing have much effect on that. The British interest is, therefore, to secure as much Community support as possible for an industrial policy that will promote the development of industry in Community countries and facilitate the necessary adjustments, which are greater in a country such as Britain that has a larger share of relatively backward sectors. The Community's budgetary problem, which requires reforms that are financially more favourable to the British, could be used as a lever to increase Community expenditure on industrial policy and hence, among other things, support for industrial policy and adjustment expenditure by member states. But the principal need, if the Community is to develop a fuller and more constructive industrial policy, is for a steady diplomatic effort to this end by the member governments that particularly want it to happen. The British have, up to now, made no such effort, partly because we have lacked any coherent concept of industrial policy on which it would be based, and partly because of political objections to strengthening the Community and its institutions. We have, in this book, considered some of the grounds for a coherent policy for industrial development; and we have concluded that neither laissez-faire, which implies no industrial policy on the part of either Britain or the Community, nor directive planning, which would almost certainly be national planning, can be successful. We have, accordingly, considered some of the policies that both national governments and the Community might pursue.

The reluctance to enhance the power of the Community is a yet profounder political issue. It is still normal for the British, including most economists, to consider our economic problems in a national perspective and to add an international element as an appendage. From this starting point, the need for co-operation and common policies in

Europe and internationally will inevitably be undervalued. In fact, the national market alone offers too slender a basis for the development of large parts of modern industry. The starting point has to be a wider perspective. We have given most attention to the Community because it offers both a large market that is securely open to Britain and a set of institutions and practices that enable decisions to be taken and executed on a wide range of policies. The Community is often criticised on the grounds that its institutions are too strong and its policies too pervasive. If the starting point is the need for a wide market and for policies adapted to the requirements of modern history, however, the criticism will be that the institutions are too weak and the policies are inadequate.

Industry would be yet better served by a still wider market which was securely open and for which common policies could be made to deal with industrial and other problems. Neither condition applies at present for an area wider than Western Europe. But the future development of industry will render such a widening of the market increasingly necessary, and it should be an aim of Community policy to make this possible.

Rapid results cannot be expected in establishing the international framework in which industry can most successfully develop. The internal free trade in the European Community and the common trade policy are remarkable achievements; but the industrial, monetary and other policies that should accompany them are still relatively weak. In the wider international economy, the trade is less free and the co-operative or common policies are yet weaker. Britain, as the most interdependent among the middle-sized and larger economies, has the strongest interest in promoting international arrangements that favour the development of manufacturing and service industries. Too often, our stance has been critical of the arrangements others have made rather than constructive in proposing alternatives; and there is the threat to opt out of the most far-reaching arrangement of all and, perhaps, to reverse the trend towards the international division of labour. Instead, the cultivation of the European and international markets, with appropriate European and international policy arrangements, should be seen as an integral part of a programme for economic development; and steady, persistent diplomacy to that end as an essential instrument of British economic policy.

Part Three
What is to be Done?

8 The Idea of a 'Least-bad' Solution

Government intervention in the economy – by tax and subsidy, by the manipulation of money, by the control of great industries and services, by the conduct of negotiations in foreign trade, by the regulation of abuses and in many other ways – is inescapable and necessarily immensely influential. In public discussion, a 'good' combination of government policies is one which moves one or more 'priority variables' in a desired direction: a 'priority variable' being the expression of a consensus that particular aspects of the functioning of the economy must receive special attention. Thus, with inflation over 20 per cent per annum, checking the precipitate rise in prices is likely to be seen as the single most important element in economic policy; with inflation down to 10 per cent but unemployment over 2 million, the provision of employment may displace the checking of inflation from its priority; with inflation at 5 per cent and unemployment below 1 million, some other variable (such as the rate of economic growth) would be used to devise the test of success in policy; while in times of national danger, the preparation of the economy for war might be seen as supplanting all other economic objectives.

This tendency to concentrate on the urgent problem or problems of the moment is of course natural, but it tends to lead to instability. Thus, in 1981-82 the Conservative Government was holding to the checking of inflation as a main object of policy, at a time when the public consensus had certainly moved towards giving priority to the reduction of unemployment. It was therefore widely expected that there would be a shift of policy; but many of the proposals being canvassed, though no doubt effective in reducing unemployment in the short term, would have been grossly inflationary, and therefore likely quite quickly to produce another swing of policy, back to the primacy of checking inflation. The wise government – though in its public explanations taking account of the worries that are at the front of the public mind – will seek partial success in a number of areas, rather than a greater success in a single area which inevitably breeds disaster in others. It will look for a 'least-bad' solution, with a mixture of successes and failures which is sustainable over a period of years, without requiring great and harmful swings in policy. It is part of the argument of this book that, because of habits and constraints which we have allowed to accumulate, the present 'least-bad' solution for the British economy is really very bad indeed; which is why there is so much thrashing about of dissatisfied groups, with simplistic ideas that ignore the constraints of the real world. If we could only get back to the problems which we thought so difficult in the 1950s and 1960s, we would be happy indeed. Plainly, then, it is the duty of government to see what it can do to alter the conditions of the economic problem so that its 'least-bad' solution gets better, and not even worse.

It is necessary to remember, however, that the priorities which we assign in economic policy relate to secondary variables. Behind them lie more fundamental purposes of government, to do what needs to be done by communal organisation to advance the happiness of individual citizens and the quality of civilisation. Inflation and unemployment threaten happiness by creating insecurity, but there are of course many other ways in which that happiness could be threatened – for instance, by loss of freedom through pervasive government regulation. It is perfectly possible to devise an economy in which unemployment is so low that it can be concealed, and in which prices are completely stable for considerable periods; such economies have existed for many years in the Communist world. But their achievement depends on an alternative sacrifice of happiness, which we would find intolerable, namely a loss of personal freedom and ability to take initiatives. In a wider sense, then, the 'least-bad' solution is one in which the impediments to happiness, and the sacrifices in the quality of civilisation, are optimally balanced. Of course we do not know in any accurate way what *will* make people happy; we rely on broad political judgements and on introspection which generalises from the state of our own feelings. But one element in individual happiness is certainly security, so that a country which indulges in wide and unpredictable swings of policy is *prima facie* less successful in its policy mix than one which can be expected to have a fairly stable policy. This is one reason why dictatorships and one-party states are sometimes not as objectionable to the citizen as the devotees of democracy would like to think.

All governments are attracted by an easy way out of the problem of choice, namely to encourage economic growth – hoping thereby to have the means to increase the happiness of some citizens without diminishing the happiness of others. But the advantages of this path are deceptive. First, in advanced countries the pursuit of economic growth may stimulate 'wants' faster than they can be satisfied, so that people end up more dissatisfied, not less. A high proportion of expenditure becomes, on a strict definition, not 'necessary', and the desire for it is governed by emulation (or envy) rather than physical need. Second, the continuous pursuit of economic growth per head of population, in a planet some of whose essential resources are limited, and which has rising population and great existing poverty, is not in the very long run a feasible policy; and many would say that even in the short run it cannot be morally justified. As William Penn wrote, 'The very trimming of the vain world would clothe all the naked one'.

Given, then, that the pursuit of a 'least-bad' solution is not easy, nor likely to yield a ready popularity, let us look at the problem in a theoretical way. Let X_1, X_2, X_3 . . . be the variables which we would like to influence, and for convenience these can be defined so that (if all else is held constant) an *increase* in one of these variables represents a move towards a more desirable state. (This involves the assumption that, somehow or other, the objects concerned can be ranked in order of desirability.) Let A_1, A_2, A_3 . . . be the instruments of policy which the government can use to alter the Xs; the As can be conceived as a list of descriptive names, like 'income tax reduction' or 'legislation against monopolies', without any assumption of universal quantification.

Some of the Xs will be bounded – for instance, if X_1 is the number of people employed, it cannot rise above the number of the highest conceivable working population nor fall below zero. Others will not be bounded: if X_2 is the rate at which prices fall (i.e. ($-X_2$) is the rate of inflation), it can in principle take any positive or negative value. But what can we say about the relation of the As and the Xs? Observation of political action over the last few decades suggests a number of propositions which, though individually they may seem obvious, nevertheless offer some significant guides for the future.

Utopia is not attainable

No policy A will unequivocally cause the Xs to increase and go on increasing. Beyond a point, a policy may be ineffective because it deals with only part of the obstacles to progress – thus, subsidising industrial development in a depressed region will eventually be ineffectual if there is a lack of entrepreneurs to conduct that development, or of other special skills necessary to its success. In many cases, policies do good in one area of the economy only at the cost of doing harm in another; thus, an effective monetary policy will reduce inflation, but at a cost, in the short run at least, of causing an underemployment of men and other resources. The relation between the good and the harmful consequences of a policy will vary through time, and with changing external circumstances, and it is not possible to say that the favourable balance of effect will be increased by pushing a policy further and more vigorously. For instance, there are circumstances in which a moderate injection of new purchasing power would get a better use of resources without grave effects on inflation, while sudden major measures of reflation would produce a runaway rise in prices.

It follows that heavy reliance on a single policy instrument is usually unwise.

The constraints affecting a policy must be clearly understood
Some of these constraints have been described in earlier pages, and arise from social habits and institutions which, if alterable at all by deliberate act of policy, can only be altered slowly. Some are administrative; for instance, proposals for far-reaching reforms of the taxation system have commonly foundered on the rocks of the sheer complexity of making big changes without grave injustice or serious new opportunities of evasion. Some constraints are best seen as a general consequence of living in a particular kind of democratic society. The British are generally good at obeying laws, but this obedience rests on the assumption that the law will not vexatiously interfere with familiar rights or freedoms. Once across the line, into a region regarded as vexatious interference, and a law will become unenforceable – or, at least, operable only with elaborate administration and severe penalties for disobedience. Thus, some of the proposals for reforming trade union law, which are relevant to economic policy because they would alter the balance of power between employers and employed, are doubtfully enforceable because they would conflict with strong ideas about rights to combine to further one's welfare. There have been signs in Britain, as in other countries, that the limits of the willingness to be taxed are being approached; attempt to go beyond these limits, and the scale of evasion (and the cost of trying to prevent it) will go up steeply. One version of the present Labour Party programme proposes massive reflation, and perhaps some sort of 'understanding' about wages, but relies on universal price control to prevent an undue rise in prices. If we lived in the sort of society in which a trader who increased prices disappeared in the middle of the night, and was never heard of again, it might be possible to enforce universal price control; but in Britain its enforcement would be a bureaucratic nightmare, resulting almost certainly in a great extension of the 'black' economy.

Policies are often weaker than they appear to be; therefore a multiple attack on a problem is necessary.

Uncertainty must be allowed for, not assumed away

The decisions about a policy will almost always be a response to facts that are imperfectly known, subject to diverse interpretations, or out of date. This imperfection of prior knowledge is to a large extent inevitable, but it is made worse by the inefficiency of governments in designing management information systems to guide their work. During the application of a policy, circumstances will change in ways which are not foreseeable and not capable of being controlled by government. Thus, every policy operates in conditions of uncertainty. This is true even of policies that look obviously virtuous – for instance, the grant of subsidies to scientific research. The facts about the national research effort are imperfectly known and out of date, and it is not at all certain that an increase in research is a necessary precondition for more successful innovation in the economy. Even if this could be established, it might happen after a period that the limit to research was set by the supply of trained manpower, and not by the availability of money. Alternatively, the reaction of industry to the grant of subsidy might, after an initial period, be to cut its own contribution to research expenditure. This example is not taken to develop a serious argument against State aid to research, but simply as a reminder that, even in such a policy, error could (in G.L.S. Shackle's terminology) occasion zero potential surprise.

The human mind deals with some uncertainties by ignoring them. For instance, the occurrence of a major nuclear war before the year 1990 would not be so surprising that we would call it 'impossible', yet most citizens go about their business without allowing the possibility of such a disaster to affect their decisions. This, however, is a reaction to an event that we feel powerless to affect; it is not a logical reaction for a policy-maker who has alternatives at his command. Thus, in investing on the Stock Exchange, few people put their entire wealth into a single 'best' share; for it is well known that investment is risky, and it occasions no great surprise if today's 'best' share performs badly tomorrow. Nor, of course, do sensible investors go for a random portfolio of shares. They 'spread their risks' in a purposeful way, seeking to have several good shares which are not likely to go badly wrong at the same time. So, likewise, prudent companies seek to diversify into a variety of products for a variety of markets; or, if they cannot achieve this, to set up their plants so that they can alter the product without too much difficulty.

This purposeful spreading of risks is more difficult to achieve in decisions about policy, because the habits of political rhetoric favour the presentation of simple, clear-cut 'solutions'. But uncertainty is inescapable, and therefore risk-spreading and flexibility are essential.

*Problems should where possible be attacked in several ways, likely to be affected
in different ways by errors of specification or by changes in circumstances as the
policies are applied. Policies should so far as possible be designed so as to be
capable of quick change if the facts which gave rise to them change.*

Time-lags, and the uncertainty to which they give rise, must be allowed for

Many policies are delayed in their effect, though they may have an
advance influence through a change of expectations. This means that
the decisions to use a particular policy A, and on the extent of its use,
have to be taken on the facts of a date earlier than that on which A will
become effective. This introduces a double uncertainty: the date of
effectiveness may not be accurately known; and the decision may prove
wrong when it takes effect, because the facts have changed. Thus, if the
Chancellor makes a tax change to encourage industrial investment,
which will not actually yield more money to the taxpayer until the ensuing tax year, he cannot know whether the expectation of the change
will immediately increase investment, nor whether the facts for the
next tax year will be such as to justify his policy. The problem is rather
like that of driving a motor car in which there is a significant but un-
known (and variable) time-lag between turning the steering-wheel and
the response of the front wheels. Such a vehicle would be accident-
prone, and it is well to admit that governments are, in the nature of
things, also accident-prone. It is, in fact, quite possible to conceive of
examples where a policy will, because of time-lags, create a harmful
fluctuation in the economy.

*The dangers arising from time-lags increase the need for devising means of quick
corrective action when things go wrong.*

The effects of policies depend on expectations of future policies

If a businessman is contemplating an investment on borrowed money,
an interest rate of 15 per cent per annum expected to *stay* at that level
will not deter him from proceeding with an investment yielding 20 per
cent; but an interest rate of 15 per cent which is expected to fall to 12
per cent in three months' time is likely to cause him to defer his investment, in the hope of increasing his margin of profit. A critical importance attaches to future dates at which expectations, now uncertain, will
be clarified. For instance, it will not be surprising if, on the run-up to
the next election, foreign investors contemplating manufacturing
investment in the United Kingdom defer their plans in order to see
whether a party comes to power which is committed to withdrawal
from the European Community.

A policy which is intended for immediate obedience, like a military command, and which is plainly capable of being enforced, can afford to take little notice of the mental state of those from whom obedience is required. Much more usually, however, policies are seeking to influence the decisions of free agents – to encourage consumers to spend more or less, to encourage wage-earners to accept moderate settlements, to encourage manufacturers to take more notice of new technology, and so on. In all such cases, what matters is how the agent, from whom action is expected, perceives the effects of the policy on him; and his perception will be greatly affected if there enters his mind a belief that next year policy will be different, or that by waiting till next year things now unclear will be, or may be, much clearer.

In a general sense, then, governments are engaged in manipulating the psychology of decision-makers. Theoretical calculations of what they *ought* to do, in response to some curb or inducement, must give way to a wise appreciation of how they are in fact likely to act, in the state of expectation as altered by the government's decision. We refer again to Keynes's celebrated words, quoted in chapter 1, about 'animal spirits'; he continued

> 'Enterprise only pretends to itself to be mainly actuated by the statements in its own prospectus, however candid and sincere. Only a little more than an expedition to the South Pole, is it based on an exact calculation of benefits to come. Thus if the animal spirits are dimmed and the spontaneous optimism falters, leaving us to depend on nothing but a mathematical expectation, enterprise will fade and die; though fears of loss may have a basis no more reasonable than hopes of profit had before'.[1]

The same dependence on feeling, rather than exact calculation, can be seen to influence the actions of trade unions and consumers, as well as business men.

It follows that, in those areas in which the needs of the economy require positive actions, such as an increase in investment, it will be important to create the expectation that policy is stable: that no extra benefit is to be found by waiting, and no present benefit is likely to be suddenly withdrawn before it can be enjoyed (though of course speed of action can be encouraged by the equivalent of a Summer Sale – a benefit which has to be taken up within a limited period if it is to be obtained at all). 'Animal spirits' do not flourish under stop-go policies. Whenever, by intention or perforce, a government gives rise to an expectation that policy will change at some future time, it needs to look very carefully at the implications of the decisions which will be made at that time – especially if a large number of them have been dammed up, awaiting a change of policy.

[1] *The General Theory of Employment, Interest and Money*, ch.12, VII.

Over a considerable area, it is desirable to create a belief in the stability of policy; but this may conflict with the requirement that policies should be flexible as circumstances change.

The British economy is suffering, not from one sickness, but from several. It was never probable that a single medicine would cure the lot; and recent economic history shows very clearly that the prescriptions to hand tend, in treating one sickness, to make others worse. No politician who promises simultaneous and rapid improvement in all aspects of economic health deserves to be given serious consideration. We suggest that, rather than concentrate on the sickness which most irritates people at the moment (with dangers that others will get worse), it would be better to aim for a balanced but moderate improvement all round. In other words, we do not accept that either of the solutions

high unemployment, no growth, moderate or falling inflation
OR low unemployment, some growth, high and rising inflation

can possibly be regarded as either optimal or stable; nor do we think that either contains an automatic corrective mechanism leading to a better solution.

What needs to be said to the patient, then, is that he is not, in the short term, going to be cured; but that it is intended to concentrate on building up his resistance, so that gradual improvement can take place. This means that *the most important policies are those which alter the conditions of the problem*: that is, which relax some of the constraints and alter some of the habits that at present make even a 'least-bad' solution very unsatisfactory. Unfortunately these tend to be policies which are difficult to put over, uncertain in their effect, and easy to postpone (because they only act gradually over a period). But it is essential that governments should give them the highest priority, and not be dominated by short-term expedients which get us nowhere. What some of these longer-term policies are, we discuss in the next chapter.

In dealing with both immediate and longer-term issues, we favour (for the reasons outlined earlier in this chapter) a multiple attack, rather than putting too much weight on one or a few instruments. In this context, we are concerned at the tendency of political parties to commit themselves in advance not to use some of the possible policies. We have laid stress on the uncertainties and time-lags of the real world, and on the subtle problems of expectations; these require an ability to be flexible, while at the same time conveying the sense of security that the main thrust of policy will not suddenly be altered.

But is there any ground for thinking that to aim for a modest but balanced improvement, achieved by the moderate use of varied policies, would give success? We think that there is. Some of the policies which yield harmful reactions probably do so only when taken beyond a threshold at which they alter people's expectations. In moderation, they may hardly be noticed, doing their good by stealth like the modest doses of homoeopathic medicine. And the discovery that the economy is full of vicious circles should not blind us to the possible existence of virtuous circles as well. If only output can be seen to rise, and unemployment to fall, without a new disturbance of the price level – so that economies of scale are regained, and investment in new technology encouraged, leading in turn to further capture of new markets at home and overseas – then there could be the conditions of confidence and optimism which would lead to further gains all round. Against this, it can plausibly be argued that the British economy is now so neurotic that its decision-makers cannot wait for a gradual improvement, but will ruin its chances by assuming failure in advance and by seeking to grab more to satisfy sectional interests. If that is really so, people may have no answer to offer except the necessity of dictatorship; but we are ourselves convinced of the potential of a free and democratic system.

What, then, is to be done?

9 Policy Proposals

General macroeconomic policy
Our main interest in this chapter is in describing policies which might help to relax or modify the constraints that have made it so difficult to run the British economy in a satisfactory way. But this will take time – and where possible we indicate in a broad way the period which we think may be needed before results are achieved. What is to be the main thrust of government macroeconomic policy while deliberate actions and unplanned events alter the conditions of the problem? Is it to be conducted on Keynesian lines, seeking to match (mainly by fiscal policy) the anticipated demand with the level of supply achievable at full employment? Or is it to be monetarist, using the control of the money supply, either direct or through the structure of interest rates, as its main instrument? Or is there some new principle to be discovered?

As may be expected from the discussion in chapters 1 and 2, we come down against the idea of using the control of money as the dominant element of policy. We do not think that there is any straight answer to the problem of defining what should be controlled, nor do we believe that control can be exercised with accuracy to achieve particular policy results. But this does not, of course, imply that the money supply should be uncontrolled. We would wish to see the Bank of England free to exercise its judgement in trying to keep the money supply in a sensible relation to the needs of the economy, as affected both by the volume of transactions and by changing habits of money use. That, however, implies that the authorities must not be pushed off course by an undue weight of public sector borrowing. This would imply, either that (by driving up interest rates) the public sector would pre-empt resources for which there is an urgent need in the private sector; or else that the needs of the public sector would be met by 'printing money', with potential harmful effects on the course of prices and costs so long as the British economy makes price responses more readily than output responses (see chapter 1). But, if public sector borrowing has to be limited, this must imply a check to government expenditures for purposes which do not strengthen the sector that produces marketable goods and services. Otherwise the economy will not become strong enough to support the welfare apparatus which government may desire to expand.

A major aspect of this matter was discussed, a quarter of a century ago, in the Republic of Ireland, in the reports of a body called the Capital Investment Advisory Committee, chaired by Mr. John Leydon; and the relative success which the Irish economy enjoyed in the 1960s and 1970s was not unrelated to the adoption of the principle of priority for 'productive investment'. The Committee defined the term in its Third Report as follows:

> 'An investment is productive to the extent that it enhances the flow of exports or produces goods which can be sold over a period at prices no higher than the prices of equivalent goods freely imported . . . An investment which does not make a net addition to the flow of goods and services is a redistributive investment. If such an investment were undertaken by the State, then the annual interest and sinking fund charges would have to be met from taxation and the physical thing created by the investment would contribute nothing. Much of the investment expenditure that has occurred in this country falls between these extremes and the individual projects can be arranged in increasing order of productiveness or decreasing order of redistributiveness.'[1]

The Committee then pointed out that, while both forms of investment create jobs, both as the asset is made and as it is worked, redistributive investment does this by measures which tend to reduce employment elsewhere; while productive investment is capable of creating continuing employment which is not offset by reductions elsewhere. An example of the first would be State borrowing (or taxation) to cover the deficit on capital account of a nationalised industry, without offering any assurance that its economic viability will be greater next year; an example of the second would be the re-equipment of that industry so that it becomes viable.

It will thus be seen that, while not placing any simple-minded reliance on monetary policy, we advocate an approach which certainly has implications for government expenditure. If a clear priority is given to measures that strengthen the ability to produce and sell marketable goods and services, then tomorrow's tax base will be able to bear some of the expenditures not directly supporting the productive sector, which we all desire. But if there is no such priority, and the demands of government remain high, the productive base will be made even weaker, whether by the pre-emption of resources or by the effects of inflation. We shall have more to say about the implications of priority for the strengthening of production in this chapter.

Subject to this priority principle, we believe that fiscal policy should

[1] Third Report of the Capital Investment Advisory Committee, (Stationery Office Dublin, 1958).

encourage, and monetary management and exchange rate policy should permit, a steady and reasonable growth in total money expenditures in the economy; and that this steady growth in money terms should be converted into a nearly equivalent real rate of growth by an effective prices and incomes policy, whose nature we discuss below. We thus broadly adopt the approach of Professor J.E. Meade,[2] though he proposes the use of wage-fixing to maximise the level of employment – which, as we have suggested on p. 97, raises some difficulties. We see it as a better principle that wage-fixing should be so guided as to encourage economic *development* (in the sense proposed on pages ix and 60) and that those who produce for the market sector should be encouraged to strengthen their position by appropriate physical investment or other development, without being outbid in the labour market by the non-market sector.

But in the short run any macroeconomic policy of this kind will be limited in its success because of the constraints which we have identified in this book. It is essential, therefore, that the longer-run measures that may help to relax the constraints should be developed quickly. This will not be easy, because governments always search for the quick-acting medicine – and, indeed, any pill or draught which is unlikely to work within the lifetime of a Parliament will tend to remain on the shelf. The consequence is that defects in the economy which have long been acknowledged go uncorrected for decade after decade. We must most strongly urge upon all who engage in a political life or influence political thinking the need for a statesmanship which can look beyond immediate advantage, forward over a long period of time.

We take from chapter 8 the need for a multiple attack on problems, for flexibility to meet new circumstances and to correct errors, and for the avoidance of change which is not so justified – since stability of policy is helpful. In line with what has been said in this and in earlier chapters, we shall seek acts of public policy which strengthen and develop the firms and units in the market sector. But we must not in this assume that more and more intervention by the State, to support this or that aspect of production, will necessarily be desirable. Sometimes the best policy is to get out of the way, to make people stand on their own feet, and to bring home to them – without any cushioning or protection – the consequences of their own decisions. On the other hand it is foolish to neglect areas in which the State is necessarily or desirably involved: for instance, education and training, or the diffusion of technology. Finally, we have to admit that in this vast field our proposals are no more than a first selection from a great number of

---

[2] See, for instance, J.E. Meade, *Stagflation, Volume I: Wage Fixing*, op. cit.

possibilities; plainly, the full discussion of policy needs several books, not one chapter. But the first selection can at least illustrate a way of tackling the problem.

Education and training
In chapter 5 we have referred to the constraint on the British economy due to the fact that its labour force is under-educated and under-trained. We have three proposals which seem to us to go to the heart of present shortcomings, though in this area of public policy results must necessarily be slow.

The first is to raise the age for compulsory education, but in a new way. The compulsory education of children is an interference with human freedom which is seen to be justified because it gives an individual benefit (perhaps not fully appreciated by children or their parents), and also a benefit to society as a whole. Exactly the same arguments can be used to support an extension of the ages of compulsion. The disadvantage of shortening working life can hardly be a heavy one, in a period in which the attainment of full employment is going to be particularly difficult. The argument that a large proportion of the population is ineducable, beyond levels now reached, has no support from research results or from the experience of other countries. The benefits, both individual and social, from loosening a significant constraint on the economy would be great.

But there is good reason to doubt whether, for a lot of children, more time spent at *school* would be effectively used. What we propose, therefore, is that the upper age for compulsory school attendance should be *reduced* to 15, as in West Germany; but that there should be universal requirement of continued education to the age of 18, expressed initially in terms of equivalence to $1\frac{1}{2}$ years of full-time education, but to be increased (say to 2 years) as soon as possible. This requirement could be fulfilled, or in some cases over-filled, in several alternative ways (or by a combination of them):

(a) continuing at school, e.g. to take A-level examinations, but with a requirement that the vocational content of courses should be increased;

(b) full-time or part-time further education, with the same requirement;

(c) an approved apprenticeship or similar training by an employer, supplemented by further education as appropriate.

There would have to be arrangements to check the adequacy and suitability of types of training proposed for credit under this scheme, so as to avoid abuse by employers who confuse the employment of cheap labour with vocational training. There would have also to be a requirement of substantial compulsory day release for further education; but that is a venerable idea, not a new principle. The main purpose of what is proposed would be to force new choices on that large part of the labour force which is failing to get adequate standards of education or training, and which in consequence is increasingly likely to be a burden, rather than an assistance, to the economy.

Such a plan should not be rejected on grounds of cost. The additional compulsory element *initially* proposed amounts to half a year, for those not already receiving it. It may be hoped that the changes of attitude induced by the requirement would give a higher expenditure than this implies. But the cost to employers should be offset by the lower rates of pay to the young and partly-trained worker, made possible by a surplus of this kind of labour and by the higher value to be obtained from better-trained workers; and the cost to the State should be tolerable in relation to the potential benefit.

A part of what we here propose is contained in the Government's 'new training initiative', which is to provide special and universal help for unemployed young people; and in particular in the Northern Ireland version of the plan, which not only comes into force a year earlier than in Great Britain, but also lays more stress on an improvement of training for *all* young people, not just for the unemployed. But it must be remembered that a lot of work will be needed on the *content* of training; an enlargement of schemes to prepare the young to practise the traditional crafts of Victorian industry just will not do. Despite the emergence of heavy unemployment, economic performance has been constrained by a lack of certain kinds of developed skill. The attainment and maintenance of a *perfect* match between people's skills and the needs of the economy is not of course possible; for one thing, the direction and rate of technical change cannot be accurately foreseen. But it is an important aspect of policy to stimulate new experiments in types of training, with particular emphasis on teaching basic ideas which can be flexibly employed as conditions change.

Our second proposal is intended to deal with the effect on the attitudes of young people of being taught by people who have no first-hand knowledge of occupations other than teaching. There is at present and will for some time remain a considerable surplus of teachers – greater than is at present admitted, since many trained married women find it useless to apply for jobs. This is a good moment to alter the basis of recruitment. We propose that preference in recruitment to teacher training and to teaching posts should be given to 'mature' students (i.e. aged 25 or more) who have undertaken, over a significant period, work other than teaching – including, in this context, the work of women in bringing up a family, since (although an unpaid job) this undoubtedly broadens the understanding of life. During the boom in teacher education, some colleges specialised in training mature students, and they were found to provide excellent material. Recently, however, initial entrants from school have had preference. We would like to see this reversed, though some entrants from school would still be needed to maintain numbers in shortage subjects such as mathematics. (The application of the same principle to further, and more especially to higher, education might also be beneficial.)

The third proposal relates especially to further education, which we see as the most important area of constraint on the economy caused by weaknesses in education and training, and it is based on the belief that the curriculum is too important a matter to be left to the professional educators alone. We suggest that, in addition to the involvement of employers in bodies such as the Business Education Council and the Technician Education Council, it should be a requirement on all public bodies engaged in further education and training (local authorities and the Manpower Services Commission) to provide a substantial representation of local employers on committees which determine the shape and application, in a particular institution, of the curriculum. Furthermore there should be a requirement to consider by what means training on employers' premises can be made more widespread and effective; and power to transfer public funds from 'intramural' further education to helping with training on employers' premises, where that seems the most effective way of using resources. (One of us has argued elsewhere[3] that there should similarly be an involvement of lay people in the control of the curriculum in *higher* education, at present left almost entirely to academics; and it is worth considering whether the governors of schools should not also join, much more freely than is the present practice, in curricular discussions.)

Research, development and the diffusion of technology

Next we consider the constraint of a backward technology, for which a possible treatment is the encouragement of research, development and the spread of knowledge of new methods and products. Large firms can be expected to do their own research and development, or to commission it in an appropriate way – though in hard times they may do or commission too little. But the size at which in-house research becomes realistically possible is such as to exclude a great many of the units of British industry and commerce, and indeed some whole industries. Some of the medium and smaller firms get the help and technical stimulation which they need from suppliers of materials or equipment,

[3] Charles Carter, *Higher Education for the Future*, (Blackwell, Oxford, 1980).

or from the customers for their final product. Others need a communal provision, and this has long been recognised in the provision of government research stations and the encouragement of research associations.

In no way, however, can the pattern of government aid to research and development which has emerged be regarded as a rational response to need. It is heavily distorted by the special needs of defence, aerospace and nuclear energy, as well as by accidents of past history. Our first proposal, therefore, is that there should be a careful review of existing programmes, with a view to making a more cost-effective use of present total expenditure. 'Cost-effective', in this context, implies making a larger contribution to the strengthening of productive industry. We think that methods of assessment could be developed which might also throw light on the potential productivity of *additional* expenditure on research and development.

We would hope that by these means some effect could be achieved in certain industries which have fallen far behind in their technology, but which the country ought to maintain, in order to have a sufficiently diverse economic base. But the effect would necessarily be slow, generally to be measured in decades rather than years. We therefore see a need for three measures which might produce a much quicker result.

The first is designed to speed up the diffusion of already known technology. It has long been the practice that in agriculture (in which Britain has become efficient and competitive), government supports, not only a research programme which is very large relative to the size of the industry, but also advisory services which (supplementing the efforts of suppliers) bring new technology and business method to the notice of the individual farmer. The reason given for this is that farming is predominantly organised in very small units, and the individual farmer would never be able to keep abreast of developments by his own efforts. But exactly the same argument could be applied to (for instance) the numerous small firms in engineering and building. It is high time we considered a major development of advisory services in all industries which have a large number of small firms, and are not adequately stimulated to achieve technical advance by their suppliers or customers. The potential is indicated, not only by the considerable success achieved in agriculture, but also by the promising effects of the government schemes for encouraging the use of micro-electronics (see p. 113). Advisory services should, however, be 'active' – going out and seeking the potential user; they lose greatly in effectiveness if they rely on a putatively ignorant small firm to take the first step.

Next, we would like to see an active campaign, both to bring to the notice of medium and small British firms the standards achieved in foreign technology, and to foster the transfer of that technology. The first object could be achieved, not only by developments of information services, but by fostering visits of investigation by British business men; one remembers the numerous points that were picked up by the 'productivity teams' which visited the United States in the years after the 1939-45 war. The second object also requires better information services about technology which might be obtained on licence, as well as ideas for encouraging joint ventures between British and foreign firms. It is worth remembering that, although Japan is now a prime source of high technology, her business men remain insatiably curious about what can be learnt elsewhere in the world. Britain needs to match that curiosity.

Finally, we propose a considerable effort to use the research resources of higher education more effectively in the service of productive industry. It has long been noted that the flow of ideas (and people) between higher education and business is much less in Britain than in other countries. Of course, there are some notable exceptions, and recent experience of financial stringency is forcing universities and polytechnics to look more carefully for business activities which can help to carry overheads. But there is a long way to go, and we think that strong measures are needed to stimulate a much more rapid change of attitudes. These might take the form of a tax benefit or grant available to any firm which places a research or development contract with an institution of higher education, associated with a special enhanced support of approved information and advice services based on such institutions. The net cost of these measures need not be great; at present, government provides many resources in higher education which are capable of more intensive use.

Industrial assistance

The impact of public policy on the finance of business ought to take account, not only of grants or loans made, but of the way in which the burden of taxation is distributed. This is a complex matter, depending (for instance) on the extent to which indirect taxation paid by the firm can be transferred to the customer. But the tax most obviously impinging on company profits, and shown in company accounts as a deduction before the appropriation of those profits, is corporation tax; and this contributed, in 1981/82, only 4.4 per cent of government revenue, the actual payments being much affected by capital allowances and revaluation. Only about 30 per cent of companies regularly pay corporation tax: others pay intermittently or not at all, and a tax with a nominal rate of 52 per cent has an effective rate of only some 15 per cent.

Payments are greatly affected by the availability of 'tax losses' brought forward from previous years, and although the system some-times offers valuable help to companies which are expanding, in other cases (for instance, new companies with no tax losses to bring forward) it can operate as a drag on development. The reform of corporation tax so that its effects on the orderly growth of productive enterprise become less arbitrary is a difficult and technical matter, on which the Govern-ment has recently invited comment through the issue of a Green Paper.[4] We think it important that the discussion should be based on the principle that taxation should not inhibit the speedy development of new types of productive enterprise.

When one turns to the assistance of industry by cash transfers, the picture is discouraging. A very large part of the money has been used in support of 'lame duck' industries, and often in a manner which gives no proper expectation that the need for support will be much less in future years. Nevertheless, it has become almost a convention of the government's expenditure plans that, each year, this type of assistance should be shown as falling sharply in future years: for instance, the 1982 projections show, for 'support for aerospace, shipbuilding, steel and vehicle manufacture', in cash terms:

1981/82	£1043 million
1982/83	606 "
1983/84	66 "
1984/85	0 "

Over the same years, nationalised industries' borrowing is shown as falling from £2018 million to £770 million; though (with somewhat more realism) central government subsidies to transport industries (i.e. mainly to the railways) are shown as rising from £919 million to £1050 million, which is not a great change in real terms.

We recognise the great difficulty of dealing with industries which have acquired an expectation of ready public aid, and in which man-agement and workers alike therefore tend to evade difficult decisions; and we acknowledge that in some places there have been, in recent years, significant moves towards realism. But there is a long way to go, and it is essential that government's attitudes should be known to be tough and realistic, granting interim aid only in response to firm plans which will make such aid less necessary in future years. (At Harland and Wolff's shipyard, for instance, the annual subventions exceed the entire wage bill, but offer no plausible prospect that things will be better in future.) On the specific problems created by public owner-ship, we make here only two points. First, the assumption that the

---

[4] *Corporation Tax*, Cmnd 8456, (HMSO, London, 1982).

main form of public ownership should be a national corporation for a whole sector seems to us to be wrong; it creates management units too large for effective control, and lacking the stimulus of a creative competition of ideas. The economies of scale have, we think, been greatly overestimated in such industries, and the diseconomies forgotten. Many (though not all) of the public industries could with advantage be split into regional or product groups. Second, the methods of bringing the public interest to bear on industries which lack the exposure to normal competitive forces seem to us to be amateurish and inadequate.[5]

This, however, is only the negative side of the matter. The positive intention must be to use State aid, selectively and wisely, to promote and speed development in essential areas. Such an intention must not take the form of encouraging permanent dependence on the drug of subsidy, nor should it discourage the use of normal market methods of finance, which we think could be improved. But it is not sufficient to rely on free market forces alone. The actions of free markets can be perverse in relation to long-run development needs, notably because they may be dominated by shorter-run considerations: an example of the perversity was the property boom of the early 1970s. Furthermore, we trade in competition with nations which make effective use of intelligent partnership between public departments and the private sector – notably Japan and France. As argued in chapter 6, there is justification for an active public policy to promote appropriate investment and development. Over five to ten years, such a policy could be seen to make a significant contribution to the relaxation of the constraint of an industrial structure which has not been adapting itself appropriately.

The instruments of such a policy could be various: 'front-end' grants (i.e. grants made when an investment is undertaken), help with development costs, specific help and advice in areas like overseas marketing, and so on. However (following the argument in chapter 6) we see particular merit in the use of interest rate subsidies (the equivalent of lending at preferential rates), associated, when appropriate, with limited guarantees to lenders. Such subsidies could be a matter of specific arrangement with large firms (and subject to conditions which we later discuss on p. 175), but available through a more general system for small enterprises (see p. 129). These are methods which are consonant with the desire for an interlocking of public and private sector policy; they enable the normal commercial channels of finance to be used; and they embody in a direct way the decision of policy that cer-

[5] See *Report of the Post Office Review Committee*, Cmnd 6850 (HMSO, London, 1977), ch. 8.

tain activities should have priority in investment, and that certain risks should be accepted.

However, an active public policy in the Japanese or French style is not consistent with administration or control by civil servants whose recruitment and career pattern make them amateurs in such an assignment, nor with close control by politicians whose interests tend to be bounded by the next election. New types of public body would be needed, operating independently and served by expert cadres with considerable analytical skills and with a commitment extending over a considerable period of time. In the British system, this is liable to be alleged to raise constitutional difficulties about accountability to Parliament; but these difficulties, in so far as they are real, must be overcome.

Industrial banking

On page 124 we draw attention to the fact that, despite the existence of a diverse banking sector (including merchant banks, foreign banks operating in the UK, and specialist lending institutions such as Finance for Industry), the British financial system is deficient in its closeness to the policy of firms and in its ability to form judgements about the risks of development. The key issue here is the creation of new attitudes and skills in the large clearing banks. What matters most is the industrial banking quality of a firm's normal or principal bankers; a deficiency here cannot be fully made good by the existence of specialist institutions to which application is normally made only on particular special matters. The large banks are exceedingly resistant to change, and it is by no means certain that their methods of recruitment give them a sufficient supply of the high ability and extensive experience needed for industrial banking as we have defined it. The government, through the Bank of England, is in a position to exercise considerable pressure on the clearing banks to adopt new structures and new policies of recruitment and training. There should be no hesitation in bringing this pressure to bear, if necessary reinforcing it by limiting the payment of interest rate subsidies to loans obtained from approved competent institutions, or by requiring a competent industrial assessment from a bank before the approval of grants or loans on special terms. Britain cannot afford to suffer the disadvantage of a banking system whose relations with business are below the best world standards.

The banks are sometimes seen as adopting a policy on the development or support of firms which is cautious and short-sighted to a degree that arouses complaint from major investors such as insurance companies and pension funds. However, we agree with those who

believe that major investors have tended to adopt an excessively passive attitude to the companies in which they invest, and by doing so
have deprived the market economy of one of the forces necessary to
make it work efficiently. The ability of investors to exert a helpful and
timely influence would be greatly increased if they would associate, in
groups, with an institution with strong industrial banking competence,
which would help to assess prospects and suggest ways in which share-
holder pressure could be constructively used.[6]

Two related points should be mentioned here. One is that the
government has, in the British Technology Group (which derived from
the National Enterprise Board), an institution analogous to an industrial bank. It should therefore be on the look-out for ways of using it to
fill gaps left by other financial institutions. The other is that the function of critical review of firms' development plans, which is part of
industrial banking, should also be undertaken within the firm by non-
executive directors. But too many firms do not use non-executive
directors, or, if they appoint them, they seek people with prestigious
names but neither time nor energy for their critical task – and often
deprive them of the flows of information which would enable them to
be really useful. The non-executive directors of a firm should be seen as
highly important, having a central function of constructive criticism of
plans and audit of results; and in doing so they would valuably interact
with a true industrial banker.

Institutional structures
Here we seek two changes. The first is familiar ground. The enactment
of proportional representation in central and local government would,
we think, check the tendency of a two-party system to produce violent
alternations of policy, with time being wasted in repealing each other's
enactments, and harm being done to the economy because of the inability to take a long view on essential matters. We are in no way
moved by the fears that proportional representation would produce a
rash of small parties. This is a tendency which can be checked by the
design of the system, and within reason a requirement to form coal-
itions would be a useful curb on the power of party politicians. We
think that the British electorate contains a majority of reasonable,
moderate and pragmatic voters who are increasingly ill-represented by
the more extreme party activists.

The second issue of structure is about the relations between the productive economy and government. Business can have no right of determination or veto even about policies directly affecting it, for govern-

[6] See Sir Arthur Knight, *op. cit.*

ment has to take account of other issues – social, international, even electoral. But there is ground for concern about the effectiveness of communication between business and government. Things are done hastily and badly, which proper consultation could have improved; consequences are not sufficiently foreseen. It is not helpful in the development of sensible policy that the two 'sides' in industry communicate largely separately, with close contacts with different political groups, and in an adversarial manner. The voice of the common interest in prosperity is little heard.

There is a 'tripartite' institution, the National Economic Development Council, which brings together management, unions, and government (and also the consumer interest). At the detailed level, and through the associated office (NEDO), it has done good work, but with only a limited impact on general policy issues. We think that, although a tripartite institution appears logical, in British conditions it leads to a sterile restatement of set attitudes. It would be, in our view, much more effective to retain the administrative and research machinery of NEDO, but to have as its governing institution a Council representative of management and labour, together with certain 'independent' members from the professions and the consumer interests, which would meet with no automatic government or civil service presence, but would have access to Ministers on request and would invite their presence when appropriate. Such a body, meeting in private and supported by a strong research apparatus, might we think develop what is badly needed in the British economy, namely a common voice of the productive sectors. It happens that there is a minor example which suggests the effectiveness of what we propose. Northern Ireland had a tripartite body, meeting under ministerial chairmanship, which was generally regarded as sterile. It was wound up, and (following a committee report) a new Council was constituted on the lines suggested above, with an associated Northern Ireland Economic Development Office. The submissions of this Council to government are on behalf of both 'sides' of industry, and in four years have involved no minority reports; indeed, it is known to us that the discussions are hardly ever polarised in the way which the public pronouncements of the TUC and the CBI, or of the parties at Westminster, might suggest. The adoption of this pattern in the much larger economy of the UK would, of course, not be without difficulty; but we do not think that it needs to be assumed that the Irish are better at reasonable compromise than the English, Scots and Welsh.

International issues
Despite all the well-known problems associated with the European

Community, it would (as argued in chapter 7) be an act of gross folly, likely to produce the most disastrous results, if Britain sought to leave the Community. The idea that we could do so while retaining sufficient bargaining power to hold some of the benefits of membership, or to replace them by reviving old trading patterns with the Commonwealth or other countries, is mere moonshine. So is the idea that the British market is large enough to achieve independent prosperity. The effects of leaving the Community would be an immediate rise in unemployment, an increase in the uncertainty which prevents sensible industrial planning, and an acceleration of Britain's industrial decline.

It is indeed our general view that, because of the multiplicity and size of its international interests, Britain should take a leading part in the development of international economic relations, whether through the mutual accommodation of national policies (eg in GATT negotiations) or through the growth of supranational policy. Some people (with Mr. Enoch Powell as their most eloquent spokesman) see harm or shame in any reduction of the unrestricted sovereignty of the British Parliament. This is not what we believe. The long-term interests of the world and of each part of it are harmed by the assertion of total national sovereignty, as national interests were when over-mighty barons fought for their share of power.

In conformity with this view, we favour entry to the European Monetary System if the right conditions can be obtained (see p. 136); this would strengthen the economy by reducing an uncertainty (namely, the exchange risk) which affects more than half our exports. We would not wish to forget the long-term aim of having a single European currency, though this would involve the creation of much more effective institutions of joint economic management. We also favour the early creation of a Community Reserve Fund, to help to stabilise the US dollar exchange rate; and we would like to see a common policy to seek to influence exchange rates with the Japanese yen. It is important not to have exaggerated expectations of exchange rate policy, because of course rates emerge from a complex of international transactions only some of which are influenced by Britain or the Community, and the costs of seeking to obstruct a major trend in a rate may be high. But equally it is foolish to allow market forces to produce a needless uncertainty, or to yield rates which for a considerable period are perverse in relation to the underlying real economic forces.

We recognise, of course, the need for major improvements in the common agricultural policy, and for a proper and just settlement of the issue of national contributions to the EC budget. But we think that the first of these would be seen in better perspective, and the second be much more readily achieved, if Britain adopted a positive approach in pressing for a stronger Community industrial policy. For instance, a common use of interest rate subsidies to secure selected industrial development is better than a competitive use of such subsidies; an understanding on interest rate subsidies will in any case be needed if they are to be used to offset particular harmful effects of the international communication of high interest rates. The Community line on competition policy is already quite strong, but needs further support if it is to prevent national devices for getting round it; and it needs also to accommodate, smoothly and sensibly, limited measures of temporary protection in pursuit of rationalisation, a matter which is further discussed below. The Community ought to exert to the full its common influence to help to remove non-tariff barriers, both between member States and between the EC and its trading partners outside – not forgetting the barriers which affect trade in services. At the right time it should also seek to extend further the world-wide reduction in trade barriers achieved by the GATT, and perhaps to consider further regional arrangements, such as free trade with the United States and Canada.

Competition policy

At various points in this book we have stressed the problem of achieving sufficient size to be able to compete effectively in international markets. But this is a problem of particular industries or parts of industries, predominantly in manufacturing (though some are in services). Unnecessary size, and particularly the attempt to bring under a single management a heterogeneous array of activities, can lead to slow and ineffective decisions. International comparisons suggest that Britain may have too many large firms, not too few. In this context we welcome the recent efforts of government to encourage the appearance of new small firms; this can be a most valuable way of ensuring that new ideas get a speedy trial. But in the general field of competition policy, we have to say that the problem is neither to unleash the forces of competition, nor to promote and encourage mergers, but to secure the right balance between competition and safety. Intense competition for short-term advantage is inconsistent with an orderly long-term policy of development; the man who is always wondering where the next order is coming from is in no position to innovate or to have a sensible investment policy. Too much safety leads to laziness of managerial thinking, and eventually to a crisis when the failure of adaptation to markets becomes evident. We have suggested (p. 74 ff) that it is proper, for the avoidance of social and economic waste, to allow the appearance of a temporary 'rationalisation cartel' to help to manage orderly change in an industry which is badly in need of adjustment; leaving adjustment solely to random processes of bankruptcy is a very poor way of achieving sensible change at the right time. The orderly change which we seek would require strong commitments to reduce surplus capacity, but also to develop alternative uses of resources.

All this underlines the need for a strong and experienced investigating body, on the lines of the Monopolies Commission, which is expected to publish full reports and to develop its own case law as to whether, in a particular industry, the weight of public policy should favour more competition or less. It would be better renamed the Competition Commission, with terms of reference which extend to situations of cut-throat competition as well as to mergers, cartels and monopolies. The Commission could have specific roles in advising on requests for tariff or other protection, in supervising rationalisation cartels, and in securing a proper relationship to EC competition policy. The power of reference to the Commission should not be limited by any rules about proportions of the market covered; but, since references to the Commission tend to put considerable costs on the industries investigated, there should be power to reimburse at least part of the costs. This would help to combat the assumption that firms or industries referred for investigation are *prima facie* engaged in practices contrary to public interest; whereas the public interest lies in sorting out the good from the bad practices, without prior assumptions about the answers. The method of enforcement of policy may generally have to rely on prohibitions of practices in restraint of trade, but with understandings about the power to grant exemptions, and on occasion a positive policy (related, for instance, to the conditions of grant of financial help) for the encouragement of 'restraint of trade' where competition is excessive and harmful.

Development programmes
In all that we have so far said, the underlying emphasis is on the right relationship between industry and commerce, and the State. Public policy can help to create the conditions for a right response from the decision units of the economy, but those units will themselves need to be the primary source of initiatives. In turning to the proposal for development programmes and development contracts, outlined in chapter 6, we deal with a matter which is essentially one for business itself; though we believe that the idea should be prompted by using State incentives or penalties, for instance by making such programmes or contracts a requirement for larger firms receiving State aid, or doing government work, or receiving any form of special protection.

What we mean by a development programme is an understanding reached after full and open discussion between the management of a firm, its workers and its financing institutions, (and, where appropriate representation exists, its customers or consumers), which sets out a plan of investment and product and market development, and the associated benefits to workers, customers and shareholders which are expected to flow from it. Such a plan would certainly need regular revision, as market conditions change; and it would properly cover the changes in work practices, and the variations of working conditions, which might arise as it is implemented.

We are not impressed by the argument that such programmes would be impossible because of the demands of commercial secrecy. It is quite possible for the employees of British Leyland (for instance) to find encouragement for a programme of change in working practices from a general knowledge of future benefits to flow from the introduction of new models, without revealing in advance precise details of the specification of those models. In any case, unprogressive business has a propensity to make a fuss about keeping things secret which any intelligent investigator can find out; more progressive firms rely, not so much on secrecy, as on their momentum in bringing new things to the market in advance of their competitors.

In some cases a development programme might become a formal contract within the firm, setting out the expectations of future development, the changes in working practice which will be required, and the policy for adjusting wages and salaries. Obviously there is need for care in avoiding a contract to deliver some result which may be found out of reach as a consequence of a change in external circumstances. Indeed, a part of a development contract would be an understanding about the means for its revision; and also about the means of resolving disputes about its interpretation or consequences, for instance by using the tribunals proposed for settling pay disputes. A development programme could gradually evolve the formality of a contract, but we suggest that a non-inflationary contract between a firm and its employees should be mandatory whenever a large firm obtains any government aid or protection, so that the aid is not swallowed up or negated by pay push. A typical case for this can be seen from recent relations between British Rail and government: it is evident that Ministers have been concerned lest aid given should be used to support higher pay, with no sufficient understanding about improved working practices which could justify that pay. It would have helped the British Rail Board if it could have been made explicit that a properly monitored development contract, containing firm agreements on practices as well as pay and investment programmes, was an absolute condition for obtaining investment aid. It would be an incidental advantage of such contracts that they could settle the method of adjustment of pay for several years, instead of reopening the contract each year. Longer-term pay agreements, such as are common in the United States, would help British industry by lessening uncertainty.

Some may think that the idea of reaching consensus on a programme or contract after full consultation would be impossibly slow and time-consuming. It is not, in fact, likely to be much slower than giving orders from on high, and finding them not obeyed. The difficulty in imagining the process arises because the habit of treating workers as equal human beings deserving of consultation is not well developed among British managers. British industry badly needs to discover that habit of constant consultation which does not appear to have inhibited the advance of Japanese or German industry. We believe that in the medium term the adoption of development programmes and contracts (by consent and with the help of official inducement, not compulsion) could considerably alter attitudes in the British economy.

Industrial democracy

We venture to say that the idea of the development programme and contract seems to us to be the right way to rescue the debate on indus-trial democracy from the sterility into which it has relapsed since the report of the Bullock Committee.[7] We see a development programme as the subject of interlocking discussions in every workplace of the firm concerned, each group of workers (and managers) being helped to see, in personal terms, how the programme might affect them. There would then be an attempt to obtain consensus at the level of the firm (though it is not necessary to conceive of a single programme covering all the activities of a multi-product firm; there could be several pro-grammes). This seems to us to be the right and effective form of indus-trial democracy, working from the individual upwards, perhaps through one or more stages of elected delegates; it is to be distinguished from 'top-down' industrial democracy, which assumes that national trade union officials on the Board can effectively represent the indi-vidual.

The 'bottom-up' principle of industrial democracy, based on works, office or department councils, has of course a wider application than just to consultation on development programmes. It is essentially the method which has found successful use in Germany. It does not dis-place the trade unions, which in practice would be a common source of candidates at Works Council and higher levels. It is democratic in the proper sense of bringing individuals into consultation and decision on

---

[7] *Report of the Committee of Inquiry on Industrial Democracy*, Cmnd 6706, (HMSO, London, 1977).

matters which directly concern them. Its successful working requires, of course, a strong understanding on the availability of relevant information: this is a matter on which British industry still has far to go. On all these matters the German system of statutory participation has much to recommend it. We think it should be used as a basis for a similar system, suitably adapted to British conditions.

Incomes and prices

By a 'prices and incomes policy' we mean one which, by agreement, inducement or compulsion, moderates rises in prices and incomes, leaving room for the profits that are a condition of development. People tend to think of such a policy in a simple way – controlling prices in the shops and money in the wage-packet: but of course it is much more complex than that. Some prices and some incomes are determined overseas, and are not subject to British control. Plainly wholesale and factory-gate prices must be involved as well as retail prices (since shopkeepers cannot possibly carry the whole burden of price control) – but what about auction prices, tender prices, one-off bargains made between individuals (e.g. on the sale of a house)? What about the professional fees related to these, or levied for functions like accountancy or legal advice? In the area of wages, salaries and dividends, what about increases which are 'earned', and fully paid for, by higher productivity? What about the profits of sole traders and partnerships, or pure economic 'rents' (such as are earned when a celebrated robber sells his life story to a Sunday paper)?

It is well to remember these complications, because they plainly make it more difficult to devise a policy which will be seen to be just or even-handed. But there is a more fundamental difficulty. The entities to be controlled are all 'prices', whether of goods, services, labour or capital, and they have a regulatory function in the economic system, giving signals of shortage or abundance and encouraging the movement of resources to shortage areas. Without such signals, the economy will work badly (and increasingly so, as its distortions increase). What we are seeking, therefore, is a means of maintaining *relative* movements of prices while inhibiting the tendency for all prices to go up together. But unfortunately there is no way by which the exercise of pure reason by controllers can be sure to stimulate what would have happened in a free market. Of course, in the constrained and manipulated markets which are common in the modern economy, the signals from prices are on occasion perverse or misleading (especially in the labour market), though this does not mean that they can be totally ignored.

This liability to produce distortions and inefficiency is of itself enough to rule out crude prices and incomes policies, except as a short-term expedient. It does not, however, rule out the application over a long period of more sophisticated policies, especially in the context which this book suggests, of a search for a 'least-bad' mixture of policies rather than a vain quest for perfection. For, although those who seek to influence or control prices and incomes will never be sure what desirable relative price movements they may have obstructed, or what undesirable ones they may have promoted, they can at least know that what they introduce is superimposed on the existing distortions of imperfect markets, and may sometimes serve to correct these previous distortions. Thus, it may be held that the exercise of trade union power has created, in some industries, an inadequate differential in favour of the skilled and experienced workers. It is quite conceivable that a deliberate incomes policy could help to correct this, and thereby improve the working of the economy by encouraging people to seek skill and regular experience. (Note, however, that a crude policy, such as allowing everyone an extra £100 a year, has the opposite effect.)

In considering what should be done, let us begin on the incomes side. One concept frequently discussed is a policy achieved by a voluntary and sensible agreement between representatives of employers and employed, and followed as a matter of custom or because of competition for those incomes which lie outside the main area of collective bargaining. (The latter proviso is important; without it one will get a transfer to the unregulated area, similar to that which created 'the lump' – labour-only sub-contracting – in the building trades.) Britain in the 1980s, however, provides a very poor environment for the emergence of such an agreement. The TUC is not authorised to negotiate for the trade union movement, which is fragmented into numerous unions organised on a variety of principles. Furthermore, to our great disadvantage, the 'sides' of industry have a close relationship to two of the major political parties, the Labour Party in particular being dependent on trade union financial support. This fact imports into any discussion of large issues of policy the adversary traditions of political debate. Hitherto, any such discussion would have taken place with one side identifying with the government of the day, and the other with the opposition. This is not a situation likely to produce a sensible agreement; it is, indeed, much easier (as happened during the period of the 'social contract') for the side which identifies with government to bargain behind closed doors with that government, perhaps seeking concessions in other areas that relate to its power and status, and leaving to government the task of enforcing the bargain. There are signs that the simple political relationship to dominant parties is breaking down, but years will have to pass before the habits of mind which go with that relationship are superseded.

The option of a compulsory universal detailed incomes policy is theoretically practicable, but nevertheless (we think) unattractive. Such a policy must be capable of enforcement, at least to a degree which ensures a general acceptance that justice is being done. It therefore needs (if it is to continue over a period) to go into innumerable details of incomes and fringe benefits. Satisfaction that even the boss is only getting five per cent will quickly wane if it is observed that his children are going to Eton at company expense, or that his yacht has been transmuted into an entertainment cost. A considerable bureaucracy will be required to ensure enforcement, and the general direction will need to be in the hands of men and women of great wisdom and saintly character, trusted to observe the general interest despite all the pressures of special groups. Even so, it is not clear how a universal policy can be enforced, in face of a determined attack.

But the most serious objection to a long-term compulsory incomes policy which attempts to fix all incomes from the centre is that it would make the signals that relative incomes ought to change indistinct and hard to interpret, and would therefore deprive the wise and saintly controllers of management information essential to the performance of their task. The signals would now be given, not by employers actually changing what is paid, but by the emergence of surpluses and shortages of labour, and the extent of these surpluses and shortages in relation to a particular skill would not generally be known. It is typical of a shortage situation that almost any deficiency appears as a desperate famine with a consequent danger of over-reaction. We would not like, for instance, to have to make a judgement, based on gossip about shortage alone, on the extent of the relative movement appropriate for the pay of computer staff.

This leads us, therefore, to consider intermediate possibilities of incomes policies of a less rigid kind, achieved mostly by inducement. There are three ways in which the probability of success could be enhanced. The first is by the use of more than one instrument (in conformity with our emphasis, in chapter 8, on using multiple instruments of control), so that the whole stress is not carried by a single policy. The second is to concentrate detailed attention on key areas, and in particular the public sector and the largest private firms, leaving the rest not unregulated but subject to a more general form of control. The third is to encourage some changes in the habits of wage bargaining which would make sensible settlements more likely.

We deal first with the last of these. We have already mentioned (p.176) the possible advantage from longer-term settlements, even if they provide (but by a stated method) for interim increases. It would also help if as many as possible of the major settlements could be reached at the same time of the year, thus discouraging the practice of having a whole series of 'comparability' adjustments. For it is of the nature of such adjustments that they are only made upwards; no one has ever been known to use the comparability argument when the comparable trade has had a low settlement. The synchronisation of negotiations would also help towards the creation, by informal means, of a national consensus on the year's settlement – perhaps by the emergence of a 'leading settlement' which others copy, as occurs in West Germany. The government could help the process of synchronisation by seeking to move all public sector negotiations to a period (such as the autumn) already used for some major private settlements.

Although our main stress is on inducement, we think that there is at least one form of compulsion which is reasonable, and would indeed be accepted with relief by most members of the public. This is that before disruptive action is taken – whether by way of strike, go-slow, lockout, or other means – there should, at the instance of *either* party, be a hearing before a public tribunal which should have power to make recommendations and (if appropriate) to publish a report. This would not be binding arbitration; the recommendations could be ignored, and the disruptive action could be taken. It could be provided that any agreement ultimately made would be back-dated at least to the date of reference to the tribunal; so the workers involved would not lose by delay. But at least the facts of the case would be in the open, and there would be some additional pressure on the parties to settle in a reasonable manner.

This concept of a cooling-off period is taken from United States practice. It offers an opportunity for the public, as well as the parties, to ponder on the facts of a dispute before the weapon of disruption is used. As we suggest below (p. 188) it could have a wider application to industrial disputes, and certain penalties or disadvantages could be attached to disregard of the requirement to go to a tribunal or of a tribunal's findings; this matter is explored more fully in Professor Meade's book cited above (p. 96). In the present context, however, we prefer to stress the value of a period for reflection, clear establishment of the facts, and further negotiation.

The compulsory hearing before a tribunal would discourage the habit of 'striking first and negotiating afterwards'. But it would not be wise to see it as a sole instrument. This would require too much weight on means for the enforcement of a tribunal's findings, and it would not touch the problem of inflationary settlements in industries with monopoly power, in which (in effect) managers seeking a quiet life can collude with their workers to give excessive increases at the expense of the captive customer. Our proposal for a Competition Commission would have some relevance to this problem, and it is conceivable that that Commission could be an alternative source of awards to protect the consumer by setting a limit to certain cost increases. But even this would do little to counter the pay push that originates at the countless points in the economy where a group of workers, formal or informal, large or small, has substantial bargaining power. As we have seen in chapter 4, this power is so dispersed and so varied that it is impossible to envisage any simple general regulation applied by a central authority, which would check the pay push sufficiently to prevent either the general inflation that follows when firms use their oligopolistic power to push up prices and thus maintain their profits, or the loss of investment, development and employment that results when this inflation is checked by restrictive monetary policy. Nor, as we have just pointed out, could the complexity of pay and bargaining power be matched by an equally complex central system of compulsory pay determination, without undermining both economic efficiency and political freedom. Yet the combination of pay push, price push and restrictive policy is probably the main cause of the stagflation that is doing such grave damage to the British economy and those of most other western countries.

A way through this dilemma may be offered by the second of our three methods for enhancing the probability of success of incomes policies: to concentrate detailed attention on key areas. The general level of prices in the British economy is strongly influenced by a few hundred big firms that account for a large proportion of production and the general level of pay is largely determined in those firms and in the public sector. We consider later how the government, as the employer, can counter pay push while improving efficiency in the public sector. Here we make a proposal for preventing the larger firms from generating inflation, while at the same time encouraging their development.

We have, earlier in this chapter, summarised our idea of firms' development contracts which was presented in more detail in chapters 4, 5 and 6, and we have suggested that a non-inflationary contract, i.e. one that enables the firm to keep its prices sufficiently stable and the employees' pay at rates which leave room for the profits to finance vigorous development, should be a condition of any government aid or protection for one of the larger firms. Where such aid and protection are important, as we have argued they may have to be during a period of revival of the British economy, this could be a decisive inducement for both firms and employees to make contracts that could be accepted by the proposed pay tribunals as both non-inflationary and developmental. If such inducement is not enough to ensure development with stable prices, a more powerful inducement, or even some compulsion, might be required, at least for a period in which inflation is being brought down and new habits and expectations are being engendered. It should after that be possible, if the experience of Japan and Germany can be taken as relevant, to keep inflation low and development strong without compulsion and even without a great deal of official induce- ment; and meanwhile, any compulsion should avoid the danger of excessively detailed intervention because it would relate to the firm's total pay bill calculated to allow both stable prices and adequate profits, and not to the pay of the individual employee. Thus the task of aggre- gating these individual interests is not attempted by the government, but left to negotiations between the firms and the employees' repre- sentatives, limited only by the constraint of a non-inflationary 'kitty' for total pay.

If this method succeeds in securing both price stability and develop- ment in the large firms, and if the government prevents pay push in the public sector from upsetting the equilibrium, a new phase of non- inflationary development will have opened for the economy as a whole because the trends of prices and production for the whole economy are set by these large organisations. But the prospect of success will be improved if there are further instruments to encourage stability in the large organisations as well as to reach out to the rest of the economy. Thus in line with the other of our three chosen ways to improve the chances of success for incomes policy, by using several instruments, we favour a further measure which would be a general discouragement of the award of increases that go beyond what the nation has earned by increased productivity, and which would reach down to the smaller firms that are not likely to be involved in development contracts or to be major subjects for the Competition Commission. This measure can be attached to the tax system.[8]

The policy would begin from the statement of a percentage 'norm' for increases in hourly earnings (or of weekly earnings, for those who work no set number of hours). Since a norm is bound to be interpreted as, for most people, a minimum entitlement, it would be desirable in the long run to set it below the expected rate of increase in the real national income. It is true that incomes fixed in money terms would not increase, and possibly certain welfare benefits would not be in-

[8] The proposal is at present known especially by the name of Professor Richard Layard (see Discussion Paper 99, Centre for Labour Economics, London School of Economics, 1981, which includes further references); but it has a considerable history, and a version was earlier propounded by Professor Michael Fogarty, in *We can stop rising prices,* (Economic and Social Research Institute, Dublin, 1970).

creased in real terms; but nevertheless a low figure for the norm, say two per cent, would be needed to leave room for such higher increases as might occur, while still preserving consistency with a zero average price increase.

Each employer would then be taxed on that part of his *total* wage and salary bill which (averaging over his work force) arises from giving increases in excess of the norm. Operating on a single 'kitty', he would be able to make internal relative changes, free of tax, if he could give some workers less than the norm and thus others more. Workers would still be able to share in their particular firm's prosperity, but at a lower rate, since a part of the fund which could provide wages in excess of the norm would be taxed away. The employer would be able to pay 'over the odds' to attract scarce labour, but would pay a penalty for so doing; however, part of the incidence of the tax might well be on the scarce labour concerned, by scaling down the size of the differentials offered. It has been suggested that the proceeds of the tax should be redistributed back to all employers by way of a reduction of national insurance contributions, thus rewarding those who are able to stick within the norm; but the redistribution might more appropriately be used to favour development, for example, by the interest rate subsidies discussed above.

Such a policy would evidently produce uneven results, but they would tend in the right direction, because the tax would alter the matters considered at the bargaining table and by tribunals: 'inability to pay' would become a stronger argument. However, there are many difficulties to be considered even in this proposal, and some are discussed below.

(a) *Increase in earnings due to higher productivity (e.g. through piece rate and bonus systems)*. It would appear bizarre to tax an employer who manages his business well enough to achieve rising productivity. On the other hand, a general exemption for productivity payments would be difficult to manage: it is too easy to devise bogus systems which yield extra earnings without adequate extra production. It is not possible to levy the tax on earnings per unit of output, because many businesses do not have any simple way of measuring overall output. In the long run, the existence of the tax would alter the terms of some productivity agreements: where workers have (in effect) said 'we will not work this new machine unless we get 50 per cent of the resulting before-tax benefit to the company', they might have to settle for 40 per cent. But this would not help with agreements already operating, nor with productivity inducements which are simply there to persuade people to work more effectively with existing technology.

A particular problem can be seen with a *loss-making* business which is achieving rising productivity – in 1981, British Leyland would have been an example. Taxing the excess earnings in such a case would simply defer the date of viability. Some help could be given by allowing the tax to be carried forward, and allowed as a charge on future profits. Furthermore, there could be an exemption for the distribution of the fruits of higher productivity when they are in accordance with a duly certified development or profit-sharing contract (pp. 92, 181). Access to low interest money, following an 'industrial banking assessment, might be limited to firms which either make a distribution covered by such an approved development contract or keep to the norm. Undoubtedly there would be a residual problem, particularly in smaller firms, and the matter requires further thought; however, the use of multiple instruments of control may make it possible to limit the harm by using a fairly low rate of inflation tax, say 20 per cent on the excess payments.

(b) *Evasion by increasing fringe benefits.* Benefits in the form of shorter hours or extra holidays are already caught, if the tax is assessed on earnings per hour actually worked. But there would be a temptation to increase fringe benefits which cost less to the employer than they would if individually bought by the employee; and especially the provision of cars, since (out of tenderness for the motor manufacturers of the world) this benefit has been taken into account for tax purposes at much below its true value. The only ultimate answer seems to be to introduce by stages a forthright policy of penal taxation of every discovered fringe benefit (assessing it, for instance, at 150 per cent of its full value) in order to drive all employers back to straight systems of remuneration in money. This would also be of value in lessening class differences in the treatment of different kinds of worker.

(c) *Professional fees.* Presumably the profits of independent (self-employed) business men and private partnerships would generally be left to find their own level; most are restricted by competition, and an ability to get an increase above the norm in a particular year has to be seen in the light of the ever-present danger of a sharp downward fluctuation in profits, or the appearance of losses. But there are certain professional fees which are earned in situations of very restricted competition: audit and conveyancing fees are examples. These might need investigation by the Competition Commission and special control.

It is a great advantage of the 'tax inducement' version of incomes policy that it allows some relative changes to occur, and thereby allows signals to be given of the pressures for change while at the same time increasing friction so that rapid imitative changes in levels of income are discouraged. In the context of policies which cannot be perfect, we recommend this one for consideration. But the tax rate must not be too high (which would exaggerate the disadvantages), nor so light as to be ineffective.

We have left to the last the problem which has defeated every recent government, namely the control of public sector pay. We must first make it clear that we do not favour the use, for large parts of the public service, of direct comparisons with the private sector as a sole means of guiding settlements. The public service is too large a factor to be dealt with in this way; the comparisons are inexact and hazardous, and prone to bias because the risks of the private sector are not readily assessed and allowed for.

We consider that there could be a limited class of workers in the public service who, in exchange for an understanding that disruptive action is to be outlawed, could have the benefit of a favourable formula for pay. This might apply, for instance, to the armed forces, the police, and *essential* health service workers. The formula might offer for ten (or twenty) years to come adjustment each year in line with retail prices *or* an index of average earnings, whichever is higher; this would have the effect of producing a cumulative increase at least as good as the average, but very probably better. The employer's side might further supplement these rates if difficulties of recruitment make this necessary.

But such protection could only be granted to a limited group. If the group is made too wide, it will stimulate pay push in that considerable number of occupations in which the public and private sectors are competing for the same kind of people. The next proposal, then, is to treat other parts of the public service as if they were large firms, and require non-inflationary development contracts whose validity could be monitored. This is certainly a possibility for some or all of the nationalised industries (for which the sanction of the withdrawal or delay of aid is a strong one). It might be used more widely, for instance if the Competition Commission or some other body were put in charge of 'efficiency audits' of sections of the public service, which could be the basis for judging the reasonableness of pay proposals. (Our view is that in government departments, local authorities, and associated services such as health and education, there is certainly scope for productivity improvement.)

Finally, it would be possible to apply to the public service a version of the 'tax incentive' proposal. The employees of central and local government could be dealt with by limiting the offer to the norm (with the likelihood that this would produce damaging industrial disruption) or to the actual average achieved in the private sector (which would necessitate a confusing time-lag, and provide no pressure for 'justifying' increases above the norm by higher productivity). A superior system, allowing genuine collective bargaining but also incentives to improve methods of operation, would be to build in the norm (and no more) into a rigid cash limit for each part of central and local government. The norm would already embody an assumption about a national average increase in productivity, and each sector would thus be challenged to see how far it could go to achieve it. A tougher version of the control suggested would be to 'tax' public departments for increases above the norm, as if they were private employers, the tax taking the form of a reduction in the cash limit.

What about prices? There is no strong case for attempting to control the prices of goods and services which are in unrestricted availability as imports, at least in the form of near substitutes. It is true that the competition so provided will not eliminate inflation, but only hold it to something like the level achieved by our main trading rivals (as modified by changes in exchange rates). However, this in the British context is enough to curb the most harmful price rises; excluding exchange rate effects, the centre of the inflation problem is to prevent industries being destroyed by rises in home *costs* which exceed the rises in other trading nations. There are some cases in which non-tariff barriers to imports exist, and might be modified; or, as in the case of automobiles, non-tariff barriers allow an internal price level much higher than that in other nations. Governments should not hesitate to use the freedom of exchange within the EC to discourage price rises.

Equally, there is little reason to use the instrument of price control where genuine and widespread competition between British firms exists. The problem is to decide at what point the restriction of competition justifies recourse to the considerable complications of price control. At one extreme, there are a few major true monopolies: British Telecom is an example. The danger with these is that they will work on a cost-plus basis, with inadequate control either of efficiency and quality of service or of the level of remuneration of staff, since they are secure in the knowledge that the captive customer can always be made to pay. Such monopolies require, not only a control of prices (requiring a special argument for increases above a permitted norm), but also some external efficiency audit, supported by power to require the production of information (see p. 168).

The most difficult area is that of restricted competition, for instance between firms which follow a 'price leader' or which have developed informal methods of exchanging information and avoiding the inconvenience of vigorous competition. But many such firms are subject to international competition. What seems to be required for the residue, therefore, is a limited system of standing industry committees under the Competition Commission, with power to investigate and to control either charges or increases in charges, having regard to efficiency and quality of service. For instance, a committee might be needed to control 'prices' in the major multi-branch banks, whose record in the control of costs may well be criticised as inadequate.

What we have suggested shows a lack of symmetry between incomes and prices, and there is a reason for this. The labour market, almost in its entirety, is exceedingly imperfect; employers are not able to hold an auction, and hire the worker willing to offer himself at the lowest wage. The market for goods and services is patchily imperfect; competition – domestic or international – has some real effect in limiting price rises, and could have more. It is true that firms which make profits at a high level may (at least if they stop growing) find themselves paying a lot of tax, but this is not analogous to the proposed tax on wages and salaries above the norm. A firm which is able to exploit its market situation to make a lot of profits will not be discouraged from that exploitation by having tax to pay: rather the opposite. In any case, the central problem is not just the earning of high 'rents' from monopoly or the imperfections of competition, but the assumption that increases in cost can automatically be passed on to the buyer, without any need to search for improvements in productivity and efficiency to offset them. In the protected parts of the economy, many firms making low profits or losses are nevertheless, by standards of good practice elsewhere, overcharging their customers.

A sensible continuing policy on prices would have an immediate effect on competitiveness, and would remove a major uncertainty which constrains the development of the economy. But, as chapter 4 has suggested, part of the problem is that a legal and institutional framework intended to favour combinations of workers (because of their relative weakness) has persisted into a period when some are strong and capable of wrecking the prospects of the economy. We cannot avoid, therefore, the problem of what to do with the trade unions.

Policy towards trade unions

Although we have been quite frank in identifying the issue as being one of changing the balance of power, this does not imply that we give priority to legal curbs. On the contrary: the first thing is to encourage in trade unions and their members a recognition of the gains to be obtained by working together according to a sensible plan. The proposal for development programmes goes to the heart of this; so does our stress on the need for industrial democracy 'from the bottom up', and for a system of continual consultation between managers and workers in the spirit so well shown in Germany and Japan. Worker share ownership and profit sharing are logical complements to this approach; and there is a place, particularly in small-scale enterprise, and given proper management, for the extension of worker cooperatives. We have noted that a possible consequence of development programmes would be agreements governing pay for considerably longer than one year; and it would be an advantage of longer agreements that they could contain cumulative benefits which would be lost if the agreement is broken.

But we are not able to join those who assert that all attempts to deal with union problems through the law are useless or harmful. The legal framework is indeed an essential part of the matter, since it gives to unions immunities not available to other associations, and this at once raises the question of what obligations are to be associated with these exceptional rights. The minimum obligation should in our view be a requirement of genuine democracy: that is, that members should be consulted by secret ballot for the election of officers, and should not be required to take industrial action unless they agree in a secret ballot. The domination of union meetings by a minority of activists is a well-known problem, but such a system of government or decision-making should not be allowed to masquerade as democracy. Further, we hold that it should be illegal for a union to enter into any agreement which restricts the right of management to communicate directly with individual employees. There are well-known cases in which management is not permitted to explain its own proposals to the workers: this is totally contrary to the close personal relationship which we see as desirable.

We have proposed above what is in effect a cooling-off period, by a right of either party to refer pay issues for non-binding arbitration, and a prohibition of industrial action while this is being done. This system could be applied to other industrial disputes. It will, of course, be argued that, if workers want to strike in defiance of the law, nothing will stop them. But they could properly, for instance, be regarded as having discharged themselves and forfeited accumulated rights to redundancy pay in the event of later discharge: this would be a considerable disincentive. Furthermore, a union which organised a strike contrary to law could be made liable to pay damages for the consequences.

Are any special measures needed to curb the monopoly power of workers in essential services, or of key groups of workers whose absence can cause disproportionate loss? The definition of an 'essential service' is not an easy one, but there may be a few groups for which the available reference to arbitration should be binding. Such groups could however properly expect special treatment, similar to that proposd on p.185 for essential public servants. It seems to us very unlikely that this would in the long run cause any disadvantage to the workers concerned. The device of withdrawing key workers (who can readily be supported on strike pay by unions) does not seem to us capable of any legal curb, because of the diversity of situations to be covered. The only obvious remedy, regrettably, is for employers to act quickly in locking out all the workers affected, so as to force the unions or their members to face the full costs of a strike; but the employers may need immunities to parallel those of the unions, such as relief from liability to compensate workers so locked out.

However, apart from the provisions affecting reference of disputes to a tribunal by either party, we would prefer to give a little time to see the results of the more positive measures suggested above (pp. 187–8), before seeking to enact any further changes in the law. The requirements of responsibility in action and of democratic consultation are simple and obvious. Perhaps British unions are capable, gradually, of reforming themselves; a limited encouragement of mergers would help, provided that the largest unions do not grow too large to be managed. We are by no means in favour of reducing the unions to an impotent anarchy; our model is rather the strong and well-organised unions in Germany, and the concern for efficiency and the long-run interests of members shown by some unions in the United States. We would like to see a greater degree of professionalism in union activities, with officials being better paid and better trained; this would imply higher subscriptions from members, and this alone might help to encourage a more lively interest by the rank and file in what is done with their money, and hence a more constructive balance between the individual and local interest and the central bodies of the unions. We believe that the need for self-reform is beginning to be better understood in the unions; but they should be left in no doubt that further changes in the law may have to be considered if, unreformed, their way of doing business continues to have a damaging effect on the economy.

Conclusion

As we warned earlier, this chapter can only be a first selection from a great number of possibilities. We have said little about social policy, and indeed its more expensive extensions will have to wait until economic viability is restored; but it is of course necessary that in the meantime social policy should be well managed and seen to be just in its use of scarce resources. We have said little about the discouragement of unnecessary class division, though measures against fringe benefits would help (p. 184); so will any measures which encourage a greater equality in the ownership of property. But if policies for a constrained economy are to work, the prerequisite must be that there is wide public understanding, both of how weak and unsuccessful the British economy has become, and of the nature of the constraints which create this situation. However, an analysis of problems is not enough; there must also be an assurance of hope. For hopelessness is itself a constraint, and a great step forward would be taken if the psychological approach of British business men, union members and consumers could be so altered as to embody a belief that economic problems are going to be conquered. Therefore we see a need for a national development programme, comparable to the programmes which we have recommended for the larger firms: that is, a coherent set of policies for development to be consistently applied over a long period, which may reasonably be expected to yield higher real incomes and the freeing of resources to deal with social problems. In order to ensure that such policies do not become the victims of adversary politics, they should be backed by the unions and employers' associations, who should be able to reach a consensus on such issues of vital mutual interest within a joint body such as we propose (p. 171). It is hard to find satisfactory terms for such arrangements. Unfortunately the brief and simple word 'plan' has become devalued, and is associated with schemes of a bogus precision which fail to work. As regards the support of the unions and employers, a national 'contract' awakens memories of the dubious bargain of the 'social contract'; a national development 'understanding' would sound better, though even this might suggest a deal between particular political groups at the expense of others. These devaluations of the vocabulary are the consequences of past failure. Somehow Britain needs to find a way of expressing a determination to achieve full employment of resources in a developing and buoyant economy, by the steady application of measures which give priority to the strengthening of productive activity and the removal of the constraints which bind it. We have used for this the name of national development programme, and we hope that it will be read without any association with the memories of earlier errors.

We look, therefore, for frankness and honesty, but also for faith and hope, from politicians, leaders of industry and the trade unions, and all who help to form the public mind. Just in case these commodities prove not to be in good supply, we offer this book in the hope that it will stimulate public thinking.

Index